# Celebrity

# Celebrity

How Entertainers Took Over the World
and Why We Need an Exit Strategy

## Marina Hyde

Harvill *Secker*
LONDON

Published by Harvill Secker 2009

2 4 6 8 10 9 7 5 3 1

First published in Great Britain in 2009 by
Harvill Secker
Random House, 20 Vauxhall Bridge Road,
London SW1V 2SA

www.rbooks.co.uk

Addresses for companies within The Random House Group Limited can be
found at: www.randomhouse.co.uk/offices.htm

The Random House Group Limited Reg. No. 954009

A CIP catalogue record for this book
is available from the British Library

ISBN 978–1–846–55259–5

The Random House Group Limited supports The Forest Stewardship
Council (FSC), the leading international forest certification organisation.
All our titles that are printed on Greenpeace-approved FSC-certified paper
carry the FSC logo. Our paper procurement policy can be found at
www.rbooks.co.uk/environment

**Mixed Sources**
Product group from well-managed
forests and other controlled sources
www.fsc.org  Cert no. TT-COC-2139
© 1996 Forest Stewardship Council
FSC

Typeset by SX Composing DTP, Rayleigh, Essex
Printed and bound in Great Britain by
Clays Ltd, St Ives plc

*In memory of Kate Jones*

# Contents

# Introduction

On the eve of the most recent Palestinian presidential elections, a televised message was broadcast to voters in the region. 'Hi, I'm Richard Gere,' smiled its star, 'and I'm speaking for the entire world . . .'

Did you miss the meeting at which this got decided? Does it seem like an encouraging state of affairs? Do you find it confusing that Richard Gere should claim not simply to be speaking for himself (debatable), but for the whole of Earth?

Then apologies for startling you, but this is your world. Try not to choke on it. In 1990 Richard was starring in *Pretty Woman*; fifteen years later he was making formal interventions into Middle East politics. The saddest part is that you weren't even in a coma for that period, so future generations are going to regard you as complicit.

Of course, we're not just talking about Richard Gere – although as planet spokesmodel, he's certainly a reasonable starting point. We're talking about the entire celebriscape, which in recent years has seemed to be expanding at least twice as fast as the universe it inhabits.

Once upon a time, you see, the entertainment industry was an industry which made entertainment. Its workforce was required to do quaint things like show up to movie sets, or make music, or go to wild parties. Today, that brief has expanded slightly. It now includes proselytising for alien religions, attempting to negotiate with the Taliban, getting photographed in a manner that basically constitutes an unsolicited gynaecology examination, and being brought in to fix the Iraqi refugee crisis.

Are you familiar with the term 'mission creep'? Mission creep is the expansion of an enterprise beyond its original goals, typically after initial successes. Hilarity does not usually ensue. What does ensue are things like the escalation of the Korean War, or the Crusades, or Sharon Stone explaining that earthquakes are visited upon Chinese peasants because of 'karma'.

What ensues is Angelina Jolie getting to visit Baghdad on some confected UN refugee jaunt, and declaring during a stroll around the heavily fortified Green Zone: 'There seems to be just a lot of talk at the moment, and a lot of pieces that need to be put together. I'm trying to figure out what they are.' To clarify: she couldn't even figure out how not to be in *Mr & Mrs Smith*. Is it OK if she *doesn't* have a say in addressing the displacement of two million people?

The celebrity situation is out of control and we need to start looking for an exit strategy. Entertainers have vastly exceeded their mandate. And – in direct contravention of the warning of Spider-Man's uncle – with great power has come great irresponsibility.

But we needn't throw the baby out with the bathwater. In recent years, disingenuous folks have traded off a lot of false oppositions – things like 'you're either for the war or against the troops'. The same argument is advanced about celebrity – either you take notice of it, and are therefore an imbecile, or you ignore it totally, and are therefore superior.

This is nonsense. There are more than two positions you can hold on the subject. It's OK to like premiere frocks and scandals and crazy dispatches from Sparkleville. But celebrity's like alcohol, kids! It's important to enjoy it responsibly.

By the same dint, those lofty types studiously ignoring the world of celebrity don't appear to be making the problem disappear. In the past two years alone, celebrities have used the New York headquarters of the United Nations as a venue from which to sell luxury goods. They have closed an entire country's borders to journalists. They have still found time to lecture you about human rights. Their cell matter has been traded on the open market. They have been unwittingly photographed in their own homes. They have made spectacularly uncalled-for, even-more-spectacularly uninformed statements on sensitive matters of science and medicine. The Russian parliament has voted on whether to send one of them to the International Space Station. This is all true.

One of the favourite laments of the modern celebrity is that 'there's no handbook for fame'. Barely a week goes by without some applause-burdened star letting this maxim trip off their tongue. But rather more affectingly, there's no handbook for the rest of us, either. The rest of us being people who don't have publicists, people who think B-movie stars should have precisely nothing to do with refugee crises, and people who believe earthquakes are caused by plate tectonics as opposed to karma. In short, people who hadn't realised they'd given Richard Gere power of attorney.

This book will serve as both: a handbook to the world of celebrity – everything from the publicists to the pets – and an attack on its most troubling excesses – the cult-pushing, the paparazzi, the hijacking of an entire sovereign state.

So, what to expect as we journey across a perilous landscape of sex tapes and birthing rituals and road maps for peace in the Middle East? Some of the biggest names will crop up again and again because their influence is immense and rising – and because the bigger they get, the more places they want to reach. You'd be amazed how soon it is after you start earning $15 million a movie that you realise that actually, all you ever wanted to be was a public intellectual. There'll be trips to Africa, and to Neverland, and we'll be calling out everyone from the UN's department of famewhoring to the repulsive magazine editors who think there's some kind of utility to pictures of celebrity sweat patches. We'll be secretly amused when Paris Hilton tries to take her pet goat on to a plane. We'll be less so when Sharon Stone explains that caffeine causes cancer.

We'll recall the days when people thought celebrities taking drugs constituted a decadent society, and we'll wonder whether today's new breed of 'socially responsible' star isn't evidence of a far more significant moral decline – a slide into a society where the entertainers are formulating aid policy, or backing bills, or skewing public health debates. There'll be a few too many war metaphors, way too many references to action movies, and uncredited cameos by the likes of John Stuart Mill and Steven Seagal.

So keep your wits about you, stardust consumers, and prepare to tumble down the rabbit hole. Above all, remember this: if the entertainment industry is the solution, then we're asking the wrong questions.

# CELEBRITIES AND THE WAR ON TERROR

'War is too serious a matter to entrust to military men.'

*Georges Clemenceau*

'My security guard is going to take me to a gun range. He says if I'm going to Iraq, I should really know how to shoot.'

*Lindsay Lohan*

Western civilisation stands at a crossroads. We are under constant threat from a complex, unknowable enemy, whose hatreds are so deeply embedded as to seem intractable. They play by alternative rules; they refuse to be narcotised by our fine reality television; and they're irritatingly resistant to our traditional tactic of arming them in return for our fighting somebody else instead. *But* we have Bruce Willis. This is called 'assymetric warfare'.

First, the science bit: Bruce Willis's ability to save the world stands in inverse proportion to his ability to keep his vest clean in the saving thereof. That's just the law. But sometimes even action visionaries like Bruce understand that it's going to take more than laundry-soiling to stop an evil-doer. Sometimes it's going to take cold, hard cash. And so it was that in 2005, having correctly identified that the search for Osama bin Laden was stalling simply due to the lack of money on the table, Bruce gave the war on terror the benefit of his strategic thinking. He announced he was personally placing a $1 million bounty on the head of bin Laden.

Emboldened by the fawning praise he received for the gesture, the *Die Hard* star added to his notional largesse by slapping a $1 million Brucie Bounty on the head of al-Qaeda's Iraqi bureau chief, Abu Musab al-Zarqawi.

Quoth Bruce: 'I want to live in a world, and so do the Iraqi people want to live in a world, where they can move from their homes to the market and not have to fear being killed. And, I mean, doesn't everybody want that? Who doesn't want that?'

He made a good point, of course. The less charitable, however, might put the actor's bounty down to professional jealousy – let's face it, bin Laden's video releases were being watched by substantially bigger audiences than those for *Hostage* or that one where Bruce voiced a raccoon – but it clearly provided eighteen-year-old US soldiers from low-income families with a much-needed incentive to take down any senior al-Qaeda member who should stray into their cross hairs.

And so to 7 June 2006, the day upon which Abu Musab al-Zarqawi was finally ambushed and killed, following tip-offs from Iraqi civilians. Can you even imagine Bruce's delight at the news? Can you imagine the speed with which he dived for his chequebook, just itching to provide the plucky resistance heroes with $1 million to spend in that lavishly stocked Iraqi market any which way they pleased? Yes. Yes, you probably can.

'It's not that it's not true,' he floundered of his earlier promise. 'It was said metaphorically to some friends of mine in the military. I said it thinking my words would not be quoted in public. Once again, I got fucked. The press are everywhere.'

Mmm. For the record, Bruce had in fact made his pledge during a live phone chat with MSNBC's Rita Cosby, in an interview which remains available to view on the Internet for all eternity – a poignant reminder that if you don't want your words to be quoted in public, don't call up TV anchors on a live broadcast.

So you've heard of war presidents – the leaders who believe they step up and come into their own in times of blood-soaked strife. In this chapter you will meet the war celebrities[1] – the showbusiness personages who refuse to be pigeonholed as multimillionaire entertainers with a romantic comedy to promote, and instead are good enough to turn their thoughts to reimagining the Iraqi reconstruction effort, or coming up with 9/11 conspiracies, or training entire fake insurgencies. Reminder: all of these things *actually happened*.

## Cherchez la femme: Osama loves Whitney

'That's what always happens if you give a confused sixteenth son billions of dollars.' Now, you might well have accepted this as the explanation for why Osama bin Laden became such a psychopath – but there are other, more tangential diagnoses.

Kola Boof is Sudan's best-selling novelist, but she also claims to have been the al-Qaeda boss's Moroccan-based concubine in the mid-1990s, during which time Osama's failure to get it on with a certain someone apparently really gnawed at him.

'He said that he had a paramount desire for Whitney Houston,' wrote Ms Boof in her memoirs. 'How beautiful she was, how truly Islamic she is but is just brainwashed by American culture and by her husband Bobby Brown, whom Osama talked about having killed. He explained to me that to possess Whitney he would be willing to break his colour rule and make her one of his wives.'

And people paint him as such a cold fish.

Given that the six-time Grammy winner was missing, presumed in a crack den, for a significant portion of the next decade, it makes you wonder how Osama managed to hold it together in his video messages to the world, when he must have known from his copy of the *National Enquirer* that his infidel fantasy was engaged in a crazy struggle of her own.

After all, one edition of that fine publication featured photographs of a hotel room just vacated by Whitney, which was positively littered not simply with crack paraphernalia, but with

[1] You may decide you'd want neither a war president nor a war celebrity in a foxhole with you.

– and if you ever adored 'I Wanna Dance With Somebody', look away now – discarded adult nappies. Do enquiring minds *really* want to know? Sometimes it feels debatable.

Naturally, had Osama simply missed that *Enquirer* issue, the subscription snafu would have gifted the US a deadly weapon in their war on terror. Imagine the scene. A Tora Bora cave, unfashionably furnished, where the al-Qaeda non-executive chairman lies hooked up to a rough-hewn, Flintstones-style dialysis machine, weeping over the final scene of his well-worn video of *The Bodyguard* and fighting – just fighting – the heartbreaking realisation that Whitney and Kevin Costner can't be together because Kevin loves her too damn much to be able to protect her properly. As the first bars of 'I Will Always Love You' falter over the images, US troops burst in armed only with the *National Enquirer* photograph, which they thrust beneath his teary eyes with the spirit-crushing instruction: 'Look at your princess now!' You sense he'd have gone quietly.

Unfortunately, our story doesn't end quite here, because the loose end in the tale is Whitney's now ex-husband, whom, as Ms Boof stated, 'Osama talked about having killed'. You had the luxury of forgetting this; Bobby Brown did not. In fact, whenever the oxygen of publicity is wafted towards him – a biennial occurrence, these days – he voices his fear.

'I figure if bin Laden wants me, and everybody is looking for him, it probably won't happen,' began one such peroration. 'But if he wants to try and find me for something so stupid, he can do what he wants. I have to leave it in the hands of my higher power. But come on,' Bobby concluded. 'If [anybody else was] threatened by al-Qaeda, they'd take it seriously.'

Damn straight. Just who is protecting our parasitic ex-husbands of pop? Is it the Bureau? Is it the Agency? Is it the Department of Homeland Security? There are some very, very frightened wastrels out here. Can we please get a goddamned answer?

## We'll always have Davos: Henry Kissinger loves Angelina Jolie

Now to the cross-discipline world of Angelina Jolie, where B-movies meet international diplomacy, and humanity is the winner.

It should totally reassure you to know Angelina is a member of the Council of Foreign Relations, a prestigious and influential Washington foreign policy think tank whose leading lights include the likes of former Federal Reserve chairman Alan Greenspan, former US Secretaries of State George Shultz and Madeleine Albright, as well as war strategist and WTF-prompting Nobel Peace Prize laureate Henry Kissinger.

Yes, Henry Kissinger is on the board of something that calls itself the Council of Foreign Relations, which naturally raises a few questions. Like, was Kim Jong Il unavailable? Hasn't Kissinger been given enough of a shot at foreign relations in the past? How many children have to die as a result of his foreign-relations initiatives before someone takes him aside and says: 'You know what, Hank? *I think your skillset lies elsewhere.*'

Whatever the magic number of off-brand infant corpses may be, we were clearly nowhere near it in the spring of 2007, when the news broke that Angelina had been nominated for the Council of Foreign Relations membership. Baffled by the bafflement, a senior figure in the council defended the decision by pointing out: 'It's not like Paris Hilton is being nominated.' Right. And yet . . . that somehow feels like a false opposition. Just because they're not nominating the star of an amateur night-vision porno to a diplomatic think tank, the outcome can still be considered sub-frickin'-optimal.

Indeed, you may have assumed this was too much realpolitik for even Henry Kissinger to handle. Yet it turned out the former comedy Nobel Peace Prizewinner – and deadly serious US Secretary of State – couldn't have been more thrilled. At a speaking engagement in New York, Dr Kissinger declared of her prospective membership: 'It's my only chance to meet Angelina Jolie.'

Isn't it encouraging to think that the future of the free world is apparently being influenced by Henry Kissinger's after-hours daydreams? It makes you wonder which Hollywood bunny Robert McNamara is currently jerking off to. Let's get her on board! Maybe the object of the former US Defense Secretary's lust could fix Afghanistan. In fact, wouldn't it be great if Robert had a thing for Jennifer Aniston, and the Council on Foreign Relations found a berth for her? Then hipster ironists could dig out their old Team Aniston and Team Jolie T-shirts – only this time, wearing them wouldn't be about who gets Brad, it'd be about *the future of global foreign policy*.

Not that Kissinger was alone in slavering at Angelina's promotion to this exalted throng. 'Bring her on,' declared council member Dr Gordon Adams, an esteemed professor in international affairs. 'The idea of having Kissinger and Jolie in the same organisation is dazzling.'

Unfortunately, 'dazzling' is not diplomatic-speak for 'cretinously star-fucking', and so it was that the *Tomb Raider* star duly acceded to at least a five-year term on the Council of Foreign Relations alongside the erstwhile Secretary of State. The details of their professional dealings remain shrouded in secrecy, but like all these clubbable arrangements, it would presumably work both ways. Given that she's also one of that most cheering of modern phenomena – a celebrity UN goodwill ambassador – Angelina could undertake covert global missions for Henry, who remains poignantly unable to visit some countries for fear of being arrested as a war criminal. In return, it will not have escaped his encyclopedic showbiz mind that Angelina has an adoptive Cambodian son. So he can regale her with tales of how he once did his best to provide celebrities of the past with a near-limitless supply of Cambodian orphans.

What's not to feel positive about?

## The Taliban Mr Ripley: when Jude Law brought peace to Afghanistan

With its bigger, brasher, Iraq-based sequel really doing the numbers, it's easy to forget the first outing in the War on Terror franchise (much as people feel *T2* really eclipsed *The Terminator*). Don't worry. Afghanistan is used to being 'the forgotten war'. In fact, the resourceful populace trademarked the name in 1981, and now every time it is used in print, the publisher has to pay for one emergency food parcel to be spray-painted with the public service announcement 'Don't forget you're at war!' So congratulations. Just by reading this you helped provide a grateful Afghan with an aide-memoire.

Ever since it was first initiated in the wake of 9/11, the allies' Afghan mission has been dogged by allegations of ill-equipment. Nowhere is this more evident than in the lack of celebrity angles with which the conflict has been furnished. (Except perhaps in the lack of adequate boots and body armour. It's actually pretty evident there.) But after a six-year red-carpet drought in the country, one man was about to change all that.

Popular opinion maintains there are only three reasons for travelling to Afghanistan:

1. You were drunk/stoned in a Wal-Mart car park and dimly recall signing some enlistment paperwork.
2. You want to go to college.
3. You want to go to college as an amputee.

In fact, there are four.

4. You just starred in a coolly anticipated Christmas romcom and it really blew. You heard they're handing out free gravitas somewhere in the shadow of the Hindu Kush. Time to pay it forward!

In July 2007, Jude Law – the star of *Alfie*, *Sleuth* and a critically underappreciated nanny-humping scandal – announced he had personally undertaken a mission to Afghanistan. Breaking off breaking up with the likes of Sienna Miller, the actor announced he had travelled to what we must euphemistically refer to as 'that troubled region' in a bid to bring peace.[2]

Of course, personal safety is of paramount importance when any peace train's precious cargo is a celebrity. But Jude had no fears for his life. 'I felt there was no way they would want the blood of a film crew from the West on their hands,' he explained on his return. Because the one thing we can say for sure about the war on terror is that our enemies really draw the line at involving the media in any bloodshed/beheadings/tortuous kidnap plots. But what precisely did he get up to?

'Obviously the situation was too complicated for us to sit down with actual members of the Taliban,' was Jude's summary of the mission. 'But we were led to believe that the effects of our conversations with the right people filtered through to them.'

History is likely to cast this incident as a watershed moment in Afghan self-awareness. This wasn't just another instance in which the Afghans realised they were unimaginably screwed. This was the moment they realised that Jude Law was a key player in their peace process. He was going to save their asses one rubbish Michael Caine remake at a time. As to the nature of the complications which prevented the actor sitting down 'with actual members of the Taliban', well, Jude never did elaborate. But if Mullah Omar won't sign a simple publicist agreement banning him from bringing up the business with the nanny, then he must learn to do without a meet-and-greet.

[2] Do you sometimes feel the terrorists *have* won?

## The changing face of conflict: from Monroe to Lohan

Where once Our Boys could sleep easily in a dysentery-ridden trench knowing they would be pointlessly obliterated in the morning, today they face unprecedented threats from an unprecedented enemy. Roadside devices, Internet beheadings, iBombs . . . thank God we still have our space-race victory to fall back on. The minute al-Qaeda opens one of its cans of whupass somewhere near Mars, we're going to be *so* prepared for them.

In this changed context, the entertainment industry has had to dig especially deep to provide the requisite two fingers to the sacrifice members of the armed forces make, and this can be usefully illustrated by an examination of the 'Forces' Sweethearts' it is fielding.

> Scene: a US Army base, 1954, during the Korean War.
> Marilyn Monroe dons a bomber jacket and gives a morale-boosting concert to troops – a performance that lives on in world-renowned stills and film footage.
>
> Scene: Baghdad, the present day, a still mysteriously unnamed date.
> Who's this insisting her rider demands be met in full before she'll ask the Green Zone if they're ready to rock? Why, it's exhaustion-prone mission tonic Lindsay Lohan! Operation Enduring Hellfire just got a new face.

It was while she was riding high on the commercial failure of *Herbie: Fully Loaded* that Hollywood's least misunderstood starlet was moved to grant an interview to *Elle* magazine, an interview in which she revealed: 'I've been trying to go to Iraq with Hillary Clinton for so long.' Yeah, well. Synchronising diaries with a war can be a bitch.

'I wanted to do what Marilyn Monroe did,' Lindsay explained of her putative Baghdad mission, 'when she went and just set up a stage and did a concert for the troops all by herself. It's so amazing seeing that one woman just going somewhere, this beautiful sex kitten, who is basically a pin-up, which is what I've always aspired to be.'[3]

There's no one way to prepare for an Iraqi mission, of course, but Lindsay had firm ideas of what kind of dry run was required. 'My security guard is going to take me to a gun range,' she explained. 'I'm going to start taking shooting lessons. He says if I'm going to Iraq, I should really know how to shoot.'

Use this, readers, as a rejoinder to people who say the headlines from Iraq can't get any worse. Tell them that they could be reading: 'Shia militia refuse to believe trigger-happy *Mean Girls* star acted alone; all-out civil war finally ensues.'

## The Rocky road to Iraq: Apollo Creed trains insurgents

Did you ever wonder what Carl Weathers – aka boxer Apollo Creed – did after he was killed in *Rocky IV*? OK, he was killed in *Predator*. But after that, it turns out *he trained an entire fake Iraqi insurgency*. Can we finally lay that 'no second acts in American lives' rubbish to rest?

Whatever, we're racing ahead of ourselves. Our story begins somewhere in the Mojave Desert, with movie convention demanding that you imagine that location description being rattled out, letter by letter, in Courier font at the bottom of your TV screen. Like this:

```
Somewhere in the Mojave Desert . . .
```

Somewhere in the Mojave Desert there lies a 1,000-square-mile facility called Fort Irwin, where the US military has constructed a cluster of thirteen mock-Iraqi villages. It's like the real Iraq, but with water and electricity and hope. Here, with the help of

---

[3] Were you aware that Lindsay has father issues?

Hollywood special-effects technology and Iraqis playing civilians and rebels, troops en route to the Great Mesopotamian Adventure are treated to a simulated, mind-blowingly elaborate taste of that most enchanting of conflicts.

Wondering where Fort Irwin sourced their Iraqis? Turns out there's an Iraqi community in San Diego. They drafted in hundreds of these expats – most of whom had family in Iraq – to act the parts of the villagers. At one point, Fort Irwin's police chief was being played by a man who had fled Iraq and ended up in California, where he was seeking political asylum. It's OK to feel distinctly complicated about this. Anyway, having secured these Iraqis' services, the US military divided them among the mock hamlets. This would be the Iraqi-Americans' home for weeks on end, day and night, from which they were instructed to mount a fictitious but continuous attack on the real American troops being trained for dispatch to Real Iraq. Think of it as faux-rilla warfare, with all that remained being to train them to act like insurgents.

Enter Apollo Creed.

For several years now, the movie actor Carl Weathers has been a principal figure in Red Tight Media, a firm which among other things makes high-level training films for the US government and military. There's one in which he effectively explains how to deploy a Patriot missile – and frankly, it's hard not to be thrilled that that kind of operational teaching is in the hands of Apollo Creed. He always gave great training montage.

And from 2006, Carl Weathers has been employed to give the Fort Irwin faux-rillas acting lessons – a sort of Defense Department version of *Inside the Actors Studio*. In turn, the students use what they have learned from this master of the craft to inflict as many simulated casualties on the trainee soldiers. Death by Rocky training montage, one assumes. You can't help feeling Fort Irwin graduates must have been a bit disappointed when they finally ventured out of the Baghdad Green Zone only to discover that real insurgents don't use skipping ropes, and would have no need to beat Sylvester Stallone in a barefoot beach running race, preferring to decapitate him on the Internet and walk it instead.

As for what they made of their method coach . . . Maddeningly, the fake Iraqi insurgents refused to be interviewed by the media invited to view the facility, terrified this would lead to their relatives in Iraq being identified and killed by real-life insurgents. Still, they did excellently in the war games. Fort Irwin being their home turf, the insurgents inflicted massive death tolls on the Americans, with many of them the subject of mock executions which were video-taped and uploaded to the base's version of al-Jazeera. And you know what? It turns out that being beheaded in Fake Iraq can be a real confidence-knocker if your next stop is Actual Iraq.

In fact, so effectively disturbing is the fake insurgency that several US soldiers have developed battle fatigue and post-traumatic stress disorder, and had their deployments to the war zone cancelled.

To repeat: Carl Weathers is basically invaliding marines out of the US military *just by his acting*. And he was killed by Ivan Drago in *Rocky IV*. Imagine if Dolph Lundgren had got the Fort Irwin gig. He could have seriously affected the coalition's ability to assemble enough untraumatised troops for the Surge.

Perhaps most intriguingly, though, this means that three significant US seats of authority have been filled by people who were in the movie *Predator*. There's California governor Arnold Schwarzenegger, former Minnesota governor Jesse Ventura, and now Carl doing his thing in the desert. Can we please try and ensure the eponymous alien gets at least a senate seat?

**Al-Qaeda and Hollywood: why our celebrities get Lost in Translation**

There are days when even the World's Most Wanted Man looks in the mirror and just feels like the world's most *un*wanted man. He stares at his grey beard, sighs wearily at a FedEx-ed package of cave-floor carpet samples Mullah Omar wants him to pick between, and thinks: is there some sharia law loophole that would let me hang out with Scarlett Johansson for a few days, as long we just laugh at funny little Japanese people together and don't get it on?

His heart says yes; logistical problems say no. But what is the point of all the senseless mass murder and crappy pieces-to-camera if he has no one to share them with? Addressing Osama's belated midlife crisis became unavoidable in 2007, with the release of one of his videos. The film's ostensible message was something about joining his 'caravan of martyrs', but its subtext was loud and clear: 'I've been manscaped. Who wants to go to a karaoke bar?'

Studying that newly dyed beard, two shades up on the Pantone chart from Paul McCartney's hair, it was possible to draw only one conclusion: an age-inappropriate woman had inspired it. Not only was Osama palpably concerned about his appearance, he was probably toying with buying a Porsche and quitting his job as al-Qaeda's CEO. Maybe even learning to surf, you know? Above all, he finally looked ready to ask Whitney out.

Alas, the global jihadist movement has the ideological manoeuvrability of a supertanker, and despite the boss's apparent new direction, bin Laden's junior colleagues are still way behind his curve. They decline to prioritise personal grooming. Their interest in high-performance German vehicles stops with Panzer. And from what we know of their likes and dislikes, they remain relatively unimpressed by the fine buffet of entertainment personalities served up by the West.

In fact, there is a bewildering amount of published material on the latter subject. In his wry book *Schmoozing with Terrorists*, journalist Aaron Klein conducted interviews with several jihadists, during which he sought their opinions on various celebrities. To summarise: holy warriors were pretty exercised about that kiss between Madonna and Britney Spears at the 2003 MTV video music awards. The one that Madonna declared she had explained to her daughter thusly: 'I am the mommy pop star and she is the baby pop star. And I am kissing her to pass my energy on to her.' (Unfortunately, Britney's downward spiral from there on in suggests Madonna is in fact a succubus.)

Accordingly, Abu Abdullah, a senior member of Hamas's military wing, has a strategy for how things will shake down come his unsparkly revolution. 'At the beginning,' he told Klein, 'we will try to convince Madonna and Britney Spears to follow Allah's way.' Did he even *see Swept Away*? Madonna can't even follow Guy Ritchie's way. The complex strands of the Qur'an might be a stretch at this difficult stage in her journey.

But Abdel-Al, a like-minded leader of the Popular Resistance Committees, concurred: 'If these two prostitutes keep doing what they are doing, we of course will punish them. I will have the honour – I repeat, I will have the honour – to be the first one to cut off the heads of Madonna and Britney Spears.'[4] He went on to say that women such as Madonna 'must be eighty times hit with a belt'.

You may have already seen that in the 'Express Yourself' video.

Clearly, though, all the indications are that militants are becoming weirdly obsessed with celebrities, the opium of the West, and – like the rest of us – they will soon be so consumed by Lindsay's rehab visits and Paris's upskirt shots, that they will forget all about their day jobs. Let's see this as a positive: it's not like anything else we're doing is working. In the meantime, have they voiced respect for any of our stars? Well, there is the one . . . they love Mel Gibson, who you may recall took the occasion of his drink-driving arrest to lecture a police officer on which religion is responsible 'for all the wars in the world'. Yes, the jihadists have a lot of time for Mel. And unfortunately, it isn't because they really liked his work in *Mad Max*.

---

[4] Can you technically be anything other than the first person to cut off someone's head?

## Celebrity conspiracy theories: Charlie Sheen

For many celebrities, conspiracy theories are the VIP rooms of history. Sure, you'll have your Warren Commissions and your senate investigations keeping the plebs behind the velvet rope, but if you know the right people, and have access to enormous quantities of self-regard, you can get through to the inner sanctum where they tell you It's All A Big Lie.

Frankly, with dentistry as expensive as yours, you simply can't afford to let The Man stamp his jackboot down on your face, and so it is that when faced with the inquiry 'Did Lee Harvey Oswald act alone?', you find yourself thinking: 'God, I mean . . . do any of us? Like, he had to have people, you know? At least an agent and a publicist.'

So when acting's Charlie Sheen was good enough to focus his mind on the official explanation for 9/11, all right-thinking civilians were commanded to listen. And you know what? He wasn't buying it. 'It just didn't look like any commercial jetliner I've flown on any time in my life,' the *Hotshots Part Deux* star told a US radio station, 'and then when the buildings came down later on that day, I said to my brother "call me insane", but did it sorta look like those buildings came down in a controlled demolition?'

You're insane. Next?

'It seems to me like nineteen amateurs with box cutters taking over four commercial airliners and hitting 75 per cent of their targets,' he continued, 'that feels like a conspiracy theory.'

But it was George Bush's assertion that he had seen the first plane hit the north tower of the World Trade Center before any footage of it had been released that convinced Charlie he was really on to something. 'I guess one of the perks of being president is that you get access to TV channels that don't exist in the known universe,' he continued, in a manner which in no way suggests he once had a monstrous cocaine problem. 'It might lead you to believe that he'd seen similar images in some type of rehearsal, as it were, I don't know.'

Oh, *right*. The 9/11 'rehearsal'. Of course!

'It feels like from the people I talk to in and around my circles,' Charlie concluded triumphantly, 'it seems like the worm is turning.'

Yes . . . It seems repetitive to restate that acting and politics are discrete career choices. As, indeed, are acting and civil engineering. But sometimes we *have* to repeat ourselves, because it's increasingly possible for the star of *Two and a Half Men* to glance up at the World Trade Center on the morning of 9/11, reckon it looks as if the towers were brought down in a controlled explosion, and have his views heard all over the shop simply because he was once in the Brat Pack. Frankly, Charlie's views on politics add as much to the debate as would Noam Chomsky saying: 'I won't be critiquing United States foreign policy for a bit, on account of I've got a twenty-two-episode sitcom to film for NBC.'

Pick a lane, Sheen.

In fact, pick a lane *all of you*.

The War on Terror may have a ludicrous name, but that doesn't mean it should have celebrity parents. That isn't the tail wagging the dog: it's the fleas running the kennel.

As a useful forecasting model, let's look at this like Vietnam. Presently we're in the Tet Offensive phase. Jude Law is holding press conferences in Kabul – while Afghan president Hamid Karzai consistently finishes higher than him on *Esquire*'s Best Dressed list. At the present rate of acceleration, by the time we get to the last-helicopter-out-of-Saigon phase, the future of the free world will be in the hands of whichever fourth-generation *High School Musical* stars didn't make the transition to a Hollywood romcom.

The only thing these celebrities are 'raising awareness of' is themselves. Face it: if you need a celebrity to explain the news to you, then you need to consume more news. No matter how badly our struggle against miscellaneous evil-doers is faring, can we at least be smart enough to realise that the solutions lie somewhere other than with the entertainment industry?

# WHEN CELEBRITIES SHARE

ALGERNON: Do you really keep a diary? I'd give anything to look at it. May I?

CECILY: Oh no. You see, it is simply a very young girl's record of her own thoughts and impressions, and consequently meant for publication. When it appears in volume form, I hope you will order a copy.

Oscar Wilde,
*The Importance of Being Earnest*

Right now we are developing other products by putting our unique twist on the kinds of snacks you would find in the pantry on the Aerosmith tour bus.

Joe Perry, Aerosmith

How many autobiographies is it acceptable to publish before the age of thirty? It's such a tough question, isn't it, because while Winston Churchill declined to address his early years until he was in his late fifties, Geri Halliwell had told her life story twice before concluding her third decade.

In recent times, we've seen a wholly encouraging proliferation in the numbers of ways celebrities can communicate with a public anxious for news. Where once a star wishing to share themselves would be limited to traditional outlets, it is now possible to telegraph one's state of mind via an exciting new range of communicative platforms. Tattoos, fragrances, snack lines ... even sex tapes. Crucially, what these forms of expression allow is for the celebrity to address their fans in a way that bypasses more outmoded routes, like waiting to be asked for such information. And in most cases, they're lucrative. Frankly, there's never been a better time to have nothing interesting to say.

Poleaxingly, though, there is a downside to this hyper-transactional way of exploiting fame. And so it is – and only the cynics would brand it inevitable – that items stars would rather you *didn't* trade in have become saleable. Of course, celebrities have been insuring their body parts for years, but we've now moved into a phase where celebrity cell matter itself has become a prized commodity.

So in this chapter we'll examine the many ways in which a celebrity can share with a fortunate public, moving through statement tattoos to deliberately leaked sex tapes to more overt ways of taking people's admiration for your talent and sublimating it into a secondary income stream.[1] Things like fragrance lines.

But we'll also be be taking a look at the way that things that have passed in and out of celebrities' hands – come to that, in and out of their digestive tracts – have become tradeable commodities. A sandwich half eaten by Britney Spears was sold for $500; while her half-full water bottle[2] received a top bid of $495. A pregnancy test purporting to come from a hotel room she had recently vacated went for $5,001.

Does it feel to you like this chapter's going to have a happy ending? Let's find out!

## Tattoos: say it with body art

Contrary to the popular assumption that she has contributed precisely nothing to the sum of human knowledge, or indeed pleasure, Elizabeth Hurley gifted the world a mirthless laugh when she revealed that she has a special way of referring to non-celebrities. She calls them 'civilians'. Civilians are like a foreign country; they do things differently. And so, in civilian hands, the

[1] Or often, a primary income stream. Talent's starting to feel like a loss leader.
[2] On second thoughts, the bottle was half empty.

tattoo is used to assert individuality, usually in the form of the Chinese symbol for 'love', which – through years of being branded on the lower backs of millions of crop-top-wearing Westerners – has now semantically shifted to mean 'I have low self-esteem: meet me behind McDonald's'.

Where stars are concerned, though, tattoos really exist for two reasons: to beam their powerful personal philosophy to the world, and to provide us with an aide-memoire of their romantic entanglements.

Falling within the former category are tattoos like Billy Bob Thornton's 'Remember the Alamo' and Robbie Williams's 'Elvis, Grant Me Serenity'. The latter category boasts entries such as David Beckham's earnestly misspelled Hindi triumph, 'Vihctoria', and Eminem's belly-spanning tribute to his ex-wife Kim, in which the words 'Rot in Pieces' sit atop her open grave.

If you're looking for 'body art' that defies categorisation, a useful starting point is the instruction 'breathe' which Lindsay Lohan had branded onto her inner wrist. Yes, branded. No ink: just searingly hot metal. But was it merely decorative? After all, celebrities are always extolling the importance of their taking time out to do things normal people do. The brand may very well have been Lindsay's way of reminding herself to regularly exchange oxygen for carbon dioxide, in the manner of less scheduled and cheaper- clothed humanoids.

And in its favour, the exhortation 'breathe' will at least remain relevant for the rest of her life, which cannot be said for the dermal stylings of many stars, who too frequently marry in haste and repent at laser. As the Spice Girl Mel B commented after her ill-fated romance with Eddie Murphy: 'You don't tattoo the person's name on your body after three days if it's just a fling.'[3]

For all that Fate conspires against them, though, many celebrities resist the siren call of the laser. Their approach can be summed up as: this is an unsightly mistake, why don't I cover it

---

[3] You do it if you're that special cocktail of needy and crazy.

up with an even bigger one? It was this school of thought that sublimated the small, italicised 'Charlie' belonging to the former Mrs Sheen – Denise Richards – into a large, ankle-hugging fairy, apparently needled on by a person with no eyes or hands.

But if we really seek to understand the palimpsest nature of celebrity 'body art', we must consider the *pensées* of Pamela Anderson, which prove again, if proof were needed, that a profound interest in zymology and being attracted to guys in Mötley Crüe aren't mutually exclusive. 'Tattoos are like stories,' she once explained. 'They're symbolic of the important moments in your life. Sitting down, talking about where you got each tattoo and what it symbolises, is really beautiful.' As anyone who saw Tommy Lee's since-removed swastika will testify.

Alas, some stories have ugly endings, which is why Pamela eventually attempted to curtail any discussion of the 'Tommy' tattoo around her wedding finger by changing it to 'Mommy'. (For those who want to remember the way Mommy and Tommy were, there's always their beautiful and symbolic honeymoon sex tape, which will still be available on the Internet when Pamela's ring finger is so gnarled fans will assume the blue scrawl to be some kind of rheumatically induced spider vein.)

Naturally, no treatise on this subject would be complete without running the rule over at the Zen mistress of tattoo affectation: Angelina Jolie, whose largest organ[4] should be regarded as the Rosetta Stone of celebrity body art.

In fact, we probably shouldn't rule out the theory that Angelina is simply adopting or biologically spawning children as backup for the inevitable moment when she realises she has no available flesh left on which to tattoo such thought-provoking statements as the 'What Nourishes Me Also Destroys Me' that sits above her bikini line, or the 'Know Your Rights' that bestrides her neck. Her young charges could provide a kind of epidermal spillover area on which these important philosophies could be expanded.

[4] Actually, her skin is not the largest. The largest is her *heart*.

Yet it seems that she will at least endeavour to fill up Brad Pitt's defaceable torso first, as her gentleman caller continues to build up quite the tattoo collection of his own. The first Brad unveiled was a forearm tattoo of Otzi the iceman – the mummified hominid discovered frozen in an Alpine glacier, and who is believed to date back to 3300 BC. This was revealed to be a deliberately arch reference, as Otzi himself has over fifty carbon tattoos.[5]

The second was a mysterious series of parallel lines that were diversely interpreted as a tribute to the great Nintendo platform games of the 1980s, and a diagram of the New Orleans levee system. As it turned out, the speculation was way off target: Angelina herself had created the cryptic hieroglyph.

'We went to Davos,' she explained. 'One night we didn't have anything to do, so I was drawing on his back. It's meaningful in that it's us making angles and shapes out of each other's body, that kind of a thing.'

No. That is not why it is meaningful. It is meaningful because the kind of people who get so bored that they doodle on each other and turn those doodles into permanent tattoos *are now attending the World Economic Forum*.

## Help yourself to my self-help: the prominent display of reading matter

Ever attuned to new delivery mechanisms, stars have recently hit on a more easily updatable way of explaining Where They're At to the public. Audacious in its simplicity, it involves the ostentatious clutching of a personal-growth tome in the vicinity of photographers.

You may be familiar with this shtick: 'Look! Someone from Television is carrying *Facing Love Addiction*. I wonder what *that*

---

[5] Otzi is believed to have made his living in the Copper Age equivalent of Black Sabbath.

means?' Though it would take Roland Barthes to extract the full meaning of what the Person from Television is saying, the upshot is that they're *addicted to love*. But, crucially, that they're *facing it*.

The central, counterintuitive point is that where celebrities are concerned, self-help books are deployed to give the public some much-needed perspective – not the star.[6]

The trend began in earnest with Geri Halliwell, formerly of the Spice Girls, now the UN's answer to the Aids epidemic and the crisis in maternal healthcare in sub-Saharan Africa. When Geri broke all our hearts by leaving the Spices, the time-honoured nine-day drink and drugs binge which the occasion demanded never materialised. Instead, she embarked on an orgy of public self-help-book reading, being photographed with M. Scott Peck's agonisingly tedious opus *The Road Less Travelled*, and something called *Feel the Fear and Do It Anyway*. Suddenly, all became clear. Geri was *feeling fear* about leaving the Spice Girls. But she was *doing it anyway*.

Think of this technique as indecent exposure of the brain – a kind of psychological flashing.

Then think of the only situation in which you could possibly conceive of seeing professional cretin Jessica Simpson within a mile radius of a book, and realise it's going to be literally minutes before the singer/actress announces her split from her husband. The book? *Dealing With People You Can't Stand*. Could you bring the sledgehammer down one more time, Jessica? There's a chance a couple of particularly backward ten-year-olds haven't understood you.

Thus it is that any celebrity wishing to engage in unmediated discourse with their rudderless public need simply pay a visit to their local Mind Body Spirit shelves. (Incidentally – a dedicated

[6] Related media: the slogan T-shirt. Largely the same as the above, only in easy-to-wear cotton jersey form, and tends to be employed by a celebrity wishing to mark themselves out as a gifted ironist. See: Paris Hilton sporting 'I'm Paris Hilton and I Can Do Whatever I Want' or Victoria Beckham in 'Bored of the Beckhams'.

Mind Body Spirit section? Surely the entire bookshop is effectively packed with product that will enrich one or more of the three? Ditto 'Personal Growth'.)

Perhaps inevitably, the neatest reminder that self-help should be about helping yourself comes from Jennifer Lopez, who once bemoaned the lack of reading material for stars who are 'in the public eye' and 'making a lot of money'. 'I might do that next,' she explained. 'Nobody writes books about how to deal with that.' She's right, of course. And it's odd. All those *Women Who Love Too Much*es, and not one *Starving Schmillions: Why Being Insanely Rich and Fabulous Is Hard Too*. Alas, in the next breath, the muse appeared to leave Jennifer. 'No, I'll make no money,' she judged. 'So it's not worth it.'

## Endorsements: when sharing means taking your share

There is, however, a common glaring drawback to the afore-mentioned means of sharing oneself with one's fans. One does not draw payment for the service. And so to the *business* of sharing. Celebrity product endorsements are a magical invention. They allow the magic of a member of the entertainment industry to be fused with the magic of a product of which you most likely have no need. And the celebrity gets paid for it! C'mon, who loses?[7]

These days, marketers have even devised an index to determine which stars are best suited to push which products. It's called the Davie Brown Index, and it brings a quasi-scientific approach to the business of celebrities sprinkling their gold-effect dust over your wares. Dreamt up by a talent agency that books stars for corporate advertisers, the Davie Brown Index employs a research panel of 1.5 million civilians to make weekly evaluations of 1,500 celebrities on the basis of eight criteria: trust, appeal, influence, trendsetting, notice (ubiquity), endorsement

---

[7] You lose.

(spokespersonability), aspiration (how much you want to be them) and awareness (how recognisable they are).

The likes of Oprah and Tom Hanks pretty much own the top spots, but beneath them teems an entire ocean of celebrities whose box-office smashes, rehab visits, unforced fashion errors and the like are being fed into a giant, constantly updating human barometer – all the better to determine whose plastic surgery is undetectably good enough to advertise a miracle face cream, which you will duly purchase at a price you cannot afford, powerless to combat this assault by the joint forces of celebrity and science.

And yet, many celebrities nurse blush-inducing hang-ups about hawking themselves quite so overtly. And that is why overseas ads were invented. Picture a child putting its tiny, chubby hands over its eyes and thinking you can't see it, because it can't see you. This is the mindset of the celebrity fronting an advert in foreign climes.

For reasons possibly related to the heady cocktail of self-regard and insecurity that propelled them into the entertainment business in the first place, most stars remain amusingly uptight about pushing someone else's product in lands where their movie or TV series does not have to be dubbed. They fear it may look tacky. They believe it will compromise The Brand. But transplant them to Japan, or Europe, and their unwillingness to sell out evaporates, as they prove they can inhabit a tacky, insanely high-paying advert campaign every bit as convincingly as they can inhabit the role of a hot housewife or a hot junior doctor or a hot DEA agent.

Take Eva Longoria's happy association with Magnum, an ice-cream chocolate bar which is not sold in the United States, but which Eva has put into her mouth, for money, in France, Spain, England, Italy ... Frankly, she's done it all over Europe. It's like the choc-ice-fellating equivalent of the Grand Tour. And as with all these furtive little outings, it's the post-rationalisation that provides the true entertainment. 'I'm happy to represent Magnum,' declared Eva in a statement she most likely prayed no

American eyes would ever scan, 'as I believe in indulgence and sensuality . . . Being part of this campaign is really fun for me.'

And with that humble 'being part of', Eva confirms that sell-out ads are the one time a celebrity actively wants you to think they're involved in an ensemble piece as opposed to a star vehicle. Our heroine may be the diffident frontwoman, but how it warms the heart to hear her tacitly acknowledge the on-set armies of unseen, muscle-tongued assistants, who perform the invaluable task of fluffing the Magnums to the brink of their indulgent, sensual peak, before Eva swans in and takes over for the money shot.

But even if your product isn't suited to dribbling down a celebrity's chin, there's still a way of getting it on their body that doesn't involve paying a film crew and buying advertising space. As long as it's a luxury fashion item – or at the very least a sub-ironic slogan T-shirt – you can simply send it to the entertainer in question and hope they wear it somewhere they'll get photo-graphed. As the cliché goes: if you're rich enough to buy this stuff, people give it to you free anyway.

This adorable notion of the human billboard taps into both the celebrity's unwillingness to pay for stuff, and humanity's increas-ingly deranged desire to copy them. Your room-mate copying you would obviously seem grounds for mental health intervention, but if she's slavishly adopting every single outfit choice of a *Gossip Girl* star, then that's completely fine. It's just *Single White Female* at a societal level.

And there are really no limits to the situations in which this device can be deployed. When Angelina Jolie and Brad Pitt sold the pictures of their newborn daughter Shiloh to *People* magazine – for a $5 million fee to charity – the little T-shirt they chose to dress the baby in had been sent to them by a PR company. With exquisite grace, the PR firm issued a press release describing the event as 'one of the most important product placement oppor-tunities in the world'.

So, just as the newborn was using its celebrity to help others the minute it came out of the womb,[8] it was also helping other people sell their crap. If it helps, imagine Shiloh emerging from the birth canal with 'YOUR PRODUCT HERE' stamped on her belly. Hey – it's the one tattoo Mommy doesn't already have.

### Celebrity product ranges: a better class of tat

Where once a star might restrict themselves to a product range related to their line of work – Michael Jordan's Nike Air Jordan sport shoes, for instance – this is now viewed as needlessly limiting. In fact, it's probably evidence of communist sympathies. Gone is any expectation of relevance, and so it is that we are gifted such unmissable retail opportunities as Kylie Minogue bedlinen – a collection of quilts, cushions and the like, apparently designed by the singer to appeal to all those who have found themselves unable to sleep until that ineffable Minogue quality was brought to a fitted sheet.

More darling even than this, however, are the stars who want you to believe they were intimately involved in the creation of their wares, and whose promotional blurbs furnish the public with the full, amazing backstory. Take Steven Seagal's Lightning Bolt, in which the action movie star turns his thoughts to refreshment, and all our palates are the beneficiaries. Or as the publicity material thundered: 'Steven Seagal can add energy drink formulator to a list of talents that already includes –' Yes? *Yes?* '– veteran actor, singer-songwriter, guitarist and Aikido black belt.' Ah.

According to this breathless account – and at some level you do have to doff your cap – the *Marked for Death* legend personally travelled to Asia to source the ingredients. In between taking down a bent cop, uncovering massive CIA corruption, fighting a bunch of tae kwon do separatists, and smashing an international drug cartel (let's speculate slightly), he managed to stuff some Tibetan goji berries and a fungus called Asian cordyceps into his

---

[8] It's really important you buy into this, particularly the element of the child's choice in the matter.

vest pocket, with the result being a drink claiming to be 'as unique as the man who created it'.

As for the name . . . 'The name Steven Seagal's Lightning Bolt was an inevitable afterthought,' the public was informed. 'When Steven Seagal finished creating a drink that holds untold natural power, there was only one equivalent in nature – the lightning bolt. Both mysterious and powerful, it's a symbol of the untold energy the earth has to offer. Such is Steven Seagal's Lightning Bolt energy drink.'

The main thing to realise is that, with the arguable exception of incontinence pads, there is no product some celebrity or other wouldn't slap their name on if they thought there might be money in it. Or as they would euphemise it, if they thought they could 'enjoy a long association with the only energy drink/razor/incontinence pad I've ever trusted'. Don't believe it? Then it's probably time we talked about the Kiss Kasket.

Kiss are not merely a rock band you could never care about, no matter how many more eternities they keep flogging their face-painted, catsuited, age-inappropriate act. They are the most rapaciously merchandising entertainers ever to have existed. Against their awesomely shameless record, even will-this-do product spewer Gwen Stefani is a merchandising pygmy. This lot have licensed their name to more than 3,000 products, from the Kiss toothbrush ('rock your teeth clean') to Kiss studded condoms (let's not and say we did) to Kiss bathroom tiles (really?) to Kiss Cabernet Sauvignon (OK, just leave now).

But in June 2001,[9] it became clear that Kiss were not simply scraping the bottom of the barrel. The barrel had a concealed basement. And so to the Kiss Kasket, the world's first celebrity-branded coffin.

Have you ever contemplated falling into death's embrace and

[9] In a couple of decades or so, when the flood has come, and your rag-clad grandchildren break off from scavenging for food to ask you where it all started to go irrevocably wrong, this date will be one to mention.

thought how much sweeter it would be if a member of the entertainment industry had ripped you off one last time before your surviving relatives began shovelling in the earth? Then let's hear some more about the product that could make that happen. The Kiss Kasket featured the faces of all four founder members of the band, as well as its logo and the immortal slogan 'Kiss Forever'. It retailed at $4,500 unsigned, and $5,000 signed. Come on: this may be a difficult time for you, but an autograph's an autograph. It's what the Kasket's kargo would have wanted.

As Kiss frontman Gene Simmons declared upon its launch: 'This is the ultimate Kiss collectible.' High praise indeed. 'I love living,' he continued, 'but this makes the alternative look pretty damn good.'

Kiss, however, are all about delivering value to the customer, and they understand that the discerning consumer will demand versatility from a coffin. Certainly, it's comforting to know that you or your loved one will be turning to dust beneath the laminated, heavily airbrushed visages of the guys who gave the world 'Lick It Up'. But what are its hospitality functions?

According to its creators, the Kiss Kasket 'can also be used as a giant Kiss cooler, enabling fans and their friends to enjoy ice-cold sodas and beer served directly from the ice-filled, completely waterproof Kiss Kasket'. You see? For those keen to milk value from their purchase during the living years, or perhaps double up its usage during those open-coffin viewing days – when, let's face it, we could all use a drink – the Kasket represented the only conceivable choice. The way Kiss saw it, fans would be literally dying to own one.

**Fragrance: smell the love**

Yet of all the high-mark-up products a celebrity can release into a fame-narcotised marketplace, one stands neck and stopper above the rest. That product is the celebrity fragrance.

In recent years, celebrity fragrance has been one of Earth's most exciting growth sectors, as personages of note explored different ways of delivering their message to you. Sure, that message was still playing very strongly in their traditional heartlands, your eyes and ears. You'd seen their movie. You'd bought their album. But what about your nose? How on earth had your sense of smell stayed untapped so long?

It hadn't, of course. The first ever celebrity fragrance as we'd understand it – widely available, marketed using faintly trampy pictures of its subject – was probably Mary Garden, created by Detroit cosmetics firm McLean some time around the turn of the twentieth century. Mary Garden was an opera singer who became a star in Paris before returning home to Chicago, where her performance of Salome apparently shocked even Al Capone. Whatever, McLean's perfume was clearly so successful that by 1910, the perfume house Rigaud launched their own Mary Garden.

And Rigaud created it for the most timeless of reasons. To allow ordinary people to experience an extraordinary world? *Please*. They needed to expand into the North American market, and since Mary was in her heyday with the Chicago Opera, it was judged she had the right mix of allure and respectability to appeal to a wide range of middle-class women. Think of her as the Sarah Jessica Parker of her day. Eventually, Rigaud exploited Mary Garden's name so ruthlessly that she was forced to take them to court, but let's not cloud her legacy, which was, quite simply, to pave the way for great moments in entertainer-endorsed fragrance.

Releasing a perfume is now a rite of passage for all zealously venal celebrities. Mary was the Emmeline Pankhurst of scented merchandise, and without her brave work, there would have been no Elizabeth Taylor's White Diamonds, which you'll recall spun off into Diamonds and Sapphires, then Diamonds and Emeralds, then Diamonds and Rubies . . . (Even now, somewhere in Bel Air, they're working on Diamonds and Prescription Painkillers.) There would have been no J-Lo Glow. No J-Lo Miami Glow. No Luciano Pavarotti's Luciano . . . Come to that, there would have been no Alan Cumming's Cumming. It had notes of whisky and Scots pine, and would eventually be supplemented by a body lotion, Cumming All Over You.

Nor would there have been some of the forgotten olfactory happenings of yesteryear, which – for whatever unfathomable reason – have failed to exert a lasting hold upon the world's nasal imagination. Forever Krystle, by Dynasty's Linda Evans. Mystique de Michael Jackson. Miss Piggy's 'Moi'.

But what of the actual product? Logically, you would assume that celebrity fragrances smelled like the celebrity themselves, and were designed with the ABC1s of the stalking community in mind. These people could simply drench their high-end inflatable Liz Taylor doll with the star's eponymous personal odour, then indulge in activity likely to cause chafing. They could indulge in it to a degree of authenticity that could only be bettered were the doll to rasp 'Use me! Use me!' into their ear.

Disappointingly, this is not the way stuff works. Which is a shame, because it happens to combine reckless consumer spending with crime prevention.[10]

In fact, celebrity fragrances smell of things like cedar and vanilla and the utter futility of all human existence. That's all irrelevant, though, because this is about something so much bigger than mere odour. This is about 'capturing the essence' of a celebrity. It is about allowing you to 'experience the magic' of that celebrity. Above all, it is about distilling that celebrity's 'philosophy' into the most cheaply manufactured, margin-maximising product that will still not actually cause permanent epidermal damage.

In short, it is about the marketing department making yet another pitch for their own specially dedicated circle of hell.[11]

And so it is that one boy-band singer launched his perfume with the declaration 'my philosophy is simple'. So, surprisingly, *not* a complex marrying of Aristotelian ethics with late

[10] Your loss, society.
[11] They currently occupy the eighth circle, sharing inferno space with the panderers and false prophets.

existentialism? 'I believe that the most important thing in the world is love,' his mission statement ran, 'especially the love of your family. I hope that one day we may have true peace on earth and that we can all help to make the world a better place for our children.' Wait! He left out wanting to work with animals. What does that smell of?

So too is it that P. Diddy's time-worn fragrance advertising motif has involved photographs of him pinning down a succession of dead-eyed women. One of them gets shoved up against a wall; another one is clamped over his knee. It's aspirational because it makes you think there's GHB in the bottle. It probably smells like victory, or, at the very least, like napalm in the morning.

Yet somehow, in a category all of their own, are the people behind Britney Spears's Fantasy. 'Britney Spears has the power of an enchantress,' their promotional literature explained, 'and her life is a modern-day fairy tale.'

Indeed it is. Grimm.


## Celebrity credit cards: Ushering in a golden age of stupidity

You know how entertainers are lodestars, and their mere association with a commodity is the absolute guarantee of quality? Well, it would seem some celebrities are no longer satisfied by simply sublimating their essence into a hair wax or a lunch box. These celebrities – liberators, in any real sense of the word – have bravely committed to crossing another Rubicon. They have actually put their name to financial products.

For reasons likely to secure all manner of people eternal damnation, celebrities tend to focus on prepaid debit cards, which banks and the like will tell you are 'well suited for consumers under-served by traditional financial institutions'. Or 'kids' for short.

Keen to ride this wave of teen enablement, self-effacing R&B star Usher chose 2004 to make an important announcement. 'As an entertainer,' ran his prologue, 'I make music for everyone, and I wanted the same mindset to apply to all my business ventures.' What followed confirmed that the rumours were true: democratised bump 'n' grinding would now come in prepaid debit card form. Or, to give its full title, in the form of the Usher Raymond IV Debit MasterCard.

The Usher card cost $15 to buy, $4.95 a month to maintain, and $3.95 each time you wanted to replenish it. Consumer watchdogs estimated that you could easily spend 20 per cent of your deposit on fees. But that seems cheap at the price, because it had a really snazzy picture of Usher on the front of it. And as a MasterCard spokesman pointed out, what the card was *really* about was giving Usher fans 'a great way to connect with their favourite entertainer'.

Connect with? Oh, MasterCard guy! Does the mirror crack when you look in it? Not that this arrant nonsense wasn't also being peddled by the great man himself. 'This gives them access to Usher world,' proclaimed Usher, opening up the dizzying possibility that when lonely, small-town-dwelling cardholders were paying for groceries, they were actually passing through some invisible portal into 'Usher World'. If any card could score you consequence-free sex with a string of women, this card was it. 'This,' Usher concluded triumphantly, 'is about empowering my fans.'

But of course it was. The sentiment was amplified by MasterCard executives, who stated that they hoped it would bring Usher fans into the 'financial mainstream'.

About time. For too long Usher fans had languished in the financial backwaters, denied the chance to be normal, profligate members of society simply because of their passion for almost elaborately unchallenging R&B. In fact, in so speaking, MasterCard conjured an image of Usher fans as a demonised band of fiscal outlaws, perhaps existing in the earth's catacombs, a bit like the rebels in *The Matrix*. The Usher Raymond IV Debit MasterCard would enable them to escape this existence, thereby ranking it if not above, then certainly alongside the polio vaccine, as one of the great emancipating advances of the past hundred years.

Naturally, Usher isn't alone in his quest to empower the financially disenfranchised. Celebrities from Carmen Electra to Hilary Duff have put their name to debit and credit cards, though the daddy of them all is, and you might already have had an inkling, the Kiss Platinum Visa Card – funding crazy, crazy nights since 1998.

You know what the Kiss Platinum Visa Card says about the person handing it over?

Yes. Yes, you do. And it's not that you are in possession of, as the promotional material would have it, 'the inside scoop on your favourite rock icons with monthly updates directly from the band'. It's not even that you 'proclaim your rock and roll passion whenever you use the card'. To be candid, it says that you are unlikely to trouble any Brains Trust meetings. And as such, it's an incredibly useful indicator. Banks and credit card firms want stupid customers, because they make money from their mistakes, and there are few better ways to gauge the stupidity of your customers than a celebrity-endorsed financial product.

'Mr Doe? Our records show you are an Usher Raymond IV debit card holder . . . In which case, I'd love to talk to you today about an exclusive opportunity we are extending toward you and other specially selected clients. Have you heard about these fantastic sub-prime mortgages . . .?'

## Sex tapes: thanks for sharing

Celebrity sex tapes. On the one hand, they're that little bit of extra access for the twenty-first-century fan. On the other, they're raising a whole generation of stalkers too lazy to do their own fantasising. In days of yore, a guy wondering what it would be like to have sex with Paris Hilton would have to use his imagination to get himself to that point where he decides to break into her home and take her hostage. These days, all he needs is an Internet download of the night-vision classic *One Night in Paris*. That, and the resilience to tolerate the director's elegiac commentary.

So where do celebrity sex tapes fit into the whole self-commoditisation game? Well, where once persons of high station would be introduced to society via mechanisms such as a debutante ball, or a role in a motion picture, it is now possible to be fast-tracked into the limelight just by performing fellatio in a memory-stickable format. Sex tapes are showreels. One no longer needs to hiss, 'Who did *she* screw to get ahead?' One already knows. One can purchase the box set.

To begin making sense of the phenomenon, we must revisit the work that started it all. Pamela Anderson and Tommy Lee's legendary honeymoon video may have been a small step for them, but it marked a giant leap in humankind's noble quest for knowledge. Specifically, knowledge about what celebrities look like when they're having sex. In 1995, Pamela and Tommy returned from their honeymoon with a richly textured, world-cinema-type record of their trip, and at some level, you sense Tommy Lee knew the tape was a totemic object of extraordinary power – an analogue Grail for which men would go to war. For which men would die.[12]

This is quite a burden for a drummer, and on his return Tommy made especially sure that he placed the Humpy Grail somewhere for safe keeping. Where? By his own account, he locked it into not merely a safe, but a 'five-hundred-pound monstrosity' safe. And that safe was not just in a cupboard. It was under a heavy carpet. And it was underground. And it was encased in . . . Look, remember the tomb in *Raiders of the Lost Ark*? It was basically like that, minus the rolling boulder.

Then one day, Tommy wakes up to discover that the inviolable underground chamber has been mysteriously violated – and the safe stolen *in its entirety*. The finger is swiftly pointed at an unnamed, never-to-be-traced former builder, who, according to

---

[12] Men would not die.

Tommy's character note, was 'an electrician who used to be a porn star' . . . But enough. The details of its theft were literally incredible.

Which brings us to the question: are we still pretending these things get stolen? Indeed we are, so each time you hear of another heist, you are formally obliged to imagine a young male freeze-framing his loot for the 327th time and thinking: this is my ticket out of the removals business. Failing that, at least admit the possibility that there could be a burglar at large in the greater Los Angeles area who only steals sex tapes, a sort of smut-seeking missile who leaves the rest of the lavishly equipped celebrity home untouched on each of his daring raids. The news networks like all villains to have a catchy name, so let's call our gentleman thief the Porn Panther.

In the meantime, though, there are sex tapes to be made, and it seems apposite to break off for a minute, and furnish any celebrity contemplating taking part in a sex tape with the definitive rules of the game.

1. Remember to press record. Obvious, you might think, but you'd be surprised how many celebrities have failed to land themselves a reality-show gig simply by forgetting to invade their own privacy. If you are under the age of twenty-five, this shouldn't present a problem, because anyone born after the year 1984 does not actually believe sex has taken place unless it has been recorded, at the very least on a mobile phone. Doing it on video is kind of like going to a fancy hotel.

2. Pick your moment. You need to be in a certain 'place' in your career. Namely, tanking. You don't see any A-list sex tapes out there, and that's not just because they have more sophisticated burglar alarms.

3. Set dressing. When a sex tape featuring Verne Troyer – aka Austin Powers's Mini-Me – hit the Internet, it revealed good use of props. In the background – and you seriously,

seriously didn't want to look at what was going on in the foreground – lay a casually placed volume entitled *The Power of the Actor*. Run that one through the sex tape parse-o-meter, and the meaning was clear. Mini-Me may have had a big tax bill to meet, but he was dedicated to his craft.

4. Lighting. Bad lighting is totally non-negotiable. You must submit to its unflattering ministrations, and make sure you adopt several uncomfortable-looking positions during the course of the shoot. This is a humanising exercise: seeing you all awkward and arrhythmic makes us feel better about our ugly, meaningless lives.

5. Commentary. A good commentary can lift a sex tape from a pedestrian also-ran to an instant classic. If you can't think of anything to say, just gloss the action taking place on camera, preferably in the most leadenly erotic manner. Stuff like 'You know you want to do *that*', or 'She's licking my –' Well, never mind what she's licking: for our purposes, she's bringing you to the attention of unscripted programming executives, who – if they like what they see – will welcome you into their endlessly versatile repertory company of fellow sex-tape alumni/dwarves/washed-up wrestlers/recidivist drug users/proven reality villains/racist bounty hunters. You've arrived.

6. Storage. On no account put the footage anywhere safe. Remember, you need to get this thing stolen. Do you know of a poorly secured set of storage units, payment upon which you could swiftly fall behind on, prompting the proprietor to prise open the shipping crate and find a single video cassette lying spotlit in the centre of the floor? Failing that, light-fingered decorators are a popular choice, but try and save them the bother of having to sift through your entire tape collection. You may want to mark it with a label reading 'My private sex tape, do not touch, keep out 4evah!!!!!!!' to help things along.

7.  Immediate aftermath. When the tape hits the news, accuse everyone of betraying you. This was between two people alone, an intensely private moment of night-vision humping and low-level humiliation/violation role play. How do you feel now? Well, you feel humiliated and violated.

8.  Distribution. Secure a prestigious distributor. The way things are going, there will soon be an annual industry marketplace for these things, a sort of meat-market version of the Cannes Film Festival[13] where the highest bidder can pick up the rights to new work. But for now, probably go with the guy who did Paris's one.

9.  Long-term aftermath. The crucial move, if you haven't done so already, is to split up with your co-star. Staying together is unthinkably tacky. No one wants to see a sequel; no one wants to see you two working at your relationship. They want to see you weeping fat tears in a TV interview and talking about betrayal. And about your new show. Because you'll most likely have one by then.

10. And finally, never, ever bother claiming that this was staged in some attempt at irony. There are those who think the celebrity sex-tape phenomenon has tipped over into social commentary – and they'd probably cite the Mini-Me sex tape as the moment the final curtain was rent. But can we agree that irony is *not* a get-out-of-jail-free card? A sex tape is not a 'satire' on the business of sex tapes. Note to Verne: you have not played The Man and won. If you need to get naked and screw in bad lighting to 'fool' a foul and rapacious media, then *you da fool, Mini-Me*! You da fool.

## The trade in celebrity body parts: Mary Shelley's nightmare?

Midnight, one Friday in early 2007, and every filament of a shorn head of hair was gathered in veneration from a barbershop floor

[13] What do you mean,'Cannes already *is* a meat market'?

in Los Angeles' San Fernando Valley. By the small hours, in the gloom of unlit alleys off Hollywood Boulevard, toothless men were dangling chemically over-treated tendrils while pawing at travellers' coin purses. 'Beholde the hair of troublede poppe princesse Brittanie Spearse!' they rasped, eyes glittering in their grime-streaked faces. 'Touch itte, wretchede sinneres, and be saved! In suche splitte endes thy salvation lieth!'

By the stealings of first light, other matted tresses were being offered for sale out of the back doors of Internet charnel houses. Some were sold strand by strand; some were alleged to be a full head of hair preserved intact. Each came with a poorly spelled certificate of authenticity.

Ever feel like some showbiz-fixated Martin Luther needs to start work on ninety-five theses *right now*? Ideally, our noble reformer would be preoccupied with the sale of celebrity indulgences and the foul idolatry of the trade in these saintly beings' cast-off body parts. His document would be nailed to the doors of eBay and various supermarket tabloids, who would in turn attempt to force its author to recant the more subversive declarations at whatever the magazine version of the Diet of Worms might be.[14]

Perhaps the author will refuse, causing dark voices to murmur that a schism in the Church of Celebrity is now inevitable.

We cannot be sure, but the trade in holy relics nonetheless grows ever more fevered. Not a week passes without some surplus cell matter formerly attached to an entertainment personality being auctioned – and with almost all the purchasers wishing to remain anonymous, a terrifying theory begins to form in the mind.

Could it be that they are one and the same person, an over-weening scientist who means to steal fire from the very showbiz gods? Could it be that he is hell-bent on accruing celebrity body parts, so that by some twisted procedure he may assemble them into a Frankenstein celebrity?

[14] Probably a new weight-loss fad.

Working simply on the basis of genuine auctions, this überbeast would have Britney's hair, Jack Nicholson's baby teeth and one of Elvis's warts. Its crudely sewn fingers would be tipped with Brad Pitt's toenail clippings, while its unholy moans would be sparked by trying to pass William Shatner's kidney stone (the latter went for $25,000, and might be regarded as crucial to the fiendish enterprise).

Even now, this creature could be tethered to a slab somewhere in the Hollywood Hills, sedated by prescription painkillers or just zoned out in front of *The Hills* like the rest of its generation.

But how soon before this composite celebrity breaks its bonds and causes its creator to flee in terror, having disowned his wretched spawn? How soon before it lumbers down the canyons into the showbiz capital of the world, in the misguided belief that it will be embraced by the degenerate society that facilitated its creation? Yet instead of being invited on to late-night talk shows, the creature will be treated with suspicion and horror. Wherever it turns, terrified townsfolk will attempt to stun it with Botox darts and refuse it work in the entertainment business (see also Courtney Love). Tormented and enraged, the monster will embark on a murderous spree, before vowing to hunt down his creator and kill him for the patchwork-bodied misery he has engendered.

Can you afford not to heed this Promethean fable, ye traders in Britney Spears hair? *Can you?*

Can any of us? Doomsayers have spun some pretty dystopian late-capitalist visions down the decades, but you have to think that 'a society trading in the cell matter of a borderline mental patient' could hold its own with the best of them.

Yet the trade in celebrity offcuts is just the logical progression from a marketplace in which billions of dollars of goods are sold every year simply on the basis that they are tenuously linked to persons involved in the entertainment industry. It's no different from the cowed, witless, hysterical and above all superstitious trade in purported saints' fingers and the like that gripped Europe for centuries, and in some cases continues to do so. Britney's hair is merely the Turin Shroud with a marginally less crazy backstory.

And in this *expandio ad absurdum* universe of celebrity products, a sex tape is merely the equivalent of a fragrance line for people further down the luxe rating scale. So where now for self-commoditisation and the slavering consumers who buy into it? After Shatner's kidney stone, you might think – or certainly pray – that there was nowhere left to go. But there's always somewhere to go. Think again of the concealed basement in that barrel Kiss keep scraping the bottom of, and prepare for the time you can knowingly purchase high-end celebrity sperm and eggs.

# CELEBRITY RELIGIONS

'... with something of the archangelic manner he told her how he had undertaken to show ... that all the mythical systems or erratic mythical fragments in the world were corruptions of a tradition originally revealed ...'

Mr Casaubon hints at his Key to All Mythologies,<br>from Middlemarch, by George Eliot

'Before I met Jeanine, my life was cosmically a shambles. I would use bits and pieces of whatever eastern philosophy would drift through my transom.'

David St. Hubbins, This is Spinal Tap

Mainstream religion is a party to which everyone is invited. Wolves lie down with lambs, princes mix with paupers, and as long as you're not gay, or into science or anything, you can be as humbly subordinate as the next speck of dust. Casting their eye over such a scene, however, any self-respecting celebrity would simply hiss 'Get off my coat' at the favela nun kneeling on their Dior, then screech the age-old question: 'Where the hell is the VIP room?'

Clearly, the whole specks-of-dust thing is incompatible with fame. A belief in the divine or supernatural may be sufficient for drones, but what happens if you yourself are seriously divine and undeniably supernatural? In short, what if you're a celebrity?

For you, traditional theological conundrums such as 'How can a loving god permit suffering?' will be superseded by far more perplexing ones. Like, how can you tell me I'm just another of God's creatures when a second-tier gossip magazine did an eight-page feature on my breasts? Which, by the way, He didn't even create.

Fortunately, there are holy facilities better suited to you. So, how do the worshipped worship? They worship pretty much the way they do everything else. They have dedicated VIP pews in which to do it. They spend a lot of money on it. They are constantly told how fabulous they are at it. And, crucially, they do not keep it private.

Isn't it striking how many celebrities effectively claim to have *personally* found the key to all mythologies? But unlike George Eliot's Mr Casaubon – a self-regarding poltroon with delusions of intellectual adequacy – they won't die leaving an incoherent jumble of stuff that had drifted through their transoms. On the contrary. By that stage they'll already have convinced countless people to join their competitively priced faiths, people who – despite being of infinitely lesser means, and wholly unworthy of the kind of benefits extended to famous adherents – will nonetheless be able to learn how water can cure cancer, how fear of blackmail can cure homosexuality, and how they'll have to pay back huge sums in 'course fees' if they want to leave.

You may take the view that all religions are full of tall tales – although it costs less to be lied to by most of them than it does to submit to the state-of-the-art bullshit-spreading technology deployed by Scientology, say, or the Kabbalah. You may decide there is much to enchant you in these faiths' cavalier blend of McWisdom and pyramid schemes. You may go as far as agreeing that there is nothing odd about a religion whose most famous church is called the Celebrity Centre. But above all, remember this: all the answers to absolutely everything in the entire universe lie within you, and the only person holding you back from finding those solutions is you.

So without further ado, let's get ready to pass beyond the

spiritual velvet rope. Please make sure you leave your prejudices with the coat-check girl.[1]

## Scientology: the religion with science right up there in the title

Our first port of celestial call is, inevitably, Scientology – the religion started by a man who once said: 'I'd like to start a religion. That's where the money is.'

Unless you have been trapped under something heavy in recent decades, you will no doubt be aware that Scientology is a many-storied thing. Yet while we could fill hundreds of pages with accounts of the money-making schemes, the grand-jury indictments, the secretive compounds, and the jaw-droppingly malicious houndings of people who have criticised the Church down the decades, we must limit our examination to the celebrity angle. We will, however, see how absolutely central to the enterprise its famous adherents are.[2]

We begin our potted history of the last 44 trillion years in 1952, because that's when science-fiction writer L. Ron Hubbard made the whole thing up.

In the interests of strictest accuracy, it all begins just a few years before that, when Hubbard devised a self-help technique called Dianetics. Alas, only a science-fiction magazine for which Hubbard had previously written stories would publish it at first,

[1] Along with your bank details.
[2] If you do want to find out even more about this delightful organisation, there are truly excellent resources out there, with special mention going to the dedicated Scientology debunkers of Operation Clambake, as well as the Rick A. Ross Institute, which is a mine of useful information and cautionary tales about all kinds of cults and kooky sects (and has much to yield on our other celebrity religion, the Kabbalah). Anyone intrigued enough to want a fuller picture should visit these organisations' encyclopedic websites – xenu.net and rickross.org – which contain huge volumes of forensically sourced material, news articles and whistle-blower testimony. Remember to come up for air every couple of hours.

but eventually his technique developed sufficient traction on readers' imaginations for it to be codified in a book of the same name. *Dianetics* became a best-seller in the United States. It introduced the idea of auditing, a sort of cod psychiatry whereby painful memories, or 'engrams', were 'eliminated' by being brought up in a two-person question-and-answer session. The ultimate goal of auditing was to get a person to go 'clear' of these engrams. If they forked out hundreds of dollars, anyone could be 'professionally certified' as an auditor, and immediately begin treating troubled people. It's fair to say Hubbard thought he was on to something. In fact, he claimed that 'the creation of Dianetics is a milestone for man comparable to his discovery of fire and superior to his inventions of the wheel and the arch'.

Others were marginally less impressed, with *Consumer Reports* (the US equivalent of *Which?* magazine) warning in 1951 that Hubbard's claims were 'unsupported by evidence or facts', that 'abuse of intimacies and confidences' was a possibility, and that Dianetics was 'a cult without professional traditions'. *Look* magazine described Dianetics adherents as 'the usual lunatic fringe types, frustrated maiden ladies who have worked their way through all the available cults, young men whose homosexual engrams are all too obvious'.

Hubbard cast all criticism as evidence that he was a CIA target.

Other stuff to know? He loathed psychiatrists, and appears to have had a lifelong aversion to paying tax. When lieutenants in his fast-expanding organisation displeased him, or he thought someone might have given his horribly downtrodden second wife the eye, he informed the FBI they were communists. FBI files show one agent deemed him to be a 'mental case', a judgement seemingly supported by the headlines which surrounded his second divorce. 'CULT FOUNDER ACCUSED OF TOT KIDNAP', '"DIANETIC" HUBBARD ACCUSED OF PLOT TO KIDNAP WIFE' – that kind of thing.

But we move on. On, in fact, to the birth of Scientology, which took place in Phoenix in 1952. Scientology was Dianetics's Great Leap Forward – Hubbard's decision to elevate it from an earthly self-help system into the realms of a religion. Assisted by a new machine he called the E-meter – a crude lie-detector device – Hubbard invented an entire cosmology, a story which he would add to and embellish over the years.

Indeed, somewhat sluggishly, it took him until 1967 to discover the secrets to the universe, on a trip to South America. These secrets appear to have been conveniently enshrined in portable document form – though the mission was apparently fraught with peril. 'Somehow or other I brought it off, and obtained the material and was able to live through it,' wrote Hubbard, a man given to portentous obfuscation. 'I am very sure that I was the first one that ever did live through any attempt to obtain that material.' He did, however, claim to have broken his back, knee and arm in the acquisition of this knowledge.

You are about to be told those very secrets, but do be aware that were you to become a Scientologist, you would have to achieve the level of Operating Thetan III before they were entrusted to you. You would also have to have spent tens of thousands – maybe hundreds of thousands – and even then would have to be invited by more advanced Scientologists who deem you ready. The Church gives the secrets to you in a manila envelope and you have to sign a waiver promising never to reveal its contents. In 1995, somebody broke that promise, which is how you come to be reading about them today.

A warning: Scientologists believe that if you come into contact with this stuff before you're spiritually ready, you could die *just from reading it.*

DISCLAIMER: The publishers and author of this book will not be held responsible if you die in a few sentences' time. Or even if you become short of breath.

OK, here goes. Seventy-five million years ago, the intergalactic tyrant Xenu had an overpopulation problem on the twenty-six stars and seventy-six planets over which he had dominion. So, aided by some psychiatrists, Xenu rounded up 13.5 trillion of his alien people under the pretext that their income taxes were to be inspected.[3] He then paralysed his subjects, froze them in a mixture of alcohol and glycol to crystallise their souls, and deported them to Earth (which was then called Teegeeack). They travelled in spaceships which looked almost exactly like late-1960s-era DC-8s. When they got to Earth, they were dumped around volcanoes – volcanoes which were promptly blown up with hydrogen bombs, which scattered their radioactive souls, or thetans. But those souls didn't escape. No, sir. They were snared in electronic traps set by Xenu, and brainwashed by a 3-D movie they had to watch for thirty-six days. All sorts of false memories were implanted in them, and when the Thetans finally got to stop watching the movie they clustered in groups of a few thousand, and occupied the bodies of the few aliens who had survived the atomic blast. These body Thetans still stalk the world, causing untold misery.

So . . . hopefully you're now clear on the secrets of the universe. If you are experiencing feelings of death, please consult a physician.

You might have spotted the odd loose end, like: whatever happened to Xenu? He is currently held captive in a mountain, penned in by a force field powered by an everlasting battery. The mountain is sometimes said to be in the Pyrenees, but Hubbard wasn't specific. Maybe Xenu's in Tora Bora with bin Laden – we just don't know.

That's about all the basics we have space for, but there are so many other fun things to find out about Scientology. If you need a few pointers, you could read up on how the Church once had its own fleet of ships. They now retain just the one cruise liner, *Freewinds*, though it was quarantined in Curaçao in 2008 due to an asbestos problem they don't seem very keen to talk about. You might also care to gen up on the Guardian's Office, which

[3] Psychiatrists and tax inspectors have always been the enemies of Scientology. You may be developing your own theories as to why.

can only be described as Scientology's black-ops sector. From this nerve centre the Church masterminded Operation Snow White, its attempt to purge unfavourable records about Hubbard from government offices, the revenue service, foreign embassies and private organisations, via wiretapping, burglary and infiltration. Among other methods. Then there was Operation Freakout, which was an attempt to have a journalist who had written an unfavourable exposé of the faith committed to a mental institution. Their campaign of harassment included successfully framing and having her indicted for sending bomb threats. The FBI only discovered the fit-up when they raided the Guardian's Office in the course of investigating Operation Snow White. Eleven senior Scientologists were convicted and sent to prison.

Scientologists today will tell you that the Guardian's Office was just a rogue unit, long ago disbanded. What they won't tell you is that the rogue unit was run by Hubbard's third wife, Mary Sue, and that Hubbard was named a 'non-indicted co-conspirator'. Mary Sue served five years, but they remained married until his death in 1986.[4]

You might also be diverted by the tale of how the Church of Scientology's obsessive litigation contributed to driving into insolvency the Cult Awareness Network, a US organisation which provided information on cults, as well as referrals for counselling and support. They were extremely critical of Scientology. In 1996, the Church of Scientology bought the CAN in bankruptcy court and retained the name. Today, if you ring the Cult Awareness Network for advice on Scientology, it is highly likely you are speaking to a Scientologist.[5]

For now, though, it's time to turn our attention back to the Church as a whole, and ask: has it always been so adorably starstruck?

---

[4] When, incidentally, Hubbard was on the run from a massive tax investigation.
[5] Don't ring the Cult Awareness Network.

## Yes. Take your seats for 'Project Celebrity'

Remarkably early on, Hubbard began hatching plans to court celebrities as a means of publicising and legitimising his new religion. In fact, if we were using the six-day Christian creation story as an analogy, L. Ron created celebrity endorsement on the second day. He even had a name for it – 'Project Celebrity' – and he went public with the scheme in 1955 in the Scientology newsletter *Ability*.

'If we are to do anything about the society at large,' he explained to his followers, 'we must do something about its communication lines. One of the parts of this plan is Project Celebrity . . . It is obvious what would happen to Scientology if prime communicators benefitting from it would mention it now and then.'

If only he'd thought to add 'though maybe not while jumping dementedly all over Oprah's couch'.

Still, at the time, Hubbard had very clear plans about how Project Celebrity should be put into action. 'Herein you find a list of celebrities,' he wrote – and we'll come to this hilarious catalogue shortly. Suffice it to say, Hubbard knew how to aim high. 'If you want one of these,' he continued of the featured names, 'write us at once, giving the ONE celebrity you have selected. We will then allocate this person to you as your game.'

His following instructions contrived to combine three of the essential characteristics of the Scientology operation: lunacy, doggedness many would class as harassment, and the extraction of funds from its disciples on the vague promise that they will be returned manifold times over, at some unspecified point down the line, via some unspecified process. All spelling and grammatical errors are very much *sic*.

'Having been awarded one of these celebrities,' Hubbard boomed via the pages of *Ability*, 'it will be up to you to learn what you can about your quarry and then put yourself at every hand across his or her path, and not permitting discouragements or "no's" or clerks or secretaries to intervene, in days or weeks or months, to bring your celebrity into a formal auditing session and deliver an amount of good auditing necessary to (1) make him much more effective, and (2) make him aware of the benefits of Scientology on the Third Dynamic.

'Finance, your pay, your expenses on this hunt are up to you. Obviously, at whatever future date, the investment will repay itself some dozens of times.'

Obviously. Was there anything in it for you in the meantime? 'If you bring one of these home, you will get a small plaque as your reward.'

Too kind. And so to Hubbard's list of suitable personages. They ranged from the sublime – Greta Garbo, John Ford, Jimmy Stewart, Walt Disney – to the ridiculous – Orson Welles, Ernest Hemingway, Pablo Picasso. Positively littering the list are people one can scarcely imagine being less receptive to Hubbard's kooky ideas. Groucho Marx. Legendary CBS newscaster Ed Murrow. Ed Murrow! Try and imagine him smoking his way through a piece-to-camera where he explains the bit about the intergalactic alien tyrant being imprisoned in a mountain by a force field ... Goodnight, Ed, but it seems you're the one in need of the good luck.

## The Celebrity Centre: if you build it, they will come

It may not send you into anaphylactic shock to learn that Hubbard was unable to recruit quite the calibre of notable personalities he had aimed for in those heady, early days. In its first incarnation, then, Project Celebrity cannot be deemed a success. Groucho never submitted to the all-seeing E-meter, and Jimmy Stewart never took the opportunity of a promotional interview to alert his fans to the menace of 'engrams'. However, by the late sixties the Church of Scientology was richer than ever. Why? Because when people do good in the world, unlimited wealth flows back towards them.

No, hang on – its coffers were overflowing because you have

to pay to worship. Or rather, you have to pay even to learn how you should be worshipping. The point is, it was time to try a new tack, and in 1969, the Scientology high command opened a new church on Franklin Avenue in Los Angeles, in a vast former hotel building resembling a cross between a French chateau and a fairy-tale castle. It was to be the Church's first Celebrity Centre.

But would a dedicated place of worship for the rich and famous not ring alarm bells with the armies of drone-believers that could only press their noses up against the glass of such places – or at best, be employed to keep it clean? Not unless they were, in the idiosyncratic parlance of Scientology, a Suppressive Person displaying an Overt. 'The world is carried on the backs of a desperate few,' was one of Hubbard's favourite pronouncements.

'Unfortunately,' today's Celebrity Centre website expands, 'it is these desperate few who are often the most neglected. It is for this reason that L. Ron Hubbard saw to the formation of a special Church of Scientology which would cater to these individuals – the artists, politicians, leaders of industry, sports figures and anyone with the power and vision to create a better world. That church is Celebrity Centre International.'

Oh, right . . . the 'desperate few' are *celebrities*! That makes sense. When *are* rich, high-profile members of the entertainment industry going to catch a break?

'There's no shame in helping the artist,' was Hubbard's justification. 'In fact, in the larger scope of societal help, we had better help the artist if we wish to advance the society at all. He operates in a rank in advance of science as to the necessities and requirements of man.'

You hear that? The movies of John Travolta have done more for humanity than science itself. Even *Look Who's Talking Too*. That beats the discovery of penicillin hands down.

Today, the Los Angeles Celebrity Centre is just one of eight star-specific facilities, after others were opened in cities such as New York, Paris and London. Tricked out like a rococo palazzo, though, the LA original still draws the most stars, and on its roof it genuinely carries a huge sign reading 'Celebrity Centre'. You know what they say: if something sits there long and unabashedly enough, eventually it begins to feel normal.

## I'd like to thank my auditor: celebrity endorsement of the Celebrity Centre

In order to promote itself, the Celebrity Centre uses testimonials from notable adherents such as Kelly Preston, wife of John Travolta. At first glance, these interviews look like standard magazine fare. We hear about Kelly's forthcoming movies, her past achievements, how great she's looking. Then we learn how it wasn't always like this, how she made some bad lifestyle choices in her teens, and how a nice Scientologist acting coach impressed her.

Then, almost out of nowhere, comes a question about a quasi-scientific-sounding process Kelly undertook soon after beginning her Scientology journey. But what is this 'Purification Rundown Procedure'? Well, it's a 'detoxification programme' devised by Hubbard – and it is weapons-grade nonsense even by his own exacting standards. The Church itself described it as 'a combination of exercise, vitamins, nutrition and sauna use', designed to shift 'drug residues and other toxins from the fatty tissue so that these substances can then be eliminated by the body'. Hardly scientific, you may be thinking, but pretty standard alternative health fare. Except that it involves huge doses, of, among other things, niacin and cooking oil, and very lengthy shifts in very hot saunas. The cooking oil 'replaces' the contaminated body fat which is being flushed out, and the niacin . . . OK, you need to stay with this. The niacin is supposed to cause everything from stomach complaints to anxiety to childhood sunburns to radiation exposure and cancer to flare up again, and then be 'run out' of the body.

Keep reminding yourself: it's the religion with science in the title.

This kind of 'purification' is not an especially difficult illusion to pull off – niacin, in worryingly high dosages, is likely to cause skin flushes and so on, leading a credulous Scientologist to believe, in contravention of all scientific laws and evidence, that epidermal damage incurred decades ago is somehow being brought back to the surface. And if that doesn't get you, dizzyingly long stretches in a sauna on a strong, unfamiliar and potentially toxic cocktail of supplements should do the trick.

This is not to be glib. It may go without saying that the Purification Rundown Procedure has been condemned by a welter of toxicology experts, as well as America's National Council Against Health Fraud, who opted to point out that the programme achieved 'the exact opposite of what Hubbard's theory predicts'.

But what does John Travolta's wife have to say about it? 'I had heard some of the results of it and thought it made so much sense,' Kelly begins promisingly, in some fancy literature to promote the faith. 'I heard about how it could improve your happiness, your memory, your career. There was also mention of the fact that it gets radiation out of the body – having been born and raised in Hawaii and having been in the sun a lot, you know, it all made sense.'

It did? Maybe she still had sunstroke.

'Then there were also all the different chemicals and drugs I was aware I had been exposed to, not to mention all of the drugs I had done years ago. All that together with the desire to handle myself and get all of this out of my system made me want to do the Purification Rundown.'

And here's what happened when she submitted to it.

'What was really cool was the running out of certain drugs. It was like, "Oh my, what's that?" I would never have thought that all these drugs and toxins would have stayed in my body and that they still could be having an effect on me. But they had and they were coming out of my system and that was really wild.'

Also, insane.

'Seeing sunburns I had had fifteen years ago turn on and come out! I remember clearly the time when I was seven years old, I had this bathing suit that I thought was so cool – with holes in the sides and a hole in the center – and I got a sunburn in it. And then, fourteen years later, while doing the Purification Rundown, I had the exact same sunburn turn on and "come out".'

But apart from the final slide into Scientology's mendacious embrace, were there any other long term benefits? 'The Purification Rundown heightened my senses greatly,' concludes Kelly. 'Colors became brighter, my hearing more acute, everything tasted better and I felt more focused. Life became more vibrant, more alive and more vital. I was happier, lighter, brighter. Things became more effortless. Wow!'

Wow indeed.


## Tom Cruise. Where do you even start?

Gingerly, then, very gingerly, to Scientology's most famous face. Everyone knows Tom Cruise is a Scientologist, but there was a time when we knew it less alarmingly, if you will. There was a time when someone could say the name 'Tom Cruise', without one's first thought being 'crazy man'. There was a time when the image of a black polo-necked Tom laughing maniacally and repeating the mantra 'KSW – Keep Scientology Working' was not branded onto the retina of an entire generation of YouTubers.

That time was during the years that the formidable Hollywood operator Pat Kingsley served as his publicist. Presumably all too aware of her client's . . . idiosyncrasies, would you call them? . . . Kingsley ran Tom's media operation for fourteen years with meticulous care and not inconsiderable force. She once told an interviewer that it would be 'un-American' to ask him about his faith. With incredible skill, she managed to preserve his image as an intensely enthusiastic, but basically likeable guy. The kind of guy Katie Holmes, the actress who gave us wholesome little Joey on TV's *Dawson's Creek*, might have had a poster of on her bedroom wall.

But you really can't keep a lid on Cruise's brand of nutty

forever, and in 2004 Tom ended his relationship with Kingsley and installed his sister LeAnne – a fellow Scientologist – as his publicist.

You may as well regard this as year zero in terms of the emergence of the Cruise you know today. The one who surfs sofas. The one who derides women suffering from post-natal depression. The one whose public behaviour caused the owner of Paramount to sever his studio's fourteen-year relationship with the actor's production company. The one who married wholesome little Joey from TV's *Dawson's Creek* and arranged for her to be fitted with Church-approved companions all of her own.

Though he eventually returned to more conventional representation, Tom had by that stage begun to speak about Scientology in every interview. As for the stuff he was coming out with . . . well, the most tactful way to summarise it is to say that people retrospectively held even more respect for Kingsley.

The *War of the Worlds* promotional tour had the flavour of a Scientology roadshow, at which the movie's director Steven Spielberg was an increasingly awkward spectator. One particularly edifying episode found the director and his star in Germany, with the respected German newspaper *Der Spiegel* enquiring as to why Tom had insisted Scientology tents were set up on set to 'assist' the cast and crew.

'The tent of a sect at someone's working place still seems somewhat strange to us,' the paper began delicately. 'Mr Spielberg, did that tent strike you as unusual?' 'I saw it as an information tent,' came Spielberg's somewhat forced reply.

Cruise evidently disagreed. 'The volunteer Scientology ministers were there to help the sick and injured,' he explained, conjuring up an image of the *War of the Worlds* set as having been some kind of field hospital.

'Do you see it as your job to recruit new followers for Scientology?' the paper asked.

'I'm a helper,' replied Cruise, with the aggressive faux humility that was becoming his calling card. 'For instance, I myself have helped hundreds of people get off drugs. In Scientology, we have the only successful drug rehabilitation programme in the world. It's called Narconon.'

'That's not correct,' countered *Der Spiegel*. 'Yours is never mentioned among the recognised detox programmes. Independent experts warn against it because it is rooted in pseudoscience.'

'You don't understand what I am saying,' bristled Tom. 'It's a statistically proven fact that there is only one successful drug rehabilitation programme in the world. Period.'

'With all due respect,' was the reporter's exquisitely polite rejoinder, 'we doubt that.'

This little exchange is an almost unique attempt to challenge, to their face, a celebrity Scientologist's espousal of 'statistically proven facts'. Time and again, you will hear this lie repeated about Narconon, the Church's drug rehabilitation programme.[6] Kirstie Alley is the poster girl, and she can be found on podiums around the world parroting its claim to have a success rate of over 70 per cent – while not a single piece of verifiable evidence of such a claim has ever been published by the Church. Public health bodies and addictions specialists who have investigated it have branded it entirely lacking in methodology, without scientific basis, potentially dangerous and a thinly disguised recruiting scheme. Still, Crazy Tom Cruise and someone who used to be in *Cheers* reckon it works, so who are the experts to argue?

### Cruise: the next chapter. In which some videos are leaked, and hilarity ensues

By 2008 things seemed to have settled down. Tom and wholesome little Joey had a toddler daughter together, and neither mother nor child appeared to be openly attempting to escape when they were seen in public places.

---

[6] Saunas and vitamins again, for our science buffs.

And then came the videos. In early 2008 – around the publication of Andrew Morton's unauthorised biography of Tom Cruise, funnily enough – a series of leaked video clips hit the Internet, featuring Tom Cruise talking about Scientology and attending Church functions. They swiftly went viral, despite the Scientologists' fearsome efforts to cow host sites into removing them. Many rolled over, but the determined refusal of the high-traffic Gawker.com meant the genie was out of the bottle, and these internal Church films will be available to view online for all eternity, or at least until Scientology has rid the planet of Suppressive Persons and/or the Internet.

The clips combined two distinct functions. First, they offered a revealing glimpse into the kind of highly produced material with which new Scientology recruits are bombarded. And second, they pretty much dispelled those baseless rumours of Cruise's sanity once and for all.

Yes, despite the fact – fact! – that the Scientologists can 'cure' homosexuality, it appears that they are far from locating the antidote to crazy. And so it was that viewers were invited to watch as Tom explained why Scientologists are 'the authority' on everything from the mind to emergency triage; to weep gently as he blinded them with cod scientific terms; and to whoop sarcastically at footage showing him receiving the Church's Freedom Medal of Valor for Achievement in the Field of Excellence.[7]

Crucially, no one who was intended to see these videos – nor the tens of millions that weren't – could now be in any doubt how central Tom Cruise is to Scientology. He is a key part of its efforts to win converts, to legitimise itself, and to continue its expansionist mission. He was described by the Church's leader David Miscavige as 'the most dedicated Scientologist I know' in the award ceremony – and he was clearly stepping it up a gear.

[7] With that many abstract nouns, it must be important, right?

## When Tom Cruise went to Ground Zero

All of which brings us to what one of the clips described sonorously as 'The Mr Cruise response to 9/11'. 'If he takes a stand,' boomed the video's narrator, 'it's pedal to the metal till the finish line, as in helping New York firemen. He first saw the dust and heard the cough when descending to the ruins, where he bolstered morale among firemen. The devastation had spread an unprecedented combination of toxins through the air – and it was lethal.' Then it's over to Cruise. 'The EPA came out and said the air was clean,' the actor tells the camera. 'Of course, as a Scientologist, you go, "That's a lie, an outright lie . . ." You know, you just go, "Liar. Fine."'

'He personally saw to the establishment of a first New York Hubbard Detox Project,' the narrator barks. 'And no: he did not ask permission.' Permission from who? Congress? His carer?

The reality is even stranger. In 2002, Tom Cruise co-founded the New York Rescue Workers Detoxification Project, a facility two blocks from Ground Zero, in which firefighters and others who had inhaled smoke after the attack on the Twin Towers would be given the Purification Rundown. The project – or Downtown Medical as it is also known – remains in existence, and hundreds of thousands of dollars in public funding have been directed its way – largely thanks to the ministrations of a city council member later rebuked by Mayor Michael Bloomberg for having accepted $100,000 campaign money from the Church of Scientology.[8]

But Downtown Medical was set up by Tom to help rescue workers, and by all accounts – or, more accurately, its own account – the results were theatrically spectacular. 'Patients have had black paste coming out of their pores in the sauna,' the president of the 'clinic' states on its website. 'Their sweat has stained towels purple, blue, orange, yellow, and black. They have reported bowel movements that are blue, or green, or that

[8] Please take two and two and make four.

have smelled like smoke – despite the fact that they had not been at a fire scene for months.' One participant is pictured holding a blue-stained towel, while the website goes on to report that 'glass shards' have been observed to be leaving the pores of participants. Nowhere is Scientology mentioned – and nowhere are the 'miracle findings' backed up by independent studies.

Is any of this actually harmful, you may be wondering, or just the kind of placebo one could hardly begrudge any of the rescue workers who had lived through the hell of 9/11? Well, in addition to the potential dangers of ingesting large quantities of niacin, New York Fire Department officials told the *New York Times* that the Purification Rundown required firefighters to stop using inhalers prescribed by proper doctors to help with respiratory problems, as well as other medication such as blood pressure pills and, naturally, antidepressants.

'This is a very hard battle to win,' the fire department's exasperated deputy chief medical officer told the *New York Times*. 'It's not our job to say [to the firefighters] you can't go. All we can do is say there's no proven evidence it works.'

Even examined dispassionately, Downtown Medical seemed to be pushing the vanity projects of celebrity Scientologists into dangerous new territory. Say what you like about Travolta's staggeringly ill-advised obsession with bringing Hubbard's novel *Battlefield Earth* to the screen, it didn't have the potential to actually damage anyone who submitted to it. Not physically, anyway. Those of us who sat through the dialogue carry our scars inside.

But perhaps the most disturbing thing about Cruise's pet project is the manner in which it addresses one of LRH's own directives – 'Casualty Contact'.

In his fascinating biography, *Bare Faced Messiah*, Russell Miller reproduces a chilling communiqué issued by Hubbard, in which he advised ambitious auditors to clip from the newspapers every story featuring people 'who have been victimised one way or the other by life'.

'One takes every daily paper he can get his hands on and cuts from it every story whereby he might have a preclear,' Hubbard instructs his disciples. 'As speedily as possible he makes a personal call on the bereaved or injured person. [. . .] He should represent himself to the person or the person's family as a minister whose compassion was compelled by the newspaper story concerning the person. [. . .] A great many miracles will follow in his wake and he is liable to become a subject of the press himself. However, in handling the press he should simply say that it is a mission of the church to assist those who are in need of assistance. He should avoid any lengthy discussions of Scientology and should talk about the work of ministers and how all too few ministers these days get around to places where they are needed.'

Elsewhere, Hubbard expanded upon the idea, suggesting auditors should trawl hospitals for new recruits.

'Don't pick on the very bad off [*sic*] unconscious cases,' he advised. 'Hit the fracture ward and the maternity ward. Go around and say hello to the people and ask if you can do anything for them. [. . .] This is a pretty routine drill really. You get permission to visit. You go in and give patients a cheery smile. You want to know if you can do anything for them, you give them a card and tell them to come around to your group and really get well, and you give them a touch assist if they seem to need it but only if they're willing. [. . .] Its [*sic*] straight recruiting!'

Why does this call to mind the appearance of Scientology 'volunteer ministers' at Ground Zero, or in New Orleans after Hurricane Katrina? In recent years, the Church has become increasingly visible at high-profile disaster sites, setting up conspicuous yellow tents often enlivened by special appearances by their celebrity adherents. Within these tents they administer 'touch assists', a sort of laying on of hands that is presumably underpinned by some impeccable Hubbard science.

Of course, the Church and these volunteer ministers state that they are only there to help, though some aid agencies at Ground

Zero voiced concern that they displayed their leaflets around the disaster site, and were operating in the restricted area without authorisation until this was pointed out to the police, who then denied them access. Two days after the tragedy, and presenting themselves as an organisation called National Mental Health Assistance, representatives of the Church of Scientology duped Fox News into running the Church's freephone number for *five hours* on the bottom of the screen, apparently in the belief that it was the official outreach hotline. Fox News removed it after an irate intervention from the National Mental Health Association.[9]

'The public needs to understand that the Scientologists are using this tragedy to recruit new members,' Michael M. Faenza, the president of the National Mental Health Association said in 2001. 'They are not providing mental health assistance.'

Yet apart from sugaring its stealth recruitment drives, Cruise's wattage remains far from underused on other fronts. In fact, the Church must be delighted at the fancy places their best-known Operating Thetan takes them. In June 2003, Tom was given face time with Dick Cheney's chief of staff to discuss Scientology-related matters, suggesting even the Hollywood-averse Bush administration couldn't resist his charms. Also in 2003, he was granted a meeting with the then Deputy Secretary of State, Richard Armitage, to which he brought along the head of the LA Celebrity Centre. On the agenda: 'human rights abuses' of Scientologists in Germany, where the Church is deemed by the government to be a moneymaking enterprise that preys on the vulnerable. And what do you know? In 2007, the State Department actually intervened, claiming that Germany's monitoring of the organisation did amount to violating human rights. The cosmopolitan Mr Cruise lobbied Nicolas Sarkozy along similar lines when the latter was French finance minister.

Income-boosting capabilities aside, then, Tom Cruise is exceptionally useful to the Church of Scientology because he is

[9] The number was 800-FOR-TRUTH. Well done, Fox News! *No one* could have smelled that rat.

able to open doors – doors that ought to remain closed, but which barely need pushing if you're famous enough. Yet it's hard to escape the suspicion that Cruise is most valuable to the Church as a recruiting sergeant. As the *International Scientology News* has been good enough to declare: 'Every minute of every hour someone reaches for LRH technology . . . simply because they know Tom Cruise is a Scientologist.'

## Kabbalah: not Jewish. Not even Jewishish

Light up your spirituality-scented candles, gird your wrists with $26 red string bracelets, and prepare to accept the mystery of Kabbalah – the Pepsi to Scientology's Coke.

Whichever way you slice it, the Kabbalah is the johnny-come-lately of luxury faiths. Sure, a whole army of irate, eminent Jewish scholars and rabbis will quibble that the Kabbalah is in fact a centuries-old discipline of Judaism, one whose mysteries are so complex that Orthodox Jews may only begin contemplating them after years of dedicated study. In fact, it's difficult to imagine a faith less suited to those fly-by-nights of the entertainment industry. Imagine these searchers' delight, then, when someone bowdlerised it into a commercialised, non-denominational mysticism that even the star of *Dude, Where's My Car?* can understand.

That someone was former New York insurance salesman Philip Berg, who, with his wife Karen, and latterly his sons Michael and Yehuda, have built Kabbalah 2.0 into the star-humping empire of overpriced accessories and fake Judaism you see before you today.

By his own account, Mr Berg has a lively CV. He claims he and his mentor used Kabbalah to 'control' the events that gave Israel victory in the Six Day War. He declines to name the organisation that awarded him his PhD. He awarded himself the title of 'the Rav', which allows for even Philip to refer to himself in the third person with a bonus definite article.

Alas, it's fair to say that Orthodox Jewish figures have often been less than enthusiastic about the pop-culture version of this most ancient of disciplines. Rabbi Adin Steinsaltz, an eminent authority on the Talmud and Kabbalah, has described the connection between Berg's Kabbalah and the genuine article as comparable to 'the relationship between pornography and love'.

Let's get in close for the money shot.

Kabbalah shares some similarities you might expect with Scientology – the pseudoscience, the centralised power, the expensive courses, the huge property empire. No fleet, as yet – but it would be nice to think the Bergs are working on it. And, of course, like Scientology it offers you 'the tools' to live an unimaginably full life by protecting yourself against the evil eye of suppressive persons using secret technology of light and rays and chanting and science and magic string and candles made to Moses's special formula[10] and promises of immortality and of cancer-curing miracles and expensive pilgrimages and weird rituals and whatever. That's only slightly paraphrased. There's some stuff about the evil of masturbation thrown in too, but which of us has the strength?

Of course, the Kabbalah Centre does also differ markedly with Scientology. You are openly advised to tithe them 10 per cent of your income. And whereas Hubbard layered pseudoscience upon pseudoscience, the Kabbalah Centre is more likely to explain away contradictions with a metaphorical wave of the hand and vague references to something called 'the light'.

In one sense, though, its stratagems for parting you from your money are more audaciously simple than Hubbard's cosmic con. Whereas some might be daunted by the amount of study Scientology requires, the Bergs found a hilarious solution. Those wishing to study Kabbalah are told it is essential to buy the twenty-three-volume *Zohar* – price: $415 – but the good news is

[10] Yes, apparently Moses had a sideline making scented candles. Who knew?

you have absolutely no need of being able to read it in either Aramaic or the Hebrew into which it has been translated. 'You don't need to read it,' Karen Berg explains in one instructional video. 'It's like scanning the price in the supermarket – same principle. All you need is the energy from the letters.'

You hear that? You just need to look at some indecipherable characters and the benefits will come. As for these benefits, they're pretty much what you'd expect from a really expensive, really cheap-looking set of mass-produced books. 'The *Zohar* is not merely paper and ink,' runs the Kabbalah Centre's product description. 'It's the truth, and as such is alive with divine energy and is the ultimate instrument for generating miracles. An amazing number of people have reported them just from housing a copy of it in their home. By simply possessing the books, power, protection, and fulfillment came into their lives. You may find that hard to believe, but that's before you owned a set. Have one delivered today and see what we're talking about.'[11]

As we will find out, Madonna presented Shimon Peres with a volume of the *Zohar* during a visit to Israel. Switch on the news and behold the difference it made to that troubled region.

## Get me *names*: the celebrification of the Kabbalah

It was not ever thus. When the Kabbalah Centre opened the doors of its LA outpost in 1984, the task of sparkling itself up looked gargantuan. Scientology was the voguish Hollywood religion, and even given celebrity weakness for any self-appointed guru who might blow through the greater Los Angeles area, you'd have placed the Bergs' chances of gaining lasting purchase on the credulous entertainer market at slim-to-none. You'd have been wrong.

In many ways, Kabbalah is the Little System of Bullshit That Could. Its star-studded, multimillion-dollar success reminds us

[11] Mind if I *don't*?

that if you are truly enterprising, there is always, *always* a market for fast-tracking rich people in the vague direction of heaven, particularly if you exempt them from the inconvenience of having to go near the eye of a needle.

But back in the day, what our parvenu religion needed more than anything were some high-profile spokesmodels to draw in the paying drones. The Bergs are not what you'd call 'marketable' people. Even their kids lack the qualities you'd look for in a messiah – and with Yehuda once being described by *Vanity Fair* as 'a bearlike, somewhat insecure-seeming man in a yarmulke', a brand-association miracle was required.

Enter Sandra Bernhard. The comedian – and long-time friend of Madonna – began attending the LA Kabbalah Centre in the mid-1990s, and in retrospect is the celebrity who bore witness to the real Kabbalah messiah, Her Madjesty herself. Think of Sandra as Kabbalah's John the Baptist figure. The analogy is certainly no less religiously confused than most of the Centre's teachings. Before the decade was out, Sandra had persuaded Madonna to experience the Kabbalah experience for herself. Could the Bergs possibly have been any luckier? In terms of faith-advertising paydirt, Madonna's mere presence at the Kabbalah Centre says: 'I was raised a Catholic but I once frolicked with a black Jesus on an altar in a video. Stigmata were involved. These days I like to crucify myself in concerts and I've dabbled in more dumbed-down mysticism than you've taken public-transport journeys. But then I found Kabbalah, and *it worked for me.*'

Perhaps most astoundingly, though, Madonna has been instrumental in casting this hotchpotch of hocus-pocus, cherry-picked fake Judaism and sharp business practice as the sceptic's faith.

'Religion is not asking questions,' she countered sternly when an interviewer described Kabbalah as a religion. 'What I call "religious thinking" is not asking questions.' Wait . . . Madonna thought she'd been asking *questions*? Mmm. Questions Madonna didn't ask of the Kabbalah Centre are things like: Would you mind if I took a look at your accounts? Why does the packaging of the $26 red string that you state has been wrapped seven times round Rachel's Tomb in Bethlehem bear the words 'Made in China'? In fact, why – when you claim that the bracelets cost that much because of the security and logistical costs involved in such a blessing – do the rabbis who are permanently encamped at the sacred site swear they have never once seen such a ritual?

Those sorts of questions. Instead, the type of questions Madonna has asked appear to have been things like 'Was I an amazingly important person in my other lives too?'And the answer the Bergs seem to have given her is 'Yes, yes, dear – of course, you were Queen Esther, and you were a total heroine who saved all the Persian Jews from annihilation with your bravery and strength of character. Purim's basically a cele-bration of *you*.'

And yet, we race ahead of ourselves. Long before Madonna found out about what a pivotal role she had played in Jewish history – long before she became Kabbalah's favourite sock puppet – she was just a spirituality-curious megastar like anyone else.

Well, in a way. Shortly after expressing an interest in goings-on at the centre, she was swiftly assigned her own special rabbi, one Eitan Yardeni, who tutored her privately. In an interview for NBC's *Dateline* in 2003, Eitan Yardeni said that many Kabbalah students 'get just one per cent of Kabbalah, which improved their life one per cent'. And Madonna? 'I can tell you that, with no shame,' he declared shamelessly, 'Madonna is under the category of the people that gets it.' See? She's great at everything.

In the interests of you keeping your Kabbalah gurus in order, you should know that this is the Rabbi Yardeni who would go on to preside over the wedding of second-wave celebrity Kabbalists Demi Moore and Ashton Kutcher. He should not be confused with Rabbi Eliyahu Yardeni, the London Kabbalah Centre bigwig who in 2005 gave an undercover BBC reporter his delightful revisionist take on the Holocaust: 'Just to tell you another thing about the six million Jews that were killed in the Holocaust,' he stated.

'The question was that the Light was blocked. They didn't use Kabbalah.'

However, please don't think that a failure to practise Kabbalah leads only to genocide. There are other outcomes, like benighted souls' failure to appreciate Madonna's performance in *Swept Away* – the 2002 movie directed by her now ex-husband, which secured Worst Actress, Worst Director and Worst Picture at that year's prestige-free Golden Raspberry Awards. Madonna glossed the critical reaction to this important motion picture in terms of 'evil eye', which in Kabbalah's somewhat clichéd lexicon denotes envy. 'I think that there's a lot of evil eye on my relationship with my husband,' she ruled. 'They weren't really criticising the movie. It was personal vendettas.'

*Dateline* viewers were also informed that Guy Ritchie's initial doubts about Kabbalah had been vanquished once he learned more about how deeply rooted it was in science. We will conduct a more in-depth examination of the peerless scientific brain of Mr Guy Ritchie elsewhere, but one can't deny that these never-fully-elaborated-upon scientific aspects to Kabbalah are quite the draw. As Donna Karan is given to saying of the faith, 'It's not a religion, it's a science.'

And Madonna is this pioneering research institute's most generous benefactor. She has donated millions upon millions of dollars to the Kabbalah Centre, both in the form of outright gifts and all profits from her depressingly successful series of children's books. In fact, revenues from *The English Roses* et al. have gone straight to Kabbalah's Spirituality for Kids programme. According to its own literature, Spirituality for Kids 'provides children with an understanding of the laws of the universe'. Which laws? Relativity? Quantum chromodynamics? Apparently not. 'Children are taught practical tools to help them experience life as a great adventure full of opportunities and challenges – not problems.'

Incidentally, have we all finally heard enough about 'tools'? Do you recognise life – in its infinite complexity, at once beautiful and profoundly unfair – as something that can be set about with some metaphorical toolbox, and that failure to be happy and successful merely marks you out as a substandard mechanic? Hopefully not.[12]

But back to Spirituality for Kids, whose reach has expanded significantly since Madonna set up her Raising Malawi foundation with Michael Berg. Raising Malawi will export the SFK programme to the lucky southern African country that caught Madonna's eye, where its principles will be applied to orphans, and used 'to raise these children up from powerlessness into self-empowerment'. As the Bergs' mission statement says: 'Spirituality for Kids gives children an awareness of themselves, of others, and of the interconnectedness of all things so that they may grow up to become caring and responsible citizens of the world.'

You can read more about how this ties in with promoting Gucci stores in the Celebrity Activism chapter. There's a whole lot of interconnectedness.

## Kabbalah foot soldiers: will no one think of the civilians?

Clearly, celebrity worshippers have been very important to the Kabbalah Centre, and for whatever reason – let's blame the evil eye – some rank-and-file adherents have found this troubling.

A real money-spinner for the centre is getting people to pay to spend festivals and holy days with the Bergs, and in 2004 a former Kabbalah student told the *Guardian* how she had started to become disillusioned. A Miami resident, she had ponied up $2,000 to celebrate Passover with Karen and 'the Rav' in LA. So how was this precious, holy experience? 'There were masses of people, you can't hear a thing, and your spiritual leader is having a conversation with Demi Moore for hours,' she remarked tartly. 'For me, that was the beginning of the end.'

It's always sad to lose a customer, naturally, but the Bergs have

---

[12] In fact, might we venture that anything claiming to give you 'tools' is merely giving you the tools to be a tool?

somehow managed to move on from it. By the next year, it cost up to $4,000 to spend Passover with them, and the holy family hosted it in Florida. As *Radar* magazine noted, the Seder traditionally ends with all gathered making a toast with the words 'next year in Jerusalem'. But don't you feel tradition can get fusty and irrelevant sometimes? The Bergs certainly did. That year, they wound up Passover by getting Madonna, Ashton Kutcher and Guy Ritchie to dispense an ad hoc blessing.

What the civilians need to realise, and need to realise good, is that it's all very well being one of the chevre – the volunteers who are packed four to a bedroom in small Kabbalah Centre-owned apartments in LA, and paid $35 a month to do things like keep house for the Bergs or sell the *Zohar* door to door. But the celebrities are the loss leaders. The celebrities come first.

When the *Guardian* interviewed Karen Berg, they found her fretting desperately about what to buy Madonna for her birthday. 'What do you buy someone who has it all?' she wondered, not altogether originally. 'A diamond E, for Esther? What do you think?' As for other indications of celebrities' top-tier importance to the Kabbalah Centre . . . Put it this way: one former student volunteer told *Radar* that her job was to help Donald Trump's ex-wife Marla Maples find her place in the prayer book during services. If Marla Maples gets that kind of attention, it's hardly surprising that Madonna is reported to sit next to Karen Berg for services at the Los Angeles Kabbalah Centre. The pair are duly concealed from the rest of the worshippers by a screen, apparently to protect them from the envy of fellow congregants. Isn't it sad when you can't even trust your own underlings?

But it was the next detail of *Radar*'s investigation that was most illuminating. 'On shabbat, after the traditional sabbath meal,' the magazine explained, 'a circle of men, all of them dressed in white, forms around a table, their arms linked. A group of women then forms a circle around the men, and they all sing and sway in tribute to the people seated at the table. The people at table, when they're all in town at the same time, include Madonna,

Guy Ritchie, Ashton Kutcher, and Demi Moore – and their hosts, Philip and Karen Berg.'

Now, doesn't that sound a whole lot like having a host of adulatory back dancers remind everyone that you're the most important person onstage, if not the planet? In fact, the crossover potential with Madonna concerts doesn't end there – on both of her last two tours, Kabbalah products have been sold alongside Madonna merchandise. Tribute leotard and a Zohar, anyone?

## Keeping the talent happy: Kabbalah moving forward

For all its impressive star roster, Kabbalah's success looks more precariously poised than that of Scientology. In its bowdlerised form, it's been going for far less long, and lacks the stratospheric funds and long-established network of Scientology, which has insinuated its tentacles into a bewildering array of institutions, and a rather greater number of human minds.

The Rav himself is old, and despite the totally convincing eternal life schtick, his $4-a-bottle Kabbalah water is not thought to be making serious inroads into repairing the neural damage sustained in his stroke.

In fact, if the Bergs want to future-proof this show to the degree anyone can in this uncertain, short-selling faith market, they are going to have to find a way to hang on to their most famous face. Given the form book, they must be aware how easily Kabbalah could turn out to be simply another of Madonna's image phases – a little more durable than the gold tooth and cigar period she went through around the release of *Erotica*, certainly, but lacking the longevity of her trusty nun-frotting act.

A plan begins to suggest itself.

Why not just elevate Madonna into a prophet? The Kabbalah Centre make the rules, after all, and what better way to hold her attention than by giving her the one thing she hasn't got[13]: holy authority? Scientology knows which side its bread is buttered

[13] Apart from a convincing English accent.

with Mr Tom Cruise, hence the confected awards and lavish birthday parties.

Would the Madonnification even be that much of a leap? After all, the old girl has already shown messianic delusions, with utterances like 'I have felt responsible for the children of the world'.

Thunderous preaching could easily be within her range. Everyone is 'going to hell', she explained during her 2004 Re-Invention Tour, 'if they don't turn from their wicked behaviour . . . I refer to an entity called The Beast . . . ' 'I think one must choose,' she stated elsewhere, probably in an electric-blue leotard. 'Even if you choose the wrong path, you're going to get to the end quicker. I don't think the universe conspires to help a fence-sitter. I think you've got to make a choice and go down either road. I think if you choose the path of wisdom, sooner or later you are going to be wanting filth. If you choose the path of filth, sooner or later you're going to be wanting enlightenment. So you end up in the same spot.'

Sadly, the magazine editor who elicited this quote from madam was too cravenly sycophantic to ask her what on earth she was on about. But with a bit of encouragement, Queen Esther's reincarnation might expand upon it in her first volume of sacred *pensées*, perhaps called *The Book of Madonna*. Don't worry if you can't understand them: just looking at the characters on the page will make you a more light-filled, spiritually complete person.

## Religions with celebrity spokesmodels: probably not a Good Thing

You might judge that celebrities[14] are drawn to the kookiness of Scientology or Kabbalah because they have a weakness for the

---

[14] It is obviously nonsense to suggest that celebrities are either Scientologists or Kabbalists – although one very rarely hears about the faith of those stars who stick to more conventional religious paths. There are a few born-again Christians like Stephen Baldwin, once known chiefly for his work in Class A drugs and Playmate outreach, but who now claims to spank his children for not knowing the Ten Commandments.

recherché, for the illusion of having been let into a more exclusive secret than, say, Anglicanism. If we can state with certitude that the rigours of Islam are never going to be for your average Hollywood star, then we might add that these same stars are particularly drawn to religions of personal empowerment – religions, we might go so far as to say, in which they are virtually the godhead. But then, do consider their fabulousness. If anyone's the Chosen One, it's them.

Perhaps these stars' greatest delusion, though, is that they have arrived at this set of beliefs because they are fundamentally curious people. 'I can assure you that studying Kabbalah is actually a very challenging thing to do,' sniffed Madonna in one interview. 'It requires a lot of work, a lot of reading, a lot of time, a lot of commitment and a lot of discipline.' Or consider Tom Cruise's genuinely terrifying sense of intellectual rectitude. 'You don't know the history of psychiatry. I do . . . You're glib. You don't even know what Ritalin is . . . You don't know and I do.'

These people are not curious: they are *credulous*. They exhibit a quite stunning lack of curiosity, yet they are given to declaring themselves – entertainers – the authority on complex matters of which they have the most tenuous grasp at best.

It would be all very well for celebrities to become involved with such obvious cults, if they kept their opinions to themselves. They are unimaginably rich, and unlikely to get sucked into the spirals of brainwashed exploitation that befall other saps. Mainly, they're more useful to these organisations as they are, which is why they are feted at their highest tables, as opposed to being ordered to serve at them. Yet despite their apparent failure to apply any of the checks or balances a properly curious person would, celebrity adherents swiftly assume the role of proselytising in public. Their success in the entertainment industry has granted them a platform, and they think nothing of abusing it to push quackery, unlicensed extortion, and 'belief systems' criticised for monumental exploitation by any number of whistle-blowers and widely respected organisations.

It should be stated in despair that the media is appallingly complicit. For every worthy and rigorous investigation there have been thousands of pictures of Madonna arriving at or leaving the Kabbalah Centre, every one of which has inched the place and its claims closer towards legitimacy. The demand for cheap space filler in the modern news media means that most of what celebrities say is reported largely uncritically – and this includes endless interviews in which Madonna makes claims concerning the organisation.

Philip Berg once said of Kabbalah water, 'If the damn FDA would just let me put on the label that the water cures cancer, like it does, I wouldn't need marketing.' But with Madonna extolling its virtues every chance she gets, does he really even need to?

This is the essential danger: celebrity endorsement is effectively unregulated advertising. This is something we can probably all live with if what is being endorsed is a luxury-brand handbag or a cosmetics range. But when it is a cult which has a track record of preying on the vulnerable, we should be seriously concerned.

Perhaps our best hope would be to hope for an LA-based religious war, in which the mighty sparkly armies of the Kabbalah Centre and Scientology's Celebrity Centre square up after some hair-trigger event – possibly the defenestration of Katie Holmes – and became mired in a pointless thirty-year conflict, preferably with debilitating numbers of casualties on both sides.

# CELEBRITIES AND THE
# MIDDLE EAST

'Of course, everybody says they're for peace. Hitler was
for peace. Everybody is for peace. The question is: what
kind of peace?'

Noam Chomsky

'We can choose to have this alternative kind of growth
that is a collective nuance of understanding. We are just
that breath away from a peaceful co-existence.'

Sharon Stone

We began this long journey through the looking glass with
Richard Gere's get-the-vote out commercial, broadcast across the
Palestinian territories on the eve of their 2005 presidential
elections. 'Hi, I'm Richard Gere,' this opened, 'and I'm speaking for
the entire world . . .'

Are we now ready to get a flavour of how the world spokesmodel's generous video message was received? Was gratitude
unbounded? Did Palestinians rush round to their neighbours to
remind them to switch the set on, then watch the infomercial in
awed silence before turning to embrace each other while
screaming the Arabic for 'OMG!!! The star of *Runaway Bride* totally
noticed us! Quick, to the polling stations!'?

You may feel confident enough to hazard a guess. The reaction
among ordinary Palestinians can be diplomatically described as
bemused. According to one soap factory worker, speaking to
Reuters, it was tough enough keeping track of the myriad factions

fielding candidates in the election: 'I don't even know who the candidates are other than Abu Mazen [now President Mahmoud Abbas],' this man sniffed, 'let alone this Gere. We don't need the Americans' intervention. We know who to elect. Not like them – they elected a moron.'

Not an unreasonable point, but it's desperately sad that Soap Factory Guy isn't aware of *Runaway Bride*. Still, having looked at what part celebrities played in our resounding War on Terror victory, it now seems as good a time as any to examine entertainers' interventions in the Middle East.

Time was when celebrities were wary of involving themselves in the complex hatreds of the region, perhaps acknowledging that the struggles of its politics were so labyrinthine and bloody that even an actor or a lead guitarist might have difficulty unravelling them. Thank pan-religious heavens, though, that these silly insecurities have been swept away by the explosion in celebrity culture, and there now appears to be not a single tenuously famous individual with whom Israeli President Shimon Peres would not gladly hold bilateral talks. The only shame is that Anna Nicole Smith's untimely death came before she could share a platform with him. 'Why would they do that?' the billionheiress ex-Playmate once wondered of suicide bombers. 'Wouldn't they think it was kind of painful?'

Fortunately, other stars live on, whose determination not to let chronic ignorance hold them back from wading in with peace missions, fortune-cookie wisdom and poorly-researched photo-calls means that we are only a heartbeat away from peace. Or a breath away from it, should you prefer Sharon Stone's dramatic, if wholly incoherent estimation. Either way, we're only one intake of breath away from a world in which the disparate factions of the region will embrace each other with the words 'I've been a fool', only for their erstwhile enemies to counter 'No, *I've* been the fool!' The argument will swiftly escalate into the kind of mindless violence that can only be quelled when each individual citizen is given a *Basic Instinct 2* DVD to remind them what they have to live for.

So, adorn yourself with religious symbols, and prepare to learn how Ricky Martin straddles the worlds of Latin pop and Israeli-Palestinian diplomacy.[1] We'll also be reminded of why the answer to the question 'What do you get an Israeli president for Rosh Hashanah?' is not 'a cult primer'. And then, of course, we'll be examining Sharon Stone's road map for peace in the region, from its glorious inception, through its faltering early stages, to the point at which it began to be loudly celebrated. By several terrorist organisations, alas. Are all nudity-based diplomatic solutions doomed to fail? You'll be better poised to make that call in just a few short pages.

## Jerusalem is Ricky Martin's

To Jordan, in 2005, which you will undoubtedly recall as the year Latin pop star Ricky Martin journeyed to the region to pledge the kind of support only the diplomatic brain behind 'Shake Your Bon-Bon' could offer.

'I will become a spokesperson on your behalf,' the singer informed a conference of Arab teenagers described by reports as 'concerned at being labelled as terrorists'. 'I have been a victim of stereotypes,' he went on thoughtfully – and though details of his personal road map were sketchy, they were understood to include offering Ariel Sharon and Mahmoud Abbas cameos in his next video, which in keeping with his oeuvre would be set in a South Beach bikini car-wash.

But the spokesperson offer wasn't all Ricky had up his sleeve – he had some lessons for the kids too, of which the most important was his declaration that 'We have to educate the ignorant'. And that education programme began immediately, as Ricky posed up for photos with a few handpicked Palestinians, during which he draped a keffiyeh scarf across his shoulders. A keffiyeh bearing the Arabic slogan 'Jerusalem is ours'.

[1] Pretty awkwardly, would you believe.

Alas, the resultant furore was such that Ricky was eventually forced to release a 'What did we learn today?' statement from the relative safety of his publicist's Manhattan office. 'I had no idea that the keffiyeh scarf presented to me contained language referring to Jerusalem,' this ran, 'and I apologize to anyone who might think I was endorsing its message. My role is entirely humanitarian, and I will continue to promote the elimination of stereotyping anyone – be they from Latin America, the Middle East, or anywhere across the globe.'

Regrettably – and it does seem rather churlish in the circumstances – some Israelis were not convinced by Ricky's ill-informed pop-star act, and continued to voice suspicion that he must have known what he was doing. What could be done? Why, a meeting with the Consul General of Israel in New York, that's what.

Within a month, Ricky had scheduled a meeting with Arye Mekel in what briefing notes described as 'an attempt to iron out the difficulties and to apologize for any preconceptions as a result of his concert'. He confirmed he wished to perform in Israel in the coming months – and informed Mekel that some of his best friends were Israeli. He then called Mekel 'my dear' in Hebrew.

Were such surreal, time-consuming posturing not enough, Mekel then proceeded to summarise the meeting thusly: 'Especially in these times, where we are busy with issues like the disengagement . . . Martin's arrival in Israel will be a breath of fresh air for issues over and above the conflict.' Issues over and above the conflict? Like what? Snake-hipped Latin pop? 'Issues that we are interested the media cover.'

And with that, a line was finally drawn under the beefcakiest diplomatic incident of the conflict thus far. It's tough not to conclude that poor, well-intentioned Ricky got in way over his head here – but compared to a certain special lady, he was gambolling in the shallows.

## Sharon Stone will tongue for a ceasefire

Our next stop is Israel, in early 2006, where as one Sharon exited, another entered. As Israeli prime minister Ariel Sharon was slipping into a coma after suffering a massive stroke, cinema's Sharon Stone was readying herself to prove that nymphomaniac ice-pick murderers and Middle East peace envoys need not be mutually exclusive. In fact, they fuse seamlessly in her very personage.

Sadly, the reductive tendency in human nature dictates that it's impossible to see Sharon doing anything without thinking of that infamous scene down at the San Francisco police station. Oh sure, it would be *nice* if you were able to look at the photographs of her kissing the Western Wall and be able to stay in the moment and marvel at one woman's crusade for a better world. It would be *nice* if you didn't see a flash of her famous flash from *Basic Instinct*, even as she puckered up to one of the holiest spots in Judaism. It would be *nice* if you could behold those prayer-stuffed ruins and not have the words 'Have you ever fucked on cocaine, Nick?' drift insidiously into your consciousness. It would be *nice* if you could think of anything else, ever, than Sharon's erstwhile lack of knickers.

But it's not happening, is it? Still, Sharon's earnest making out with the Wailing Wall was nowhere near the most excruciating moment of her peace mission. That honour undoubtedly belonged to her joint press conference with Shimon Peres – words you probably never anticipated reading. 'I admire you, sir, so greatly, it's beyond discussion, or I would just sit here in a puddle of tears,' was Sharon's measured opener to Peres. 'That I can sit beside you here is my greatest achievement.'[2]

Next, Sharon explained that she nearly hadn't made it to the post-apocalyptic conflictscape that is Tel Aviv. Celebrities are so informed about the Middle East, aren't they? When they land in this thriving tourist metropolis, they think it's as dangerous as

[2] Better even than *Catwoman*?

wandering through Gaza wearing a sandwich board reading 'Mazal tov, underlings'.

'I said I was going to go to Israel,' Sharon revealed, 'and a lot of people went "You can't go there! You can't go to Israel! You can't! What are you going to Israel for? There's a war!" And I called my publicist, who is this great Jewish woman . . .' Well of course she is. Unfortunately, she's also thousands of miles away, which later gave Sharon the chance to demonstrate why there should always be a minimum of three handlers on-site before any celebrity goes off-script. '. . . and [my publicist] goes "Please, they invented security. They have the Mossad. Let's go. Fantastic. Love you. You're great."'

But it wasn't just Jews who work for Sharon who would get a mention during the trip. 'I've always been attracted to Jews,' she later told *Ha'aretz* newspaper. 'I like dark men who are drawn to study, to art.' 'The fact that I married two Jewish men,' she informed another publication, 'is related to my obsession with studying and eating, which are two pillars of Jewish culture.'

Even at this early stage, you may find yourself overcome by a powerful urge to commit to Sharon's vision of a Middle East accord, but holding back simply out of the fear that comes from having been hurt before. That's OK. Sharon was keen to offer more detail. 'I don't think because I am a celebrity that I have the power to do anything different than you do,' she revealed to those members of the press who had gathered to listen to her – perhaps so that one day they could tell their grandchildren that most magically humble of historical boasts: *I was there.*

'I just think that because I have fame,' Sharon continued, 'I have the opportunity to sit here and reflect back to you anything that you have or desire to see happen. The only power that I have is the opportunity to be a mirror back to you of something that you may be thinking and need to be reminded of. So the only power that I have is to remind you of something that is alive in your own heart. If you want to have something change maybe I can remind you of that.'

Was there much more of this to come? Yes. Yes, unfortunately there was.

'So if I can be the mirror of that truth then I have power,' Sharon elaborated. 'If you can wash away reactionary behaviour and be in the present then my mirroring will have power. It is up to you. It's really not up to me . . .'

Is any part of Shimon Peres embarrassed when his hand-picked envoys come out with these geopolitical brainwaves? Who knows, but he certainly sat beside her and smiled wanly when even the most bloodthirsty of boxing trainers would have thrown in the towel in horror at what was taking place out there on the canvas.

The next body blow came when Sharon indicated that her aversion to no-nudity clauses might stretch all the way to geopolitics, as she made the sensational claim: 'I would kiss just about anybody for peace in the Middle East.' Oh Sharon, Sharon, Sharon . . . Is it OK if we *don't* channel the entire peace process through your libido? Things are usually fragile enough without the world turning its thoughts to Fatah divisions and finding an image of you uncrossing your legs lurch unbidden into its consciousness yet again.

It's not that you can't believe that Sharon would lock lips with anyone for peace in the Middle East – although it does remain an inadequate excuse for *Sliver*. It's just . . . well, it somehow feels like this one is never going to be solved by air-kissing. But she did make good on the remark by puckering up to Peres, a guy she could totally have caught wrinkles from.

As for Ms Stone's subsequent engagements, Prime Minister Ehud Olmert managed to spare the time to give her a tour of Jerusalem, before the actress theatrically planted a 'peace tree' with her bare hands, having declined the offer of a hoe. She needed to feel the land against her bare skin, apparently. 'I do this for love,' she explained to reporters. 'You can tell I am a farm girl.'

But that, alas, was not the last the world would hear of the visit, as Sharon began giving glowing accounts of her efforts to secure an end to the violence the minute she docked back on American soil. It's bad enough having to sit through other people's holiday photos. Imagine having to hear about their *soi-disant* 'peace mission'.

'It was really wonderful to be asked,' she expanded, on some red carpet or other, 'and to get to talk to people principally on the subject of peace and humanity, and holding your own dignity, being in your own spiritual elegance, and knowing if you have an idea, do it. And don't stop at trying to be good. Go ahead and be great!'

## Phase two: in which the Stone Road Map loses its way

It seems like only the previous paragraph that we were all feeling so bright and optimistic about one woman's attempt to bring peace to a war-torn region using only her vagina and a highly acclaimed gift for incoherence. How quickly our hopes turn to dust. After such a strong start, the question was whether Sharon was going to be able to maintain the pressure on warring factions to submit to her elegantly truth-mirroring, horny-for-Jews vision of a way out of the mess in which they find themselves. You should be warned that it all faltered somewhat in the second act – a sensation that will not be unfamiliar to those of you schooled in Sharon's cinematic oeuvre.

What went wrong? Well, Sharon would have probably got away with her decision to return to the region later that year on what she termed a fact-finding mission (it was in fact the Dubai International Film Festival, and she reportedly did not stray from the luxuriant confines of the emirate). However, granting one particular interview to a pan-Arab newspaper was, in retrospect, the key strategic error.

Explaining that the September 11th terror attacks should not have been used as a pretext for launching wars in Afghanistan and Iraq, Sharon confessed: 'I feel at great pain when the spotlight is on the death of 4,000 American soldiers, while 600,000 Iraqi deaths are ignored. I feel sad,' she added, 'when I realize how much truth is being changed or obscured in the American media.' Not desperately controversial, you may judge, but one should never underestimate an enemy's ability to revel in any perceived admission of imperial weakness – even if the person making it is cinema's not-altogether-respected Sharon Stone.

No sooner had the comments been published than a heavenly host of terrorists queued up to give Sharon reviews she could only dream of in her day job. 'I think this lady is smelling and seeing the dangers for the future of America,' gushed Abu Islam, the leader of the Gaza-based Islamist extreme movement Jihadia Salafiya, whose credits include accusations of bombing a UN school that had allowed boys and girls to participate in a sporting event together.

'We feel satisfied with Stone's quotes,' was the gracious verdict of Jihad Jaara, who directed the blood-soaked siege of the Church of the Nativity in Bethlehem in 2002, 'which prove we were right and the policy of wars will not lead anywhere.' Wait . . . a random Sharon Stone digression *proves* they were right? Let's adopt this new logic in our own evidence-based legal system. 'We see she is a woman who understands well what are the risks of American foreign policy,' Jaara continued, perhaps making a coded admission that his mental faculties had finally gone and it was time for his subordinates to stage a leadership coup. 'If you don't follow Stone and if you renew the Republican regime [it was 2007], you cannot blame anyone besides yourselves for the dangers this new Republican regime will bring unto you.' Were the vision of a world in which we are required to 'follow Stone' not nightmarish enough, there followed a direct shout-out to Sharon from Muhammad Abdel-Al, senior leader of the Popular Resistance Committees terror group.

'What Stone said strengthens what we have been saying all along – that the Bush administration and the American evangelical Christians who control US policy are leading America to defeat,' gibbered Abdel-Al. 'I say to Stone, if the American policy continues, it will be the beginning of the end of your empire of evil.'[3]

Incidentally, Abdel-Al was the media-friendly evil-doer who contributed extensively to the book *Schmoozing with Terrorists*, reviewed more fully earlier, in which he appeared to be inviting the world to judge him on the calibre of his enemies. 'If these two prostitutes keep doing what they are doing,' he ranted edifyingly about Madonna and Britney Spears's bromidic kiss at the 2003 MTV video music awards, 'we of course will punish them. I will have the honour – I repeat, I will have the honour – to be the first one to cut off the heads of Madonna and Britney Spears.'

Has the clash of civilisations come to this? A face-off between Britney and Madonna and a guy who appears unable to get his gander up without trawling the gossip websites like some embittered, sexually confused red-state teen blogger? Frankly, if they didn't have military hardware and a total disregard for human life, it would be impossible to take these guys seriously.

## Reincarnation of Queen Esther takes steps to rescue the Jews once more

In case you weren't up to speed on the manner in which Israeli President Shimon Peres ushered in Rosh Hashanah in 2007, it's a pleasure to inform you he did so with a two-hour meeting with Madonna and her then husband, Guy Ritchie. As leading practitioners of fake Jewish cult the Kabbalah, the Ciccone-Ritchies had journeyed to Israel to celebrate New Year, and naturally a staging post of that journey would be the schmooze with Peres.

By all accounts, the meeting got off to a flying start, as the pair presented each other with gifts of holy books. The President gave the singer a copy of the Hebrew Bible, and Madonna presented him with a copy of the *Zohar*, the mystical text that serves as the

---

[3] Sharon Stone's empire of evil? You need to work on your grammar, terrorists.

basis of Kabbalah. What a shame she didn't give him her misunderstood *Sex* book. After all, what better way to say 'L'chaim!' than with pictures of oneself being spreadeagled by long-forgotten rapper Vanilla Ice.

But a *Zohar* it was – and to recap, the *Zohar* is the one the revenue gatherers at the Kabbalah Centre tell you is 'the ultimate instrument for generating miracles. An amazing number of people have reported them just from housing a copy of it in their home . . .' The president's gifted copy was inscribed, according to reports, with the words 'To Shimon Peres, the man I admire and love, Madonna'.

'You don't know how popular the Book of Splendour is among Hollywood actors,' Madonna was quoted as telling Peres. 'Everyone I meet talks to me only about that.' What a peculiar friendship circle she must have. And then came the really great news, as Madonna informed him: 'I am an ambassador for Judaism.'

It would be nice to be able to report that upon hearing this, Peres sat Madonna down and furnished her with a couple of home truths, and maybe the odd new year's resolution. Like: 'I resolve not to make absolutely everything, including the entire Jewish faith, about me.' Alas, no such report can be made.

Instead, you should know that President Shimon Peres toasted the new year with Ms Madonna Ciccone and Mr Guy Ritchie, and nobody found anything in the arrangement remotely preposterous. In fact, they took the opportunity to discuss how to move forward towards the era of peace which can only be round the corner if productive summits such as this one are scheduled on all available high days and holidays.

'The president and Madonna discussed how to advance the peace process, and conciliation and tolerance the world,' elaborated presidential spokeswoman Ayelet Frish. 'Madonna told the president she wants to promote those messages in her songs and books, and how important it was to educate children with those ideas. She also said that meeting President Peres and welcoming in the new Jewish year together with him was the fulfilment of a dream.'

A dream she'd stumbled upon all of ten minutes ago.

Others found themselves in less of a reverie. The Orthodox Jewish community has long fumed at the appropriation of their sacred mysteries by a red-string-pushing insurance salesman and a self-crucifying Catholic gym bunny,[4] but the whole 'ambassador for Judaism' thing proved the final straw.

In the days following Rosh Hashanah, the director of one of the most respected yeshivots (Orthodox rabbinical schools) in Jerusalem informed the *Jerusalem Post*: 'It is a known fact in Kabbalah that impurity and evil are inherently attracted to sanctity. That's why people of Hollywood,' he went on witheringly, 'a place of iniquity and lasciviousness, are naturally attracted to the holiness of Kabbalah. Wherever there is holiness and sanctity there is also evil. That's why someone like that lady – I don't even want to mention her name – is so attracted to the Kabbalah.'

The director then revealed that during a previous visit to Israel, That Lady had repeatedly attempted to contact his institution, but that he had declined to return her calls. And that about concluded the diplomatic end of Madonna's mission. The rest of her trip was taken up with attending a Kabbalah 'conference' at the Intercontinental Hotel, along with fellow Kabbalists Ashton Kutcher and Demi Moore. Were the latter couple Peres snubbers or snubbees? Impossible to guess.

## The DiCaprio Code: a Middle Eastern thriller

And so to March 2007, when both diplomats and Middle East analysts were beginning to voice scepticism that the Bush administration was seriously committed to pursuing peace in the Middle East.

---

[4] Note: these words may not accurately reflect those used by the Orthodox Jewish community.

Yet after six years of inertia, it was once again Shimon Peres who reminded us how thoroughly on track the peace process was, by scheduling talks – his word – with none other than visiting Hollywood actor Leonardo DiCaprio. Yes, yes. We *all* loved him in *The Departed*. No doubt he'd have some really interesting stuff to say on West Bank disengagement.

The actor's visit was by most accounts a roaring success, marred only slightly by an incident at the Western Wall, when Leonardo's bodyguards hit two snappers for trying to photograph him. Why do people persist in thinking of this holy site as a public space? Can't they just designate the wall the equivalent of a velvet rope and turn the entire Temple Mount/Haram al-Sharif area into a VIP enclosure? It *is* supposed to be a sanctuary, guys.

Naturally, though, no celebrity's visit to Israel would be complete without their being summoned to a high-level summit with gossip-hungry President Peres Hilton himself. Ideally, these talks would take the form of some trainwreck press conference, but if the president's men can't persuade people who know next to nothing about the region to demonstrate that conclusively in front of the cameras, Peres's spokesman always makes sure the world knows as many of the details of the summit as possible.

'The meeting was pleasant and interesting,' the spokesman averred, after pictures had emerged showing Peres grinning next to DiCaprio, who was wearing a back-to-front baseball cap. 'Shimon told Leo about his joint Israeli-Jordanian-Palestinian economic development plan.' But of course he did. No doubt he received invaluable counsel in return. The spokesman went on to say that Peres requested the *Titanic* star's help with the Middle East peace process, which he conceded had not made much recent progress.

Time to consider it out of the doldrums.

No sooner had he been asked to assist in bringing peace to the troubled lands than Leonardo promptly embarked on a whirlwind round of multilateral diplomacy, ultimately finessing all the main players in the region and overseas into signing a historic accord.

Oh no, hang on. He went back to Hollywood. But he did shoot a movie in which he and Russell Crowe play really hard CIA guys who smash terror cells in the Middle East ... so that's sort of helping with the peace process, right? It's certainly helping remind people what the Middle East is all about.

So just sling another chair leg on the fire and synthesise delight that the peace process has such a hot A-list star attached to it. Let's accept that celebrity endorsement works. Let's picture people coming to their senses all across the world. 'Oh, I was having a really tough time working out which of the many stalling global peace processes to back. I was going to go with those guys in Banda Aceh, but now Leo's endorsing that one in the Middle East, I'm so in! *Titanic*'s, like, my favourite movie of all time!'

Let's concede that there are no hatreds so historically complex that they cannot be untangled by exposure to a physically attractive actor, and look forward to the day when the country is sufficiently forward-looking to call for Leonardo to address the Knesset, and Shimon to be offered a role in *The Departed*'s sequel.

Above all, let's be optimistic.

# CELEBRITY ACTIVISM

'A model talking about a nuclear power plant is going to capture a different audience than a nuclear scientist will.'

Christie Brinkley

'Most of the trouble in the world is caused by people wanting to be important.'

T. S. Eliot

The practice of Putting Something Back is such fragrant, fragrant celeb-nip that Anne Hathaway could barely contain herself during one soliloquy about her 'incredible' boyfriend, Raffaello Follieri. 'One of the most untouted aphrodisiacs in the world is charity work,' the actress gushed, hinting that suffering effectively exists to get stars in the mood for sex. 'Seriously, you want a girl to be impressed, vaccinate some kids, build a house.'

As various august bodies would discover – bodies like the IRS, the New York State Attorney General's Office, the Vatican and Anne Hathaway's publicist – her boyfriend was *literally* incredible. He eventually pleaded guilty to multimillion-dollar real estate fraud, conspiracy and money laundering. He is currently out of the kid-vaccination-and-construction game, having been sentenced to several years in a federal prison.

Did Anne's ex do a lot of this simply to enchant a celebrity, and thereafter to live an enchanted celebrity lifestyle? Perhaps we'll never know, although his lawyer worked a 'celebrities made me do it' line when it came to entering a sentencing plea. Either way, the suspicion remains that Follieri knew exactly the way to the celebrity heart: through highly publicised acts of philanthropy. Or fauxlanthropy, in his case.

When celebrities care, they find it excruciatingly impossible to do so with quiet dignity. Entire camel trains flit through the eye of a needle with more ease than a movie star keeps a lid on their generosity. So blurred have the boundaries between performance and philanthropy become that their very lexicons seem interchangeable. Time and again we hear how an actress's latest cause 'may be her most inspiring role ever' as though her romcom filmography was up against stiff competition from caring about sick kids.

Our business in this chapter is less with individual acts of charity – though Mariah Carey's decision to mail a couple of furs to Mongolian nomads remains an inspiration. It is rather with the manner in which entertainers have become an institutionalised part of charitable aid and activism, and are now a virtually unquestioned element of the response to intractable global problems. The Red Cross has a 'director of celebrity outreach', while Oxfam and Amnesty International have similar departments. The UN, of course, is forever swelling the ranks of their famous 'Goodwill Ambassadors'.

In the following pages we'll be looking at celebrities and suffering, and asking where that particular marriage was made. We should probably also try to get a hype-free idea of the real effects of celebrities on charitable and political causes.[1] Along the way, the rule will be run over fund-raiser economics, as we wonder how much foie gras is *de trop* at a famine-relief benefit. We'll marvel at the new Scramble for Africa, and at the story of how the death rattle of the *Rambo* franchise brought about the end of military rule in Burma and ushered in a new era of bandanna-wearing democracy.[2] And we will learn how one of the

[1] We already know the glowing effects of charitable and political causes on celebrities.
[2] This happened, didn't it?

Backstreet Boys isn't even *close* to being the least expert celebrity witness invited to speak before a congressional committee.

Unfortunately it's a little hard to joke about this stuff, so prepare to experience a certain amount of discomfort, distaste, and disbelief. In the sainted words of Martin Lawrence in *Bad Boys II*: this shit just got real.

## Phase one: getting your voice heard

You might, by this stage, be on the point of suspecting we hear quite enough from celebrities these days. So it might come as a surprise to learn that many entertainers actually feel *disenfranchised*.

'You shouldn't be discredited because you work in Hollywood,' runs the spectacularly point-missing thesis of comic actress Janeane Garofalo. 'No one would stand up and say that because people work in the food service industry, their opinions aren't worthwhile.'

That celebrities are able to retain a victim mentality about their purchase on the public discourse is a tribute to their . . . strong sense of self. When was the last time you heard from someone in the food service industry on anything – including the food service industry? In fact, if it's amusing homilies about life waiting tables that you're after, just comb the interviews of someone who makes major motion pictures. They like to throw in screwball anecdotes from back when they worked in a bar, because it makes them sound just like us.

Shortly before the invasion of Iraq, *USA Today* began soliciting ordinary people's views on celebrities 'speaking out' – and unearthed a certain frustration among folk who felt that when celebrities speak out, other people don't get heard.

'Their profession is acting,' one Texan woman told the paper. 'That does not make them any more qualified to comment on the war than I am. As a matter of fact, I think that I am more qualified. I am married to a soldier, live on an Army base and have a lot more at stake than they do if war does break out. They spend most of their adult lives pretending to be someone they are not.'

But we live in a celebocracy, which means that a celebrity's voice is worth approximately 10,000 times what yours is. And it's easier and easier for them to get that voice heard. In days of yore celebrities would have to do something fairly kooky or, you know, *protesty* to get the media's attention. Now they call their own press conferences – which often serve the joint purpose of publicising both their cause and their next movie.

Likewise, for all their hot air about 'taking a stand', there is minimal risk involved in today's starry protest. When the American sprinters Tommie Smith and John Carlos raised their fists in a black power salute on the podium at the 1968 Mexico Olympics, it would not be twenty-four hours before they were stripped of their medals and expelled from the Olympic Village. They returned home to abuse and death threats, and years of struggling to find even menial employment, and yet they had guessed the odds when they made their protest. What does Angelina Jolie risk depriving herself of when she calls the US government out for spending money on weapons that could be used for aid? Certainly not the chance to get paid millions of dollars in her next shoot-'em-up.

Yet still we're encouraged to applaud the part-time heroes and heroines of aid drives and awareness programmes. Above all, we are encouraged to succumb to the implicit suggestion – whatever Garofalo says – that entertainers are somehow more qualified on most subjects than anyone else.

When the Screen Actors' Guild got itself a new president in 2005, actor Alan Rosenberg marked his accession with a suitably understated mission statement. 'We're Americans,' he addressed his fellow actor Americans, 'and if we don't speak out, who will? I have more faith in what an actor has to say, if they're well informed, than any politician.' Quite a claim, even if it is mirrored by Barack Obama's constant refrain that *Friends* would have been so much more credible if they'd only given Joe Biden a shot at the Joey role.

## Fund-raisers: in which we clamber inside the generosity simulator

*Fund-raiser (noun): a way of extracting charitable donations from rich people whose convictions and/or hearts are so small that they require the device of an expensive party to separate them from their money.*

Typically, a fund-raiser will be funded by corporate sponsors. This simulation of generosity is in fact a voguish concept known as 'cause-related marketing'. We have entered a new age where even the most venal corporations recognise the need to be 'socially responsible',[3] and as such it makes just as much sense – maybe even more – to spend money on associating yourself with half thought-out gestures towards saving kids with flies round their mouths as it does to spend money getting Scarlett Johansson to pose like she wants to have sex with your It bag.

These corporate sponsors will lavish extraordinary sums on creating a spectacular event. The food will be high-end restaurant quality, the marquees will resemble big tops or New England beach clubs or enchanted forests. There will be armies of serving staff. There will be living statues; there will be ice statues. The attendees will likely buy new designer outfits, and get their hair all did, and arrive in limousines. Oh, and the parties will often be sponsored by diamond firms, in order that celebrities might approach the 'Let's Help Sierra Leone and Stuff' benefit looking like they personally fund every warlord in West Africa.

Imagine it like a balance sheet. In the Costs column go all those outlays. And in the Revenues column goes money raised by ticket sales and auctions. Subtract the second from the first, and whatever's left over goes to people who are traditionally referred to – with neat understatement – as 'those less privileged than us here tonight'.

---

[3] Do the air quotes gesture.

This is called *care-o-nomics*. And if you're asking why they don't save the cost of a party and give all the money to the underprivileged, then you are formally referred back to the first paragraph of this segment.

Fund-raisers are performative. No cocktails and networking, no food for the kids with flies round their mouths. Sorry, but those kids need to realise that it's an imperfect world out there. What do you mean you think they already do? Well, that's great. Knowledge is power, and we are working to empower these children.[4]

Now you understand benefit nights, let's do a case study and see how the marquee isn't the only ludicrous 'big tent' at most of these things. We lay our scene at a fancy Aids gala in Washington in 2005, where Hillary Clinton, the then US Secretary of State Condoleezza Rice, and Angelina Jolie were all on the bill. Over the course of the evening, the three happily posed up for pictures together and flattered each other's work, suggesting that they had put partisan differences aside to face this universal problem.

At the podium, Condoleezza Rice gave a speech in which she submitted that the Bush government was making great progress on Aids in Africa, and pledged to continue its unprecedented work.

When it was Hillary's turn, the then New York senator made a largely platitudinous speech, but criticised the Bush administration for its stance against condoms and its promotion of abstinence-only sex education programmes, which she held responsible for unnecessary deaths the world over.

For Angelina's part, she was given a hastily confected humanitarian award, but has repeatedly suggested that money funding the Iraq war should instead be spent on saving Africans.

So, these people disagree profoundly with each other. What on earth is the point of them sharing a stage and handing awards to each other? To remind a few punters paying $5,000 a plate of that

---

[4] There is a discomfort bag located in the rear pocket of the seat in front of you.

old adage 'something must be done'? Way to change the world! Pass the caviar, and don't screen any footage of dying Africans when we're eating, OK?

## Goodwill ambassadors: the best way to show goodwill?

Ah, UN goodwill ambassadors. They change so much: primarily the definition of goodwill. The skillset requirements of this rapidly proliferating modern role remain shadowy, but it seems to have been created as a way to say 'sorry about the bombing/famine/pestilence – we've sent you a celebrity as a goodwill gesture'. Or perhaps it was created out of a belief that the only way to emphasise the utter desperation of a people is to suggest they'd be glad to see Geri Halliwell.

Naturally, *naturally*, the erstwhile Spice Girl is a goodwill ambassador, with special responsibility for the Aids epidemic and maternal healthcare in sub-Saharan Africa. Never say we don't put our best people on this stuff.

The UN have been validating Geri's delusions about herself since 1999, when her departure from being the shouty one in the band left a yawning gap in her schedule. The Spice Girls' gain would be the global aid debate's loss. In fact, one has to double-check to ensure the recollection is not a malevolently implanted false memory, but in 2008 Geri really did dress up in what she no doubt saw as a cute twist on a Jackie Kennedy outfit, and travel to Washington, where she was scheduled for talks with *actual legislators*. Luckily, some celebrity magazines were on hand to take pictures, and one of them characterised the Spice Girl's mission thusly: 'It was a case of Ms Halliwell Goes to Washington.'[5]

In the magazines, we learned that madam had held a series of meetings about African maternal healthcare and Aids relief 'with

[5] In the movie referenced, of course, Jimmy Stewart plays a guy who talks away the possibility of something happening simply by banging on and on and on until everyone else but him is asleep. The filibuster: possibly the perfect metaphor for Geri's entire career.

various power players in Congress'. Pictures of Geri with a couple of humpy-looking congressmen were duly provided, and the publications drew inevitable comparisons with – yes – Jackie Kennedy.[6]

One of these Washington power players described Geri as 'a shining example of how one woman can make a difference for the health and dignity of women everywhere'. In answer to your question, yes. It *is* OK to say, 'Not in my name.'

Then without further ado it was over to Geri, who blathered at length about 'the work I do for the United Nations'. Oh, Geri! . . . You do nothing for the United Nations, and they do even less for themselves by signing up people like you.

Yet on it all goes, amid utterly unsubstantiated claims that it's raising awareness of these issues in some meaningful way. More worrying still, somehow, is the suggestion that the goodwill ambassadors might have genuine authority. Take Nicole Kidman. Nicole is goodwill ambassador for the UN Development Fund for Women, but served as an example in a discourse on celebrity advocacy by Donald Steinberg. Mr Steinberg is deputy president of the International Crisis Group, an NGO dedicated to global conflict prevention and resolution, and averred: 'It's going to be hard for a foreign government to say no to Nicole Kidman.'

And yet, on what grounds is it? On what bewilderingly screwed-up grounds is a foreign government going to show compunction about saying no to a movie actress? In 2008, Forbes rated Kidman as the most overpaid actress in terms of the ratio of her fee to how much her films gross. Can we add 'most over-rated public intellectual' to her awards haul? Of course, in the manner of many stars keen to augment their achievements with – what? Something that might bring that elusive sense of self-worth? – Nicole has made plenty of statements about it being famous folk's 'duty to give something back'. Maybe she could just

[6] God, if only Geri would hurry up and 'end up on the yacht of some arms dealer', as Charles de Gaulle almost accurately predicted would be the fate of John F. Kennedy's widow.

settle for putting money back, and keep for herself the belief that she can bewitch repressive regimes into playing nice.

## The new Scramble for Africa

Apart from the plundering, and the atrocities, and the racist pseudoscience, and that stuff Leopold II of Belgium's guys did in the Congo, what was wrong with the late-nineteenth century Scramble for Africa, in which competing European powers laid claim to all but a couple of African countries? Correct: it wasn't sparkly enough. Happily, that earlier, dowdier model of expansionism is today being refurbished by a whole host of stars, who in recent years have moved to assert if not literal, then certainly *moral* ownership of various parts of the continent. It's the new New Imperialism.

These days, you have no hope of being a celebrity superpower unless you're involved in the Scramble for Africa. Cast the roles of Livingstone and Bismarck and Rhodes as you see fit, but do make sure a plum one goes to Angelina Jolie, whose 2005 adoption of an Ethiopian child arguably precipitated the run on the continent. Whether Madonna actually wanted to adopt an African child is irrelevant. Strategic rivalry meant she'd have had to acquire one anyway, so in the Queen of Pop swooped from the eastern front.

At this point, Hollywood realised it was every celebrity for themselves, and confusing things began to happen. Things like a huge advertising campaign starring Gwyneth Paltrow. In minuscule print below the vast image you could just make out the name of an African charity. But mainly, it depicted Gwyneth, arguably the most WASPish-looking woman in Hollywood, facing the camera in a beaded tribal necklace with a dash of blue warpaint across one cheek. The caption? 'I AM AFRICAN'.

Finally, a reason to care about the continent. Of course, hilarity ensued. However, this gave way to the suspicion that Gwyneth might have been attempting to make a point, which after long contemplation it became crystal clear. She was parking her grass-skirted tanks on the sub-Saharan lawns of her celebrity rivals.

A few years previously, such an audacious landgrab would have been unthinkable. That, of course, was before Angelina colonised Namibia, which she and Brad Pitt earmarked for the birth of their first biological child. Of the Namibians, Angelina gushed 'everyone was just so lovely'. In recompense, she bestowed upon the land that most precious of late-capitalist gifts: a swarm of photographers. Can you believe Namibia didn't have paparazzi before then? It's so sad. You have to turn off the news when you hear stuff like that.

Clearly, though, Angelina's annexation of this grateful country produced two distinct effects. One, it prompted every failed state on the continent to pray that she uses them as a birthing pool or adoption catchment area. And two, it threw down a gauntlet to Madonna, who subsequently announced she had finally found 'a big, big project' for herself. Which is one way of categorising Malawi. So committed was she to sorting out that country's psyche that she confirmed she even planned to visit the continent for the first time later that year. She did, and the rest is history. Positive effects? Well, Malawi immediately saw a sharp upturn in its child acquisitions market, as Madonna obtained an orphan-effect infant and took him back to live with her in London. It's still too early to say what her Little Red Kabbalah School project will do for the African nation's health.

Before long, even Paris Hilton wanted a slice of the stain on the world's conscience, and following a spell in the Century Regional Detention Facility in Lynwood – it's LA's Robben Island – she knew exactly what to say to begin the laundering of her reputation. She pledged that she would visit Rwanda. 'There's so much need in that area,' Paris explained vaguely. 'And I feel like if I go, it will bring more attention to what people can do to help.'

Really? Because it sounds like it's adding insult to injury. Or rather Hilton to genocide.

'I know there's a lot of good I can do,' the heiress continued, 'just by getting involved and bringing attention to these issues.' Yes, Paris was 'raising awareness'.[7]

But Paris's mooted Rwandan mission – continually postponed and as yet undelivered upon – merely marked the latest phase in Africa's journey. It is now the must-mention for any star seeking to come back favourably from a period of bad publicity.

'I'm planning a trip to Africa in the second week of December,' Lindsay Lohan told various interviewers, shortly after her 2007 arrest for drunk-driving and drug possession, which itself came minutes after she had embarked upon a late-night car chase of her former personal assistant. 'I'm working with the American Red Cross.'

Ah, Africa . . . Sometimes you get the feeling it only exists to help celebrities put all their crap behind them. Nevertheless, Lindsay was good enough to suggest that even Africa couldn't preclude the possibility of a relapse. 'Temptation is always there,' she quavered.

And with that, the world feared an evening beneath the African skies, when Lindsay would once again succumb to her demons and override her alcohol-monitoring ankle bracelet. Immediately, the starlet would realise she had just a few hours of sweet, sweet freedom before her automatically alerted sober sponsor caught up with her – freedom which she would use, on the form book, to carjack a passing Red Cross vehicle, before embarking on a high-speed chase of some underling, and all with someone else's coke in the pocket of her anti-landmine skinny jeans. Still, if the episode warned just one African child of the perils of developing a prodigious coke-and-clubbing habit, then God knows it would have been worth it.

Beautiful vision though that is, alas, it's time to pull the needle off the record. As it turned out, Lindsay was indeed scheduled to 'work with the Red Cross' around that time. And in compliance with the conditions of her DUI sentence, she duly completed her two days of community service at one of the charity's facilities in Los Angeles.

[7] You know what 'raising awareness' is? Cheaper than 'giving money'.

Where will it all end? A post-celebrity-colonialist nightmare of war and corruption? Looking at the map (and hey, how cool is it that they made us look at a map of the place?), Madonna could get her Africans to march across Mozambique, Zimbabwe and Botswana to mass on Angelina's eastern border. Lohan's reaction is tough to predict. But let's go with some kind of bead sanctions.

## Seeing RED with Bono

If you ever require a reminder of why you should always, always listen to Bono, the events of one week in November 2006 are quite the eye-opener.

It was during this time that the U2 frontman launched a new phase of his Product (RED) scheme, bringing Red Motorola phones to the United States with a display of self-deprecation convincing to anyone who has never seen a U2 video. The scheme involves various big-business partners bringing out ranges of red-branded products, and pledging to donate a percentage of the profits to fighting Aids and other diseases in Africa.[8] But allow Bono to gloss it. 'Sometimes when I'm walking down the street,' he wrote around the time of the Motorola launch, 'a passer-by will say "love your work on Africa, Bono, great cause". No doubt, no doubt. 'Sometimes they wish they hadn't,' continued our hero. 'I'm Irish, I love to talk to strangers. I love to talk about Africa. It can be hard to get away ...'

Yet let's not permit this self-effacing tableau to crowd out everything else – because Bono's *other* achievement in that November week in 2006 was his landmark legal victory over a former stylist to his band. And after a costly case that had rumbled on for several years, a Dublin high court judge finally ordered this Lola Cashman to return a pair of trousers, a Stetson, a sweatshirt and some earrings – 'memorabilia', as Bono would have it – to the U2 frontman.

[8] Because branded consumption is *so* the route to a better world.

At last, a liberation case that prestige junkies could actually give a toss about. Having been left totally cold by campaigns involving Mordechai Vanunu, underage Guantánamo Bay detainees and the Guildford Four, it was the plight of the wrong-fully en-wardrobed garments that finally touched some hitherto untested fibrous matter they believed to be a heartstring. There was, of course, a measure of sadness that the human rights lawyer Gareth Peirce had never felt moved to take up the case, and that we had thus been denied an impassioned declaration of vindi-cation on the steps of the courtroom.

But at least Bono had held back on the emotional appeals during the court process itself. 'They sound like trivial items,' he explained to the judge, 'they're really not. They are important items to the group and we take them seriously.' Almost as seriously as they take themselves. Bono and chums declined to pursue costs against their former stylist, which they no doubt assumed made them look quite the gracious victors.

And yet, given how long the case had dragged on, and that they had declined to settle, a contradiction seemed to loom rather large. You've probably lost count of the number of times Bono has claimed with mysteriously acquired moral authority that the problems Africa faces puts things into perspective. Is it not fair to say that lavishing vast sums of money on this stag-geringly petty little case puts his claims of moral authority into perspective?

In fact, his preachings had sounded the first hollow note rather earlier that year, around the time he and his band decided to shift their tax affairs from Ireland to the Netherlands. For many years, this chap worth hundreds of millions had enjoyed the tax-free status extended to artists in Ireland, driving around on roads paid for by teachers and nurses and plumbers – the very people to whom he'd appeal for donations when an African village needed a well. Or, indeed, a road. Anyhow, do imagine Bono's horror when the government decided that artists' tax-free income would be capped at $625,450. He and his band promptly decided to move their tax affairs to the Netherlands, which offered a yet more favourable rate.

Without wishing to sledgehammer home a point even a rock star should be able to understand: offshore tax avoidance has huge implications not simply for the charity that begins near home, but for international aid and development. That Bono should still feel able to sit on Ireland's Hunger Task Force and pressurise the government to spend more taxpayers' money on aid is a tribute to selective myopia. How significant is this little tax-evasion scheme, which Bono insists is within 'the spirit' of Ireland's laws? The Tax Justice Network estimates that rich individuals avoid paying a collective $255 billion a year by protecting it in offshore havens, more than five times the amount needed to fund the Millennium Development Goals trumpeted by Bono. These goals include halting the spread of HIV/Aids, reducing extreme poverty by 50 per cent, and providing universal primary education by 2015. Tax havens undermine all nations' efforts to help the world's poorest people – so maybe Bono's task force could take a look at that particular problem. While they're at it, they may care to know that the African Union has stated that tax-dodging schemes by foreign companies costs it $150 billion annually. The African Union receives approximately $50 billion in aid annually.

Right now, you'll be thinking just one thing: please, God, tell me the poor guy got his trousers back. And remind me how crucial this lengthy and expensive legal drama actually was.

Alas, Bono was never pressed into having to outline the relative importance of the principle at stake in the epic case of the missing pantaloons – and that's just one of many tantalisingly unanswered questions. Such as: did the trousers even still fit him, given they dated from the band's 1987 Joshua Tree tour? Clearly, it had been years since Bono would have been able to squeeze his swollen head into the ten-gallon hat, but was he attached to the leather trews in the manner that some women cling on to a pair of jeans from their 'thin days', in the futile hope that they'll one day be able to get back into them? Or perhaps some vast Bono archive is being planned.

But examining all of this holistically, doesn't a brainwave begin to suggest itself? How about establishing Litigation (RED), so that every time a celebrity launches an incalculably fatuous legal case, 5 per cent of the eventual costs will go to a starving child?

## Madonna raises the profile of Malawi, Gucci

The stated aims of the United Nations are to facilitate cooperation in international law, international security, economic development, social progress, human rights and achieving world peace.

Can you believe they left 'promoting Gucci' off that list?

This decades-long oversight was remedied in early 2008, and the universe's most starstruck league of nations had Madonna to thank. In early February of that year – the very week of New York fashion week, would you believe – the singer fronted a hugely ostentatious celebrity benefit for her Raising Malawi foundation; a benefit which turned out to be a cross-promotion for Gucci's new Manhattan store. This actually happened! And guess where? *On the lawn of the UN building in New York*, prompting the question: what's more troubling for the UN – a rogue dictator parking his tanks on its lawn, or Madonna and Gucci parking their star-humping, It bag party on its lawn?[9]

How, you may ask, did a fashion house and a pop star get to host their party on soil officially classified as international territory? The answer's in your question. As the organisers' lofty press release explained: 'Gucci and Madonna selected this prominent location because of its connection to Unicef and to represent neutral ground where people of different nationalities, religions, and backgrounds can come together under one

[9] If you answered 'I don't know – how big are the tanks?', you may continue reading.

impartial roof to support a global crisis that affects all nations: the HIV/Aids pandemic.'

But they can also come together to hawk luxury products, a fact heavily underscored by Gucci's branding being the most visible at the event. After all, as the much more prominent first paragraph of the press release had stated: 'the event will celebrate the opening of Gucci's New York 5th Avenue Flagship store'. Tom Cruise, one of Madonna'n'Gucci's guests, laid bare the ludicrous nature of the tie-in when he told reporters: 'I'm here because it's a fascinating cause and a great label.' Don't you love the way he balanced that statement? It's like there's an equivalence between Aids babies and well-cut tuxedos. He should have added that he supports clean drinking water and snaffle-bit loafers.

But it would be wholly unfair to single out Tom. Almost everyone in this historically inappropriate clusterfuck conducted themselves with total disingenuity and utterly distasteful self-regard throughout. Just occasionally, it's worth anatomising such a horror, so let's count the culprits:

First to shuffle into the dock is the Kabbalah Centre, who deny that Raising Malawi in any way benefits Kabbalah – despite the fact that Raising Malawi was co-founded by the Kabbalah Centre co-director Michael Berg and Madonna; was at the time not a registered non-profit organisation and operated entirely out of the Kabbalah Centre; and is underpinned by the sect's Spirituality for Kids Programme. The latter, oddly, remains something Madonna's camp are distinctly reluctant to acknowledge. 'There are no religious lessons being taught to the children of Malawi,' her long-time publicist Liz Rosenberg insisted to the media. According to Michael Berg's own lengthy discourses on the matter, however: 'We will be training local Malawian teachers to offer a curriculum based on the principles of Spirituality for Kids (SFK), formulated to address the specific challenges in Africa.' So, not making them pay $26 for a red string bracelet? 'We will be building the Kabbalah Community Orphan Care Center, which will be a place where children can come to eat, learn, read, and play in a safe, nurturing environment. This will also be the headquarters of our activities in Africa and the location where the children will be taught the principles of the SFK curriculum.'

Our second defendant is Gucci, who retroactively attempted to claim the opening of the new store was just 'a coincidence', perhaps forgetting their triumphalist press release of about ten minutes previously. Unwittingly, though, it was the label's creative director Frida Giannini who crystallised the situation's preposterousness. 'When our PR team proposed it I didn't think it would be possible,' she said of the event. 'I mean, why would they let some stupid fashion party inside the United Nations?' Why indeed? In front of the invited guests, Frida was way more on-message. The association with Raising Malawi, she quavered, 'is about Gucci's commitment as global citizens to doing what is right'. Cue big-screen footage of children stretching out begging bowls. Fun fact: the new Gucci store launched that week with its 'heritage collection', featuring an alligator-skin jewellery box which retailed at $33,250. Corporate social responsibility never looked so darling.

In the dock next to Gucci is Madonna, for stretching her conviction that she is an 'agent of change' to new levels of fatuity. 'I would especially like to thank Gucci and Unicef for making this evening a reality for me,' she announced blithely. How much you can actually expect from a singer is debatable, but if Madonna wishes to make the transition from pop star to lobbyist, her activities need to be judged by loftier standards than you'd apply to, say, the 'Express Yourself' video. She no longer gets to refuse to engage with detractors – and yet, that's exactly what she did. In the days leading up to the event, questions were asked about the vast tented edifice that was being erected on the north lawn, and why a shop was using UN property to push its wares. 'I don't really pay any attention to that,' she sniffed, with the clear-sighted smugness of someone who last heard the word 'no' in 1982. 'I am grateful that Gucci has underwritten this event – that's all that matters to me –

their generosity.' And then came the disdain. 'There's always controversy surrounding anything that involves change.'

For the record, then, those leading the enquiries were not cynical entertainment reporters. The enquiries were being made by a not-for-profit reporting organisation called the Inner City Press. The Inner City Press don't normally have any cause to engage with celebrities. As well as being accredited at the UN, they cover the US Federal Reserve Board, banking and insurance regulatory agencies, the Federal Communications commission and various courts. Their mission statement is to 'engage in investigations and journalism regarding human rights, transparency, corporate accountability, community reinvestment, predatory lending, environmental justice, fair housing, social exclusion, and related topics'.

*So* unglamorous.

The Inner City Press do what most entertainers would probably judge very boring things, like turn up to every one of the UN's interminable press briefings, and ask questions about humanitarian pullouts in Sri Lanka, or why Western insurers are permitted to underwrite aviation and shipping in Burma. They are not 'resistant to change'. They just wonder who is setting the rules and why, and so it was that they asked of the United Nations communications department: 'Why does [the UN] not prohibit commercial use in advertisement of the UN affiliation, for a luxury leather goods store?'

And so to the UN, our fourth defendant. Oh, they claimed to be feeling a bit down about it all, with secretary general Ban Ki-moon's people saying that 'Gucci went a little too far', and that they 'should have investigated more fully' before allowing the soiree. Frankly a tweenage Googler might have discovered that the 'charity' was administered by the Kabbalah Centre founders in LA, but that the Church's $4-a-bottle 'holy water' is very reasonably priced, and as Madonna has triumphantly pointed out, it cured Guy Ritchie's verrucas. The Kabbalah bigwigs claim it cures Aids.

If the UN really didn't know exactly what sort of event was

being planned, then they should have. It would have taken minutes to discover. They later revealed that Gucci had sought to use the UN logo in their branding but had been denied. As for why the alarm bell didn't tinkle at this point, one can only conclude it was because of the presence of a celebrity. So in thrall is the UN to the idea of goodwill ambassadors and the like that it appears institutionally blinkered to celebrities taking monstrous advantage of its own goodwill, and the failure to ask anything approaching adequate questions is particularly telling. This nonsense *appeared normal*. Certainly, Madonna was openly stating that she was using the UN for gravitas. 'I want to put Raising Malawi on the map,' is how she classed the event. 'I want credibility as a philanthropic organisation.'

Probably the most depressing thing about the muted outcry was Madonna's glib assumption that it was somehow distracting from the big picture. What she can't see – or doesn't care to – is that this no-questions-asked glitz-chasing *is* the big picture. There is a clear causal link between the way the UN conducts its business or allows itself to be used by big corporations and celebrities, and their efficacy in helping people around the globe. If things are out of whack here, then it's a fair guess to say the problems are systemic. Equally, it's not enough for Madonna to resist attempts at scrutiny, effectively on the vague promise that children will be saved with this money.

Doutbless such carping marks us out as party-poopers, though, so let's wind up this edifying episode by saying that a good time was had by all, and that the goody bag provided to guests contained an $800 Gucci bag. According to the most recent UN estimate, the per capita GDP of Malawi is – can you guess this one? – $800. So at least the hosts provided their own punchline.

## Sylvester Stallone liberates Burma

During a particularly lively TV interview concerning her divorce from Paul McCartney, Heather Mills segued seamlessly into mention of her aid work. More specifically, she claimed she was 'responsible for nine countries'. Alas, the erstwhile Lady McCartney did not elaborate which nine countries enjoyed her stewardship, and their identity remains mysteriously undisclosed. But crucially, she revealed herself to be in no doubt as to the scale of her good deeds.

She is not alone. You'd be surprised how many celebrities are geopolitically significant.

Did you see *Rambo*? Not *First Blood* – the original outing for Sylvester Stallone's bandanna-swaddled Vietnam vet – but the final instalment of the quartet.[10] *Rambo* is set in Burma, and prior to the movie's release, it received what studio bosses would doubtless have viewed as a marketing boost. To wit: hundreds of monks staged peaceful protests in various Burmese cities, which precipitated a brutal military crackdown, in which an unknown number of people were beaten and killed. You really can't buy that kind of advertising.

And if you had opted to read just one piece about the political and humanitarian crisis engulfing the country, you should have made it the Associated Press's interview on the subject with Sylvester Stallone, which offered a moving reminder that one of the most vital things we do with our Western freedoms is demand a celebrity angle on every single story, no matter how palpably inappropriate. Thus the news agency cast its eyes over the murdering of protesters, the brutalising of monks, and asked the essential question. Namely: what does Rocky think? No doubt he'll have a fascinating take on the UN's approach to negotiations with the junta.

Sly had been shooting the latest instalment in the *Rambo* series in Thailand, had spent a period filming on the Salween River, which forms part of the country's border with Burma. So while he hadn't actually been in actual Burma . . . oh, whatever. Let's not split hairs. 'We hear about Vietnam and

[10] It has to be the final one. Doesn't it?

Cambodia,' he told the AP reporter, 'but this was more horrific . . . It would be a white-washing not to show what's going on over there,' the actor continued. 'I think there is a story that needs to be told.'

Yes. But was it the story of one man, ripped on human growth hormone, saving some Christian missionaries with his ragtag band of mercenaries and still managing to disembowel some evil-doers? The argument felt unconvincing. Could we please consider at least an uncredited cameo for Aung San Suu Kyi?

As for how he'd picked Burma as the backdrop for John Rambo's latest mission, Sly was frank. 'I called *Soldier of Fortune* magazine and they said Burma was the foremost area of human abuse on the planet.'[11]

So what the violent suppression of the monks' protests did was to retroactively justify Stallone's decision to set his movie there. 'I was being accused, once again, of using the Third World as a Rambo victim,' he huffed, clearly anxious to set the record straight about the long-running franchise that began with the human-rights classic *First Blood*, and most recently led to *Rambo III*, where our hero teamed up with the Afghan mujahideen. That film is dedicated 'to the gallant people of Afghanistan', who have been saying 'thank you, America' ever since.

'The Burmese are beautiful people,' Sly went on to say. 'It's the military I am portraying as cruel.'

Indeed. Once again it had fallen to Sly to don Rambo's bandanna and pall of nihilism to liberate missionaries held captive by Burmese militia. He punches a guy's head clean off in one scene. It's awesome. But even more awesome, according to Sly, were reports that the Burmese had 'gone crazy' over bootleg copies of the film, and the line 'Live for nothing. Die for something' was being used as a rallying cry by real-life dissidents. 'This movie could fuel the sentiment of Myanmar people to invite

[11] Yes, mercenaries genuinely have their own trade paper. Subscribe your ass *today*.

American troops to help save them from the junta,' one Yangon resident is said to have told Reuters.

Can you imagine anything more mind-blowing than the fourth iteration of the *Rambo* franchise being the catalyst for Burmese self-determination? It's like the uncalled-for-sequel theory of history. Maybe a Zimmer-assisted Rocky could fight in North Korea next. Whatever, Sly was in no mood to wait and see whether there was any substance to these reports, preferring to make declarations that suggested the overthrow of the junta was a done deal. 'These incredibly brave people have found a kind of a voice in American cinema,' Stallone announced. 'That, to me, is one of the proudest moments I've had in film.'

Oh, please! What about getting Sharon Stone to strip in *The Specialist*?

As the weeks went by, though, Sly seemed remarkably unattuned to the possibility that *Rambo* might not have quite the historic impact he supposed. In fact, he kept digging, issuing a message to the Burmese government. 'Why don't you invite me over?' he enquired via Reuters. 'Let me take a tour of your country without someone pointing a gun at my head and we'll show you where all the bodies are buried.'

Alas, while any Western politician would jump at the chance, the Myanmar junta are not believed to be quite as star-struck as their democracy-crazed counterparts. That said, their grainy pirate copy of *Rocky Balboa* was marred by someone's head obscuring the screen right at the point where it's explained why and how in the name of sanity the 61-year-old Rocky gets back in the ring with a heavyweight champion of the world three decades his junior.

So one day their curiosity might get the better of them. Here's hopin'!

## Are celebrities hard-wired to get charity wrong?

A bright September day in 2005, and a small dinghy attempts to navigate the flooded streets of New Orleans. Its mission is to ferry to safety stranded survivors of Hurricane Katrina, and its unofficial captain is Sean Penn – actor, director, philanthropist. Alas, the boat is sinking under the weight of its passengers and crew, and so it is that Sean is attempting to bail it out using a small red plastic cup. Various passing news photographers capture the image, and over the next few days eyebrows are raised at the discovery that the craft also contained a photographer and a reporter covering Sean's efforts for *Rolling Stone* magazine.

Make no mistake, Sean Penn cares about Katrina victims and all kinds of other causes. But contemplating the above tableau in its entirety, we have to ask: are celebrities just hard-wired to get this stuff wrong?

You can argue all day about whether excluding Sean's Boswell would have left one more space on each journey back to dry land, but the basic story is familiar. A celebrity heads in the direction of admirable, but an inevitable swerve means they end up in the realms of absurdity.

Take the first Playing for Good International Philanthropic Summit[12] – billed by its organisers in 2007 as an opportunity for prominent activists to gather in the cause of global philanthropy. That's something we can all agree on, right? How can you *disagree* with supporting the cause of people supporting causes? Especially if it lasts three days, is hosted by 'actress and philanthropist' Eva Longoria, and takes place on the beautiful Balearic island of Mallorca. And you'd have to be certifiable to disagree with this cause once you discovered it ended with 'an elegant black tie gala dinner and the presentation of the 2007 Awards of Charitable Excellence'.[13]

[12] Spoiler alert: the first annual Playing for Good International Philanthropic Summit was also the last annual Playing for Good International Philanthropic Summit. Bonus fact: Playing for Good were the crew who were going to dispatch Paris Hilton to Rwandania. Rwandaland. Whatever. Following what is described as a 'restructuring', that trip ended up de-prioritised – just another casualty in the Great Ennui Wars.

[13] The 'Awards of Charitable Excellence'? At some point, is the Self-congratulatory Charity Award Name Generator actually going to run out of random combinations?

Paris Hilton was in attendance, making, as the organisers pointed out with somewhat misplaced pride, her first formal appearance since being released from jail.

Or take Marlon Brando's famous Oscar protest in 1973, when he decided to draw attention to the siege of two hundred Native Americans by the US Marshals Service at Wounded Knee in South Dakota. Brando was favourite to win Best Actor for *The Godfather*, but declined to attend, opting to make alternative arrangements. When his name was duly read out, an Apache woman named Sacheen Littlefeather went up to the stage, where she refused the Oscar on his behalf.

Unfortunately, those eyebrows were raised again when it emerged that 'Sacheen Littlefeather' was in fact a Californian actress called Maria Cruz, merely dressed as an Apache – presumably because the costume she'd worn when she won Miss American Vampire three years previously would have looked out of place. And eyebrows met hairlines when, by the end of the year, Sacheen had appeared in *Playboy* in no costume at all. A cautionary tale, then, embodying a couple of lessons for the celebrity activist. One: if you want to make a memorable protest about, say, the Iraq war, get your people to dredge up an Iraqi amputee, rather than some slightly tanned former Saved By the Bell extra willing to hop.[14] And two: *maybe you're just not cut out for this stuff.*

An awful lot of famous people – probably most famous people – were drawn to the entertainment business partly out of a desire to be liked. They will often admit this openly, which is creditably honest of them. There's little more wearying than having to listen to a three-chord boy band telling you it's all about the music. But bound up with this desire is a tendency towards self-regard. And when these kinds of personality types attempt altruism, things inevitably go awry. Are celebrities capable of truly selfless good deeds? To frame the question more starkly: are celebrities in need of work capable of truly selfless good deeds?

---

[14] Remember, if all else fails, every tenth statuette is coated in a substance which turns the holder into a gibbering, lachrymally incontinent halfwit anyway.

Listen to this for a blurb: 'The organisation Reality Cares was founded with the support of the reality-television industry to respond to some of the most critical issues facing the world today.' Really? *Really?* 'We help raise funds and awareness for important causes such as Aids research and education, disaster relief, creative arts, drunk-driving, and much more.' So when you can't get on TV any more, remember there's always another arena.

But these individual shots at parlaying one's fifteen minutes into sixteen are less concerning than the general trends. In their relentless quest for gravitas, stars no longer want to be just the face of a problem. They want to be seen to be solving it. Yesterday's star, like Brando, sought to draw attention to issues. Today's celebrity sees themselves as actively involved in the resolution process. Yet the problems over which they are sprinkling their stardust are extremely complex, and non-experts can tend to simplify them. At worst, a celebrity's 'call to arms' will both degrade the suffering they are attempting to highlight, and give the impression that outside silver bullets are the answer. Over again to Donald Steinberg, the deputy president of the International Crisis Group, who has stated frankly of celebrities' engagement with causes that 'there is a tendency to treat these issues as if it's all good and evil'.

Celebrities tend to react emotionally to problems. There is nothing wrong with this tendency – in fact, it's likely to make them much better actors or musicians. But these are absolutely not qualities you'd look for in a public intellectual. Complex problems like the humanitarian fallout from counter-insurgencies need to be approached analytically, not emotionally.

For an example of an analytical celebrity in action, let's steel ourselves to return to what was classed as Geri Halliwell's 'fact-finding mission to Zambia'. When the former Spice Girl was asked what the most memorable part of this mission was, she cited: 'Seeing light in the children's eyes when they see they are not forgotten and that people care.'

Do we really want to solve this one? Or do we just want to look like we want to solve it, and appease a few messianic actresses into the bargain?

## Some statistics: in which we let daylight in on magic

One useful way to measure charitable giving is as a percentage of household income after tax. The Giving USA Foundation is America's leading institution devoted to the research, education and public understanding of philanthropy. We've seen an explosion in celebrity advocacy in the past decade, so how has that affected things?

Well, in 2005, Giving USA's statistics placed average charitable giving per US household (after tax) at 2.2 per cent. Interestingly, 2.2 per cent is also exactly the forty-year average for charitable giving per household (after tax). In 2006, Giving USA placed it at 2.3 per cent. In 2007 it was 2.3 per cent. Regression towards the mean being what it is, we'll be due a couple of below-average years soon enough.

Crucially, then, the amount of money being raised hasn't altered in material terms: only the manner in which it is solicited. The mania for celebrity advocates is just a new way of getting attention – and it is a way which conflates entertainment with aid. But before we become dazzled by the glamour, those statistics should remind us that celebrities did not fill a vacuum. It was dedicated activists and charity workers whose efforts had managed to extract, on average, precisely the same level of charitable donation from people for forty years.

Yet you will struggle now to find a charity that isn't desperate for a celebrity spokesperson, simply because it has become the norm, and without a famous advocate it is hugely difficult to get one's voice heard in the marketplace. This is an utterly screwed-up marketplace that needs a serious correction.

It needs a correction not least because celebrities tend to be drawn to what are perceived as glamorous or fashionable causes, presently Africa and Aids. In a couple of decades these might be entirely different things. But they're highly unlikely to be unsightly skin diseases, or mental illness that can precipitate violence. If we hold in our mind that concept of a finite, unchanging percentage of income being available to charitable causes, then it's difficult not to conclude that celebrities don't just skew the debate: they monopolise funding that in a less febrile atmosphere might have found its way to a needier cause.

## Sharon Stone knows best, again

Would it really kill Hollywood to cast Sharon Stone in so many movies that she didn't have the time to 'save the world' in her own special way? The exercise would likely turn out to be so beneficial to the unsaved world that the studios could legitimately write her fees off against tax as charitable donations. It's a thought. For now, though, gird your loins for a couple of zingers from our beloved Sharon, the Where's Waldo figure in the annals of celebrity activism.

For the first, we journey to Davos, for the 2005 World Economic Forum. One of the plenary sessions concerned African poverty, and during the course of speeches from the platform the Tanzanian president extolled the virtues of mosquito nets impregnated with insecticide as a simple but effective weapon against malaria in his country.

Then it came to questions from the audience. And who was first up but Ms Sharon Stone – a bewildering presence in the first place, perhaps, but even more so when she opened not with an enquiry, but with an unsolicited pledge of $10,000. Some people in attendance felt she was grandstanding; rather more agreed when her next act was to raise her hand above her head in a manner *Time* magazine described as 'like an evangelical preacher'. Sharon then turned to the audience and began demanding 'Would anyone else like to stand up and help? Just stand up! Stand up and people will take your name!' A little time and a lot of awkwardness later, $1 million in pledges had been extracted.

'These were people with a lotta cash,' a satisfied Stone explained to the press that evening. 'I thought, "I really have to get it now", and that's why I made an ass of myself.'

And made an ass of herself she had, because it wasn't long before experts were criticising the actress for reacting emotionally and without proper research.

In terms of sorting the facts from the drama, the greatest service was probably done by Xavier Sala-i-Martin, an eminent Columbia economics professor, who had been sitting five yards from the actress. The prof bided his time – in fact, he waited until the next year's World Economic Forum – and only then did he enquire after the money apparently raised by Sharon. Turned out that a mere $250,000 of the $1 million pledges were ever actually honoured, obliging Unicef to make up the shortfall by diverting funds from other projects – other projects which Unicef had presumably deemed more worthy. But that's star power for you. Years of painstaking *Sophie's Choice*-style dilemmas over how to allocate aid budgets had been trumped by the gut reaction of Ms Sharon Stone.

Inspired by the saga – or rather distinctly uninspired by it – Professor Sala-i-Martin was moved to write an article on 'the negatives of celebrity-driven benevolence' for the *Wall Street Journal*, and it's worth reading as an exquisitely measured demolition of the misplaced actions of so many starry humanitarians.

'First,' he stated in this article, 'it is not clear that they base their decision to embrace a particular cause on rational and informed thinking. Miss Stone reacted instinctively to the moving words of President Mkapa. She did not carefully research the causes and consequences of malaria, she did not compare them with other problems in the region, she did not consult public health experts on potential solutions other than the free distribution of bed nets and, more importantly, she did not ask the citizens of Tanzania if that is what they wanted. Had she done so, she might have been surprised: some African governments do distribute free bed nets through public hospitals. The trouble is that many people take the free nets . . . sell them in the black market, and use the money to buy something they really want.

'When Sharon Stone raised her hand at Davos,' the professor continued, 'I was sitting next to a prestigious doctor. He whispered to me that yes, one million children die of malaria every year . . . but two million die of diarrhoea. He wondered if Sharon Stone would have been equally moved had the speech been about intestinal diseases and other affections with little aesthetic appeal.'

Maybe she'd have been moved to give us another of her karmic explanations for these afflictions. But what Sala-i-Martin identified as the third and most troubling problem is any given celebrity's total lack of accountability.

'If the funds raised by Sharon Stone are wasted,' he reasoned, 'she does not get expelled from anything, she does not have to pay back the donors, and worst of all, if her action turns out to cause harm (perhaps because she diverted funding away from other places where it could have saved lives), she will not be legally liable.' Sala-i-Martin went on to point out that were any celebrity aid drive to have negative net effects on recipient countries, the stars behind it would suffer no legal consequences. 'Contrast this with what would happen to a CEO of a corporation that pollutes a river!'[15]

Yet littering the public statements of entertainment personalities is their claim that they are using their fame in a positive way, using their glamour to draw attention to something unglamorous. This is facile. Apart from the fact that it effectively amounts to a shameless admission that they are skewing debate, it confuses the entertainment industry with human suffering in a way that is at best jarring and at worst utterly degrading of the issue at stake.

[15] Maybe the CEO should bridle at the criticism/fine/possible prison term, on the basis that without his important intervention, no one would have heard of this crappy little river anyway. He really 'raised awareness' of it.

And so to our second chance to gaze in slack-jawed horror at Ms Sharon Stone. You heard more about this earlier, but you are cordially invited to consider again the actress's meeting in Israel with Shimon Peres in 2006, from which she proceeded directly into the promotional tour for *Basic Instinct 2*.

During her excruciating joint press conference with Peres, Sharon addressed the following opening remarks to reporters: 'People are just sitting there going, like: "I don't care what she's saying, I just want to know, does she get naked in the movie? Is she naked? Nude, nude, nude, naked. Do I see her boobies?" So let's just through to that,' the actress giggled. 'Yes!'

Do you find this a) mind-bendingly inappropriate, or b) something that 'raised awareness' of the need for peace in the Middle East?

## Send in the clowns: celebrities at congressional hearings

In case you thought we couldn't tumble any further down the rabbit hole, we can. We've looked at the strange spectacle of celebrities playing like lawmakers and aid agencies; it's now time to cringe as lawmakers and aid agencies attempt to adopt show-business customs into their own worlds. At Davos in 2005, for example, Lionel Richie was presented with an award. What for? Oh, for co-writing 'We Are the World' twenty years previously. But the question we should really be asking is: why on earth does the World Economic Forum need an award ceremony?

The answer is probably because everyone else has one. Philanthropic awards are everywhere. When even Paris Hilton is doling them out, it's hard not to suspect that these gongs are like those qualifications people send off for in the post, then display prominently as a means of legitimising themselves and their activities. 'Yes, that's my Most Excellent Philanthropist Who Would Turn Up to the Award Ceremony award. Now stand aside while I use it as an excuse for all manner of diva-like behaviour.' Indeed, with hundreds of celebrities holding humanitarian awards of some stripe, it seems philanthropy is no longer its own reward.

Way more troubling than this, though, is the desperation of legislators to hitch their wagons to a star. Near the start of this chapter, we heard about the congressmen who agreed to sit down with Geri Halliwell. Regrettably, they are merely the tip of the iceberg.[16]

Congressional committees regularly call stars to testify. According to Harry Strine, author of an intriguing academic paper entitled 'Your testimony was splendid: the treatment of celebrities and non-celebrities in Congressional hearings', the trend is gaining speed. Congress has been summoning celebrities to draw in the crowds since the 1940s, but the idea didn't come into its absurdist own until 1985, when the House Agricultural Committee tabled a hearing called 'The plight of the family farmer'. Among those called to testify were Jane Fonda, Sissy Spacek and Sally Field. It should be perfectly obvious why. They had all played farm wives in the movies.

Skip forward to the present day, and it's positively common-place for the laughably unqualified to pop up on Capitol Hill – and according to Strine's analysis of a representative sample of the 400-plus celebrity appearances before committees since 1969, members of Congress 'are far more deferential to celebrities than non-celebrities'. And let's not forget that by non-celebrities, we tend to mean *proper expert witnesses*.

Strine adapted something called the Bales Interaction Process Analysis, a system for measuring the dynamics of group activity by noting whether a questioner shows solidarity with the questionee, how many times they interrupt them, observing whether they ask for or give orientation. That kind of stuff. Put briefly, Strine's analysis of the committee transcripts concluded that 'almost 25% of the questions or comments made to celebrities are statements showing hospitality, sympathy, and

---

[16] Good sense will take the role of the *Titanic*.

high regard whereas only 8% of the non-celebrities receive similar comments at the hearings. Ironically,' he mused, 'most of the non-celebrity witnesses appearing in these hearings are well educated and accomplished individuals, clearly deserving of praise, while the celebrities are in attendance simply because they are famous, or are from Hollywood.'

Yet on this farce goes, with more and more celebrities summoned to be fawned upon with each passing year. Standout moments? It's always so hard to pick them, but special mention ought to be made of the occasion in 2002 when the Senate's Environment and Public Works Clean Air Subcommittee hearing was graced by the presence of Kevin Richardson – a singer with the boy band the Backstreet Boys.

The committee was examining a controversial mining technique which involved mountain-top removal, and Kevin had been invited to testify by Al Gore's former presidential running mate, Joe Lieberman. 'Mr Richardson is here as more than a well-known celebrity,' Lieberman declared. 'He is knowledgeable on this issue and has in fact worked to protect the environment in his home state. I believe his voice will add to our understanding of the issue.'

Also: *loved* his harmonies in 'I Want It That Way'.

Bewilderingly, Lieberman's endorsement wasn't enough to persuade another member of the committee of Kevin's invaluable expertise, and so it was that Ohio Senator George Voinovich flatly refused to attend the hearing in protest.

'It's just a joke to think that this witness can provide members of the United States senate with information on important geological and water quality issues,' he told reporters in exasperation. 'We're either serious about the issues or we are running a sideshow.'

By this stage in his career, Kevin ought to have been used to dwindling attendance figures, but he declined to see Voinovich's absence as anything other than the senator's loss. 'It's unfortunate that he's not here,' was the Backstreet Boy's self-effacing retort. 'I could have taught him something.' That something turned out to be vital field evidence collected via a technical process best summarised as 'looking out of the window of a private jet'.

'I am not a scientist,' intoned Kevin, for those under the illusion that he combined a successful career in getting off a stool for the second chorus with a sideline in advanced geohydrology, 'but I do know what I've seen in flights over the coal fields.'[17]

But if you think that was the star-struck committee system's lowest moment, think again. Beside our next witness, Kevin looks like Isaac Newton. At least he was a member of the human species.

## Elmo goes to Washington

In 2002, anxious to solicit his opinions on school music education, the House Appropriations Subcommittee on Labor, Health and Human Services, and Education called Elmo to testify. *Sesame Street*'s Elmo. Elmo. *A muppet*. It would be so great to be able to tell you the inquisitors led with 'Will you apologise for the fact that you ruined *Sesame Street*?' Or that they followed that one up with 'Do you accept that you're *Sesame Street*'s Scrappy-Doo – if not its Jar Jar Binks?'

Unfortunately, that didn't happen. Instead, the committee listened, enthralled, as Elmo used his traditional third-person styling to deliver several aperçus.

'Elmo loves to sing and to dance and to make music with all his friends on *Sesame Street*,' the perpetual three-and-a-half-year-old informed the committee. 'It helps Elmo to learn ABCs and makes it easier for Elmo to remember things. Sometimes it makes Elmo excited, and sometimes it calms Elmo down – Elmo's teacher really likes that.'

Elmo was invited by the Californian Republican Randy 'Duke'

[17] Bonus fact: Kevin used to play one of the Teenage Mutant Ninja Turtles at Disneyland. *Still* think you can ignore his thoughts on the ecological impact of mountaintop mining?

Regula – sadly no longer a congressman, after pleading guilty to mail fraud, wire fraud, tax evasion and accepting millions of dollars in bribes. He is currently serving the longest jail term ever handed down to a former congressman.[18] But that was all waiting round the corner the day Elmo came to Washington, when Duke endorsed another attendee's testimony that 'Elmo, in many ways, speaks for all children everywhere'.

No. Elmo is a puppet. You are Capitol Hill lawmakers, elected to serve the people, and in whose hands lies the educational future of millions of children. And you are asking questions of an expert witness who is *made of fun fur*. It feels kind of depressing to have to explain democracy to you, but you are asking questions of this puppet on behalf of those very children. Why don't you just mail them a turd and hit the golf course? It'd be marginally less offensive.

Of course, politicians don't really want to know what a glorified glove has to say about the role of music in a child's development. They know that booking stunt witnesses is an easy way to draw cachet and cameras to the hearing, thus getting their faces on TV, and thus upping their precious recognition factor.

If lawmakers think so little of themselves, is it any wonder that people share that view? What we might unfashionably class as 'the proper legislative channels' are now openly disparaged by film stars who find the mechanisms of democracy incompatible with their schedules. 'Much as I would love never having to visit Washington,' Angelina Jolie has explained, 'that's the way to move the ball.'

And yet, tempting as oligarchy might seem to the *Tomb Raider* star, there are those who still cling to the quaint idea that getting stuff done should require legislating. It should require active agents to be accountable, as legislators are. But the slide to a celebocracy has meant that celebrites are able to wield enormous influence without having been elected, without having to be

[18] Elmo has never been investigated.

subject to proper scrutiny, and without having to go via normal legislative channels. And unlike NGOs, it's not even their day job. Many of the celebrities who describe themselves as 'working with the UN' are engaged in obfuscation on a grand scale. A few afternoons a year becomes 'working with the UN', much as your Saturday paper round became 'managing an information-delivery system' when you came to write your first CV.

But then, who needs dogged, self-effacing experts, when we have Christie Brinkley to address the United Nations on nuclear power. 'You may be thinking,' she hazarded before the assembled throng in 2007, 'what does a model have to do with nuclear weapons? Why me? I am certainly not an expert on nuclear weapons, or global politics.' Remind us why you're here then? 'But I am an American, a woman and a mother,' declared Christie, 'and I'm pretty sure that even with my supermodel powers, that I would be pulverised and disintegrate right along with the rest of you in a nuclear disaster.'

That was literally her best point. Still, the apocalypse might have its upsides.

When and why on earth did we decide to mortgage the future of aid on the entertainment industry? You may wonder who is really losing out under this model – and the answer is that we all are. Making diplomats and aid spokesmodels out of celebrities doesn't just over-empower entertainers – it edges other, more committed people out of the frame. In times past, international progressive forces created their own celebrities. The world came to know people like Desmond Tutu or Aung San Suu Kyi – people whose full-time occupation was attempting to change a grievous status quo, as opposed to people who doubled up as designer-clad multimillionaires.

There tended to be little dissonance between these people's lifestyle and the causes they were championing. These days, though, it's all too easy for a celebrity's lifestyle to entirely undermine the moral seriousness of their message. During a promotional tour for Leonardo DiCaprio's environmental documentary, the film's directors were asked how on earth the actor could preach this stuff when he continued to use private jets. 'Leonardo flew commercial to the Cannes Film Festival and they lost his luggage,' was their painfully inadequate justification. 'He knows he probably shouldn't fly private any more . . .'

Equally, it's not just heroes who will remain unsung, but whole arguments. For all their synthesised rebel posturing, celebrities tend not to be anti-establishment. Celebrities are largely conservative: they tend to pick overseas issues that will not alienate their paying public back home. They are wary of the kind of radicalism traditionally associated with any struggle for change, and so it is that you find them tucked up in uncontroversial arrangements with the UN. But their high-profile nature beams attention onto this middle ground, and onto these mainstream ideas, leaving other more radical types of political argument in the dark. To some degree, then, they legitimise the status quo – and often in a way which incenses those who toil daily rather nearer the coalface of the problems.

Take a 2003 statement by Bob Geldof, whose original Live Aid changed the face of celebrity activism, but who is not immune to drawing simplistic conclusions with the best of them.

'You'll think I'm off my trolley when I say this,' he told reporters following him on a visit to Ethiopia, 'but the Bush administration is the most radical – in a positive sense – in its approach to Africa since Kennedy.' Begging Sir Bob's pardon . . . but there was no shortage of aid agencies ready to voice irate bemusement that he should have ignored the Bush administration's advocacy of abstinence as a means of fighting Aids, or the strengthening of already ruinous American farm subsidies.

Orthodoxies are there to be challenged, so let's stick our necks out and hazard that the relentless seepage of celebrity into these areas is not a Good Thing, that it dangerously skews debate, that it encourages engagement with political issues in emotional, non-analytical ways, and that if we don't start calling entertainers out for it, the world's problems are going to get worse, not better. Currently, the message we are sending to younger generations is that solving those problems is a jobshare with making motion pictures. Let's review that as a matter of urgency.

# CELEBRITIES AND THEIR PETS

'It is the knowledge of necessary and eternal truths which distinguishes us from mere animals, and gives us Reason and the sciences, raising us to knowledge of ourselves and of God. It is this in us which we call the rational soul or Mind.'

Gottfried Wilhelm Leibniz

'I loved all the Aaron Spelling shows, *Beverly Hills 90210* and *Models Inc*. At that time, I had pet rats I was raising and I always named all the baby rats after the characters in the shows.'

Paris Hilton

If it seems odd to devote an entire chapter to celebrity pets, then you're still way, way off getting a handle on your own place in the universe. The primary purpose of these animals – the VIPets, if you will – is to give the public a sense of perspective. It makes you aware that there are dogs living more fabulous lives than you. Actually, there are ferrets living more fabulous lives than you. Paris Hilton has repeatedly been accompanied on the red carpet by one of her two ferrets, and the realisation that socialite weasels are more aspirational guest-picks than you should start to bring home your irrelevance.

Of course, accessorising with animals is nothing new, but has historically been a contributory factor in decisions to do stuff like overthrow long-established monarchies. Marie Antoinette dyed her sheep to match her outfits, for instance, and France's failure to see how winsome that was yet again underlined how tragically before her time the celebutante queen was.

Today, that kind of behaviour – far from being viewed as an argument for parting Marie from her head – would have catapulted her to the enthralled attention of reality-television executives, who would have swiftly ushered her into one of those fish-out-of-water formats that sublimates aggressive indolence and rank stupidity into huge ratings. Whatever our prime-time reality offering would have been called – let's just run with *Le Simple Life: Let Them Eat Cake* – it would have enabled the misunderstood French queen to engage with a series of hand-picked, heavily screened peasants, all the while winning over a slack-jawed public with her prototypic 'That's hot' catchphrase, 'C'est chaud'.

Today, any serious look[1] at the new breed of celebrity pets has to ask: are they not just the story of our times writ another way? Whereas the headline-grabbing animals of yesteryear were celebrated for their talents and accomplishments, today's celebripets are merely – yes – famous for being famous people's pets. Often, they are famous for being people-famous-for-being-famous's pets. While Lassie could carry a movie, your standard celebrity chihuahua seems incapable of scampering from A to B, preferring to make the journey in an It bag. You have to wonder: how long before the first celebripet sex tape? It's not like that chihuahua army over at the Hilton mansion isn't practising.

How long, indeed, before the first celebrity pet misery memoir, perhaps authored by Tinkerbell Hilton, the trailblazing handbag dog whose early public appearances soon gave way to ferret usurpers, and kidnap dramas, and whispered rumours that she'd grown too big for this season's bag?

Before long, we'll see how Paris Hilton is nothing short of the Beverly Hills Dionysus, if one whose faun retinue has been replaced by an apparently randomly assembled menagerie whose

[1] And what is this, if not the most serious of looks?

internecine power struggles rival those of a Renaissance papal court. We'll also be examining the first celebrity pet power list, and congratulating everyone involved in bringing such a deeply pointful exercise to the mass media.

But darker times await us too, as we look at the famous pets who buckle under the weight of expectation, or the partying, or the addiction to prescription chews. And in passages of almost unbearable poignancy, we will recall the career of one of the most enigmatic primate sidekicks, Bubbles, before wandering through the ghost zoo that is Neverland, being mindful not to put our fingers through the cage bars.

You should probably find out when you last had a tetanus shot.

## Paris Hilton: the animal kingdom's Angelina

When it comes to the old 'a dog is for life, not just for Christmas' line, the celebrity community pretty much gets the message. Even when the handbag a dog was purchased to fill starts looking dated, most stars are altruistic enough to realise you do not have to throw the baby out with the bathwater, or rather the chihuahua out with the Chloé. You can work with what you have. Yes, it'll yap a little when the bandages come off, but it's nothing that can't be shushed with the words 'Does Mitzi like her new pointy ears?'[2]

Unfortunately, many celebrities regard dogs as just too civilian, and, as such, an inadequate mirror to their own startling originality. This leads to outlandish animal purchases, and that is where the problems can start.

We've touched upon Rascal, one of a pair of ferrets who accompanied Paris Hilton down various red carpets, and who had been given access to the kinds of glittering soirees of which you can only dream. Award ceremonies, fashion shows – he's seen them all. But as it turns out, Rascal represented a relatively

[2] If Mitzi still won't shut up, give her a Bonio-flavoured Xanax.

conventional choice of date for Paris. What she'd *really* hankered after was a kangaroo.

'She wanted to buy one,' her sister Nicky told reporters, explaining that the pair of them had seen baby kangaroos on a visit to Queensland and realised that their Los Angeles home was one hopping house guest short of perfect. 'But then they told us that kangaroos get as tall as humans,' concluded Nicky ruefully, 'and then start punching you in the gut.'

Surprisingly, for a woman whose entourage has at varying times included a shaman and an MTV-sourced fake best friend, Paris had no career openings for a marsupial bodyguard. But the episode would appear to mark the moment when the heiress decided to be bound no more by society's narrow-minded views of what does and doesn't constitute an acceptable pet. It was time to go to Las Vegas and win a goat.

Not literally, of course – though if they can fill those claw-crane vending machines with teddies, there's no earthly reason they can't substitute horned livestock for plush bears. But in this particular instance, it seems that Paris won some money on the tables, and spent it the best way she knew how: on a ferret, a goat, and a creature she described as 'like, half-monkey, half-raccoon', all of whom would be coming home to live with her in Beverly Hills. And that would have been that, had our heroine known the answer to a single, familiar question. Namely: are you aware of the restrictions that apply to carry-on baggage on commercial flights?

In a perfect world, that laminated card that sits atop the check-in desk, and features pictures of bombs, guns and other things that ought not to be in your hand luggage . . . well, that card would also feature a picture of a ferret, a goat, and a 'like, half-monkey, half-raccoon'. Otherwise, how are you supposed to know?

Or as Paris told the world after her travel plan ran up against this glitch: 'I tried to take them on a plane, and the flight attendants thought I was insane. They were like: "This isn't a travelling circus – you're not bringing a goat on a plane." So I ended up having to drive back to LA in a limo by myself for six hours with the animals.'

But of course you did. And which of us doesn't well up just picturing Paris and her plucky fellow travellers, hastening towards LA in a long-wheel-based, minibar-equipped litter tray. It's like a way more inspirational reworking of *The Incredible Journey*.

Naturally, though, the return would have a prodigal flavour to it. Just as Angelina Jolie never tires of telling the world about the difficulties of introducing new child acquisitions to her ever expanding brood, so Paris would have been aware of the pain that would surely flicker across Tinkerbell's tiny face the minute that limo pulled into the drive, and disgorged not simply her absentee mommy, but a kind of farmyard buffet with a side of raccoon/monkey hybrid.

Can you even imagine Tinkerbell's jealousy issues at this time? Let's hope they upped her doggy meds: none of us would have wanted her to have to go through this unassisted by the good folks at pharmaceutical giant Eli Lilly (selling you dog Prozac since 2007, kids!).[3]

But because there is no end to the torments the showbiz deities will visit upon young Paris, there were even more perilous times to come for the elite chihuahua force that she continued to assemble – an army which, at one count, boasted seventeen crystal-collared foot soldiers. 'They keep having babies,' a loose-lipped Paris told an interviewer, 'and I feel bad to give them away because I feel like, if I had a baby and someone gave it away, it'd be mean.'[4] Alas, before Paris could usher the dogs into planned parenthood classes, this disclosure prompted a visit from the Los Angeles Department of Animal Services, LA law stating that you are only allowed three dogs per address.[5]

---

[3] It's actually called Reconcile. You can get stuff for canine separation anxiety too.
[4] Debatable.
[5] That's some more of that 'small government' Americans are always hearing about.

'I only have ten dogs now,' a not-very-convincing Paris soon claimed via various news outlets – the standard manner in which one responds to a subpoena from the Department of Animal Services. 'Some of my dogs had puppies, so I gave some of them away to people I really know and trust,' she continued, adding that she was having an exact replica of her mansion built for the remaining dogs to live in. 'I gave some to my stylist and to a few of my best friends, so now I'm down to ten.' Or at least she was until she found out about the frantic round of break-up sex that took place before the dogs went their separate ways.

There followed a further interview in which she claimed to have retained the services of a personal zookeeper. Then another detailing a mass dog exodus to a ranch (coordinates unspecified). Who knows how long these attempts at misdirection can succeed in frustrating the LA dog-catcher? The main thing is that someone has at last recognised the Hilton menagerie for what it is: a looming Malthusian catastrophe, whose chihuahua population looks certain to increase too quickly for its resources, leaving weaker, less well-represented species – like monkeys and goats – at risk of poverty and starvation. It's all in *An Essay on the Principle of Population*, dog-purveyors. Let's stay up to speed.

## Tinkerbell Hilton: the Patty Hearst de nos jours

Tinkerbell was Paris's first chihuahua, and, as we have seen, she lived quite the life – recognised everywhere, VIPed for all the best nightspots, and dripping with jewel-encrusted collars.

Then, one morning in 2004 – gone. Vanished, disappeared – and her mistress reported to be inconsolable. Within days, flunkeys were seen sticking up 'lost' signs all over Beverly Hills. Fashioned from hot-pink card, and bearing a magazine shot of the millionairess with the misplaced hound, their message was devastating in its simplicity: 'Please help,' they read. 'This dog is like a child to me.' A commensurate $1,000 reward was offered.

However, there was some surprise when a Hilton assistant

insisted that the missing dog was not in fact Tinkerbell, but one named Napoleon – a hitherto unheard-of member of Paris's four-legged entourage. What was going on? This being a fast-moving news event, it wasn't long before Paris succumbed to reporter pressure and confessed the truth to *In Touch* magazine. It *was* Tinkerbell who was missing – and the Napoleon ruse had merely been a last-ditch attempt at outwitting the evil-doers responsible.

'If they find out Tinkerbell is my dog, they'll hold it to ransom,' Paris told the publication, at the same time as increasing the reward to $5,000. 'Everyone knows I'm rich, so they'll want millions.'

And naturally, the prevalent assumption *was* that Tinkerbell had been kidnapped, both for ransom and the publicity her elevated position in modern American society would bring. Was she even now, like some canine version of Patty Hearst, falling under the evil spell of her captors, and preparing to rob a bank toting a small machine gun and wearing a miniature beret? Was the tiny mutt imprisoned in some dank cellar, being coached to make a series of unrealistic demands, such as for all police Alsatians to be carried in handbags?

Briefly, no. It was eventually established that Paris had in fact left the dog-child at her grandmother's house a week previously, and just forgotten about it. Look, it happens, OK?

By way of a heartbreaking coda, readers should know that the pair were only reunited for a short while, for Tinkerbell grew too large for Paris's liking, and was subsequently replaced with a younger, hotter, smaller version called Bambi. Tinkerbell now lives in seclusion at the Hilton family mansion, perhaps watching old paparazzi videos of herself solicitously lapping Mommy's vomit from the pavement after another mistimed nightclub exit. It's too bad there isn't the space for a full Norma Desmond analogy – but in any case, Paris was already sketching out her next mammal-based project. 'It's been my dream to have four babies by thirty,' she informed the news media, before wheeling out arguably the most well-worn celebrity category mistake: the ascription of pet characteristics to children. 'I look after animals,' the heiress explained, 'so I think I'd have a lot to give my kids.'

And having established her pet-care credentials, we can only hope Paris is as fertile as she is committed to swelling the ranks of our humankind.

## Bubbles: bow your heads to the trailblazer

It's all too easy to think that Tinkerbell was the breakthrough celebrity pet, whose red-carpet appearances would pave the way for a host of other loosely domesticated creatures to share in promotional events too long the sole preserve of the human species. In fact, the glass ceiling was breached nearly two decades earlier, by a certain star companion whom the world would come to know as Bubbles.

Bubbles was the ur-celebrity pet, the Michael Jackson associate who refused to be pigeonholed by the body that Nature had given him. Frankly, those who wrote him off as a chimpanzee revealed more about their own prejudices than they ever did about this plucky little primate. Bubbles was not a chimpanzee: he was a close friend of Michael Jackson who just *happened* to be a chimpanzee.

But how did this taboo-busting association begin? Well, according to something Michael said in the 1980s – which is pretty much like saying according to a magic pixie – Bubbles originally came from a cancer research clinic. The temptation is to assume that Bubbles 'came from a cancer research clinic' in the same way that your childhood dog 'went to live on a farm'. You may find it's best not to ask too many questions about a beloved pet's provenance – or its final destination.

Yet Bubbles, we must surmise, grew tired of laboratory life, with its quotidian ear-grafting and experimental doses of chemotherapy. When the ennui became stifling, the starry-eyed chimp must have requested a transfer to Neverland, the sprawling Santa Barbara ranch whose introverted owner just yearned for a little foundling to soften his heart. If you think of it as an interspecies version of *Annie*, it's less likely to give you nightmares.[6]

And for so long, Bubbles did seem the perfect lightning rod for Michael's radical nurturing tendencies, as the pair showed that despite all that wealth and fame, it was possible to raise a chimp with a grounded value system and at least an intermediate grasp of red-carpet etiquette. How could the sceptics feel anything else as Bubbles stole the world one heart at a time, turning up to awards ceremonies in outfits that exactly matched the singer's, accessorised with a big nappy.

Of course, the rumours and the myths swirled around him, same as they do around any high-profile primate. He was said to have his own bodyguard. It was sworn he had a personal assistant. He sat in on production sessions for *Bad*.

Yet gradually Bubbles began to scale down his public appearances, and it was assumed that he was withdrawing into a twilight world, no longer entranced by the bright lights of premieres, or the screaming attentions of fans. As for Michael, he appeared to be turning his attentions to less hirsute hominids. Your Culkins. Your Feldmans. Your ones we don't talk about any more.

But for all his lower profile, Bubbles continued to live at the ranch, with out-takes of Martin Bashir's disrespectful little documentary even showing him using Michael's private toilet.[7]

Then came the bombshell. During Michael's molestation trial in 2005, a former personal assistant – possibly even Bubbles's former personal assistant – confirmed that the chimpanzee no longer resided at Neverland. And so it was that the stories started up again. He had become irascible; he had bitten people. The intimation was that Bubbles had developed some kind of anger management problem. Why does one imagine him nipping a

[6] In a way.

[7] He still wore a nappy, though, perhaps out of an attachment to the old ways.

social worker in frustration after they completely failed to interpret his mime for 'I have grave concerns about the contents of the Jesus Juice cans'?

Whatever the catalyst for his exile, this American tale has been told many times before. You'd expect that once Bubbles had been cast from Camelot, he'd have been forced to survive on his wits. Perhaps he passed his days propping up low-life bars, telling embittered stories about his time with the King of Pop in increasingly slurred sign language.[8]

Conflicting stories of his whereabouts persisted. On a Canadian wildlife documentary, the respected primatologist Dame Jane Goodall claimed that 'the original Bubbles' – what on earth was she implying? – now 'lived in Florida with Patti Reagan'. The president's daughter and Bubbles! Was there some sort of tear in the eighties space–time continuum? Had the Cold War somehow collapsed into *Thriller*? No, alas – the Patti Reagan was another one entirely – and by that stage one Bob Dunn, the owner of an animal ranch in the Sylmar suburb of Los Angeles, was insisting that Bubbles was now in his custody.

'He's in his twenties now,' Bob told a magazine. 'We don't know his exact age because we don't know his early background.'

You see? Proper animal people know that sometimes it's best not to ask too many questions. Bob knows Bubbles probably doesn't want to talk about the cancer research laboratory. But for a feted chimp who once had his own PA and bodyguard, Bubbles has faced the challenges of downsizing with bravery. 'From his pen,' Bob continued, 'Bubbles can see giraffes, monkeys and chimps which we've trained as extras for Hollywood films.'

Truly, it was the pictures that got small.

[8] In fact, the chimp sign language for 'Don't you know who I am? I used to be Bubbles, man' involves the animal repeatedly smacking itself on the head, so you can imagine the special poignance that would layer upon the moment.

## Neverland: how many others were there?

No matter how far the charmed, mysterious world that was Neverland recedes into the past – no matter how long the Ferris wheel is allowed to oxidise – certain questions will always remain, questions that right-minded people should not shirk. Namely, were there more of them? How many more were there that we don't know about?

*Chimps.* We're talking about chimps. And the answer is that it's hard to say precisely. We do know that Bubbles was certainly not the only chimpanzee who got to lounge around in a handmade tuxedo with the world's highest-selling recording artist. According to the actor and former sleepover regular Corey Feldman, he met 'all kinds of chimps' during his visits to the ranch. But the clearest picture of what was going on up there emerged in Bashir's 2003 documentary *Living With Michael Jackson.* During the making of the film, Bashir noticed that several chimps appeared to be employed around the grounds, with duties ranging from dusting to window cleaning. Was that, he wondered, normal?

'The chimpanzees are very smart,' was Michael's reassuring reply. 'Their DNA is identical to humans' when you look under a microscope.'

By the time of the trial, however, several of Michael's human staff were intimating that their primate co-workers were less entranced by their life of indentured servitude than had previously been believed, and were given to staging regular dirty protests.

Still, we mustn't limit ourselves to what was going on within the mansion walls – because Neverland was so much more than a Peter Pan-themed house-without-boundaries, kept clean by an army of chimp maids. The property came complete with its own fairground, wherein negligent, congenitally grasping parents were once given to dumping their offspring for the afternoon, before occasionally bothering to collect them at park closing time, telling them to quit babbling about this Jesus Juice stuff, or so help Momma, she swears she'll ground their asses for their next two chemo sessions. Just memories today, alas, as the wishing tree stands empty, the bumper-car rink is condemned, and fragrant flower beds of childnip lie shrivelled and untended.

But our business here must be with the other element of outdoor fun at the ranch – Michael's personal zoo, whose denizens included elephants, giraffes, crocodiles, and all manner of other creatures difficult to source from the average neighbourhood pet shop. Quite the species smorgasbord it was, and in the good years, this private animal park ticked along perfectly well. Then in 2006: meltdown. No sooner had Michael been cleared of child-molestation charges, you see, than he tired of Santa Barbara life, and promptly uprooted his young family to live in Bahrain, leaving little more than a petty-cash tin to fund the estate's management.

Finally, a reason to raise an eyebrow about what was going on within its confines, and it wasn't long before a news reporter filed a hard-hitting report suggesting conditions at the zoo had deteriorated dramatically. He conjured an image of biblical suffering, of a whole menagerie of glassy-eyed animals too weak to cry, too wan to howl, too listless even to ride on the slowly rusting carousel. What ailed these creatures? Did they pine for their absentee master? Did they sniff repossession on the wind, and sense their community would soon be dispersed, co-opted into the world's freakiest garage sale? No. They were hungry. In fact, they were starving.

How could this be? How could a man who had made so much of loving all his exotic creatures leave them without even a Dear John letter, one perhaps reading 'your dinner is in the dog'? Many of us are still struggling to make sense of this glaring contra-diction, but it's difficult not to feel driven towards an unpalatable conclusion. It was almost as if Michael hadn't loved the animals at all, but had just pretended to love them, regarding their upkeep as expensive but necessary to draw in human pets. Sweet suffering Jesus Juice! Had the Neverland zoo been a loss leader all along?

Who can say for sure, but news that animals were suffering galvanised the public into getting angry, which in turn galvanised the news media into running regular stories on the scandal. That's right: a decade of molestation rumours with nary a murmur of concern for what was going on up at the big house, and where do people draw the line? At news of a peckish llama.

The animals, naturally, were subsequently taken into care. It goes without saying that the Jackson progeny – Prince Michael, Paris and, of course, little Blanket – remain in the custody of their highly eccentric father, and will no doubt do so no matter how many balconies they are dangled over, no matter how long they are photographed being forced to wear scarves over their faces in public, and no matter how palpably nonsensical Michael's claims to be the biological father of three Caucasians may appear.

But please: sleep easy about the llamas. Their body mass index has been returned to acceptable levels.

### Great milestones in reverse evolution: the first celebrity pet power list

The only mystery, really, is how it took so long, but in 2008 the magazine *Animal Fair* finally sensed the way the world was going, and published the first celebrity pet power list.

'All the time we hear about the sexiest men alive, the best- and worst-dressed celebrities or the most beautiful people,' explained the publication's editor. 'What about the pets?' Thus *Animal Fair* dared to ask the question literally tens wanted the answer to, and drew up a list of the animals that your pet should have been wanting to do it with in 2008. Species restrictions may apply.

Sharing the number-one spot were the canine charges of *Hannah Montana* star Miley Cyrus – Roadie, a Yorkie, and Loco, a shih-tzu; and though we won't get bogged down in the rest of the list, you should know that it also showcased Glenn Close's terriers, Jake and Bill. What it did above all, though, was provide an invaluable stalking resource for those pushy owners who just knew their little half-breed was right for a big hitter, but needed guidance on who constitutes the ultimate quarry.

All over the world – or rather, in highly localised pockets of the decadent West – dog owners were no doubt kicking themselves for forcing neuter surgery on their hot little poodles. Those bitches could have been getting knocked up by Hannah Montana's Yorkie by now had they only let them pursue their showbiz ambitions.

Still, while their on-the-make owners continue to make urgent calls to Brazil-based plastic veterinarians – what was that still-trialling 'spay reversal' operation they vaguely remember reading about? – the rest of us should probably mull over the idea of an 'eligible' pet. Of course, the term eligible has undergone a distinct semantic shift. The original, Jane Austen-ish sense of the word has long slipped out of use, and it is now a truth universally acknowledged that a single man in possession of a good fortune must be in want of a vaguely fetishy sexual encounter, with the whole event recorded and stored on a memory stick for subsequent viral distribution.

Times have changed for household animals, too. Today, the only way to check that your pet is normal is to place on the floor in front of him pictures of the species-appropriate stars of any given year's celebrity pet power list. If your furry charge does not slaver over at least one of them, then as a responsible owner you may need to start asking yourself some tough questions. Like, is he freebasing? Who are those strange dogs at whom he barks furtively in the park? And why won't he tell you his Facebook name?

## Pet in Arcadia ego

Faux abduction is not the only peril facing the out-of-control celebrity pet. Indeed, if one were to pick the moment at which the world detected trouble even in the Edenic existence of the famous fur balls, it would not be the kidnap of Tinkerbell – watershed moment though that undoubtedly was.

It would be the discovery that Pete Doherty's cat had a coke problem. That's right: even celebrities' pets are on better drugs than you.

The coke-hound was in fact just a kitten – one of a litter birthed by Pete's cat Dinger – and when it became ill, the Babyshambles singer took it to the vet. The latter discovered cocaine in its bloodstream. 'It is a police matter', ran an official statement by the Royal Society for Prevention of Cruelty to Animals, which confirmed the kitten had subsequently been taken into care. 'It is very important to protect animals from substances that can do them serious harm.'

You will likely find yourself torn over the tale. On the one hand, how typical of those RSPCA establishment lackeys to fail to realise that the Doherty feline was in fact a classic creative soul, driven to squeeze itself through the catflap in the doors of perception, before returning to its basket for disconnected and joyless sex with any member of its species willing to help stave off the comedown.

On the other, its too-much-too-soon lifestyle is achingly familiar.

And bafflingly, in the circumstances, celebrity animals are still largely left to deal with these kinds of things alone – or perhaps as outpatients of some vet who may be sympathetic but has no experience in the specialist arena of treating animal addiction.

Isn't it time drug-dependent pets had the option of somewhere residential? In short, isn't it time to establish Pethab: a rest facility where hopped-up showbiz animals could be encouraged to yap or mew about their feelings before 'taking responsibility' for their recovery?

There are so many celebrity pets who need not our judgement, but our love and understanding. Think of little Baby Luv, the kinkajou who was hopelessly enabled by Paris, until she spiralled troublingly out of hand and did something that made Mommy require a tetanus jab.[9] Or think of any one of the heiress's 437

[9] *So* Drew Barrymore.

dogs, a kind of Brat Pack of teacup chihuahuas who doubtless spend their days tapping messages to each other on Swarovski-encrusted BlackBerrys with perfectly manicured claws: 'OMG I heard Tinkerbell caught a tick off Britney Spears's new puppy!! I think U can guess how LOL!!!! she's such a little skank!!! What bag R U riding in tonight?'

In fact, casting our eyes back to Tinkerbell's disappearance, isn't there a very real possibility that the episode was a cry for help, and that – had things been allowed to take their course – the chihuahua *would* have found a way of escaping her gilded cage, even if it meant joining some revolutionary liberation army? Aren't the adventures of these pets really a microcosm of celebrity society, only with fewer brakes on behaviour? After all, no matter how wasted you are on dogatinis before getting into your $2,000 Gucci ride, you will never be sent to high-security kennels.

And yet, the suspicion that early death is written in the stars hangs heavy in the air. For a long time, it was rumoured that Paris had purchased a cemetery plot near that in which Marilyn Monroe is buried – in the name of 'Billy Hilton'. Now to you, that goat may be just another screw-up statistic in the Hilton menagerie, but to Paris, Billy is clearly a beloved charge who just lacks the tools to cope, and whose woefully untimely end is already being planned for.

With Pethab's help, could stories like Billy's could be a thing of the past? Who knows. But God, how many more have to go the way of Pete's kitten before we realise they're a stain on all our souls?

# CELEBRITY SCIENCE AND MEDICINE

'Science is the great antidote to the poison of enthusiasm and superstition.'

Adam Smith, *The Wealth of Nations*

'I'm a sex addict. It's my cross to bear. It's a proper disease, with doctors and medicine and everything.'

Chazz Michael Michaels, *Blades of Glory*

'I'm not a doctor, but I play one on TV . . .'

This line was first delivered by Robert Young, star of American medical drama *Marcus Welby M.D.*, in a television advert for aspirin. It was not parodic. The commercial ran for more than seven years, spanning the late sixties and early seventies, and it proved so successful in shifting pharmaceuticals that the formula has been revived at least twice, using different daytime soap stars. Whether it was Dr Larry from *One Life to Live* hawking headache pills, or Dr Cliff Warner from *All My Children* pushing cough syrup, the drill was the same. A white-coated actor would turn to the camera and utter those immortal words . . .

'I'm not a doctor, but I play one on TV.'

And thousands would buy the medication. Depressing enough for you? Then you may wish to medicate yourself, because it's going to get a whole lot more depressing, as we don the lab coat of authority and observe celebrity forays into the arena of science and medicine. Or rather, celebrity forays into the arena of 'science' and 'medicine'.[1]

Celebrity quackery is on the rise, and it's never been easier for stars to get their crazy ideas about science heard. Your quacks of yore would have to trudge from village to village with their snake oil and nostrums, living with the fear that the people from the previous village would catch up with them and demand their money back. Today's celebrity quack simply makes appearances on prime-time chat shows, and nobody ever catches up with them.

It's time to examine some of the kooky therapies and bogus science that celebrities peddle in the pursuit of gravitas or esoteric authority – and to remind ourselves that their extraordinary influence means that talking bullshit is not a victimless crime. We'll see how celebrities don't limit themselves to making modest claims – claims such as that a fringe treatment could *prevent* cancer. They're willing to go far bigger, claiming that it can *cure* cancer. Come to that, they're willing to claim that some can reverse the second law of thermodynamics, or neutralise nuclear waste.

Before you proceed, you should realise that only the scared, or the hopelessly uncreative cling to the idea of evidence-based medicine. An entertainer saying 'it works for me' trumps any damning study that the scientific community can come up with. And so it is that anyone who counters a celebrity's attempt to raise the nonsensical into the realms of the arcane will be dismissed as a cynic, or a person of closed mind, or simply unwilling to embrace the light. Or the energy. Or any other stuff that just has so, *so* much to do with the medical advances of the past eighty-odd years, which have given us everything from antibiotics to heart surgery, and prolonged life expectancy in ways that would have been unimaginable to even our immediate ancestors.

[1] You'll probably have to do the 'air quotes' gesture quite a lot in this chapter. Look for words like 'energy' and 'toxin' and 'can definitely cure Aids'; then deploy the mannerism accordingly.

We will note that though Isaac Newton's humility was such that he described himself as 'a boy playing on the sea-shore . . . whilst the great ocean of truth lay all undiscovered before me', Tom Cruise has professed himself 'the authority' on subjects as diverse as psychiatry and emergency triage. We will get seriously depressed that there is a significant overlap between this chapter, and the Celebrity Religions chapter.

And just to ease ourselves in gently, let's begin with a look at how important advances in celebrity medicine have led to things like anti-Semitism and homophobia being recognised as proper diseases, with doctors and medicine and everything. Even heroes can be cut down by these sicknesses, and they are treated behind closed doors, in the place we have come to see as a kind of entertainment industry Valhalla. The place that is rehab.

## Rehab: not really for drug addicts

The first immutable law is that there is a finite amount of mental equilibrium in the celebrity world. If a previously dissolute star is in recovery, another must relapse, and so it is that, say, Lindsay Lohan leaving rehab would precipitate David Hasselhoff to fall off the wagon. It's just science and there's nothing any of us can do about it.

The second immutable law is that only civilians say 'sorry' for reprehensible behaviour. Celebrities identify the disease to which they have fallen victim, then take the courageous step of committing themselves to a treatment programme. That treatment will perhaps involve sitting around in a circle, or petting horses, or going on hikes with other patients, many of whom will have pretentious facial hair and tattoos they refer to as 'battle scars'. It will also involve regular calls to one's publicist to enquire: 'Did this one blow over yet?'

The third immutable law is that *no one* goes to rehab because they have a drug problem. The textbook celebrity rehab dash will be presaged by a few unscheduled collapses, either in a nightclub bathroom stall or occasionally on the set of a movie being held up by the star's refusal to work while giant pink space cockroaches are crawling all over their trailer. At this stage, the celebrity's publicist will be maintaining that their client is suffering from a 'mystery illness' or 'exhaustion'. Eventually, the patient will get really very exhausted indeed. This is why they need to go to a 'rest facility'. In the case of people who need to 'rest' quite often, the 'exhaustion' is usually preceded by an 'undisclosed medical emergency', so-called because it sounds prettier than 'OD'd while attempting to persuade a homeless gentleman to participate in sex on Hollywood Boulevard'. And the same quaint tendency towards euphemism takes a heroin problem and repackages it as an 'addiction to sleeping tablets'.

But enough of the confected bogeyman of drug addiction, which as we've already established is a hopelessly outmoded diagnosis. Thanks to recent progress in celebrity medicine, rehab facilities can and do now treat a whole range of ailments. Here are some of these ailments:

• *Being homophobic*. When he referred to one of his *Grey's Anatomy* co-stars as a 'faggot', actor Isaiah Washington was evidently unaware of the furore that would erupt. After the storm had raged for a few weeks, however, it became clear that Isaiah's period of being in denial would have to come to an end. And so it was that his people announced he had entered 'a residential treatment facility'. 'I regard this as a necessary step toward understanding why I did what I did,' ran Washington's statement, 'and making sure it never happens again. I appreciate the fact that I have been given this opportunity and I remain committed to transforming my negative actions into positive results, personally and professionally.'

• *Being anti-Semitic and a misogynist*. It's often said that problems run in families, and little Mel Gibson grew up in the care of a father who was very much in denial. About the Holocaust. Never happened, according to Gibson *père*, and one can only guess what his boy might have gone on to achieve had he not been held back by the suffering and shame of living with a bullshit-dependent parent. Of course, there were the insanely high-grossing movies, the casually dismissed charges of anti-Semitism levelled at his 2004 boreathon *The Passion of the Christ* . . . But Mel didn't want to talk about any of that when two Californian traffic cops pulled him over on the Pacific Coast Highway. He failed a breathalyser test – a result perhaps presaged by the half-empty bottle of tequila in the passenger seat – but it wasn't until he was formally arrested that the *Lethal Weapon* star began to exhibit signs of sickness.

Having enquired of a female officer at the station 'What are you looking at, sugar tits?', he proceeded to inform the police that he 'owned Malibu'. Next, he demanded of a male officer 'Are you a Jew?', expanding upon his interest in the matter by explaining 'Fucking Jews . . . Jews are responsible for all the wars in the world.' There followed a smorgasbord of abuse, threats, promises to get even . . . and the police report was somehow made public. After it had led various news bulletins for a while, Mel realised he was unwell, and announced that he was entering treatment 'to ensure my return to health'. Was there anything concerned well-wishers could do? Yes. Yes, there was. The patient wished to discuss 'the appropriate path to healing' with Jewish leaders.

Would they really have had experience of his disease? After all, you'd think relatively few Jewish leaders would have taken to their beds with anti-Semitism – but an undeterred Mel declared he had 'asked the Jews to help me on my journey through recovery'. 'I cannot do it alone,' he quavered.

• *Being a shoplifter*. Once upon a time – December 2001, to be exact – and armed with only a pair of scissors and a bulky coat, Winona Ryder entered a Beverly Hills department store and began perhaps the most misunderstood 'research for a forthcoming project' ever.[2] Security guards observed her removing tags from a variety of garments and hair accessories, and placing them in her

[2] Apart from that business with The Who's Pete Townshend.

bag. According to testimony at her subsequent trial, Winona informed staff that 'my director informed me to shoplift for a role I was preparing'. Alas, it was never made clear precisely which role Winona was preparing for – the movie may still be in turnaround to this day – but from what we can piece together of her actions on that fateful afternoon, it must have been the story of a girl who needed a whole lot of Marc Jacobs stuff. You might class it as shoplifting: Winona would probably see it as a retail-sector method-acting incident.

The treatment? Well, following her conviction for grand theft and vandalism, her lawyer successfully argued that she should undergo counselling in lieu of a custodial sentence. As for Winona, she later reminded people that the case had come to court just a few months after 9/11, and should not have been paid attention to by anyone – thereby appearing to make a direct causal link between the media's decision to cover a trial and the continued failure to subjugate Afghan warlords. Bin Laden was on the loose but people were choosing to persecute her for expanding her collection of Alice bands. Incidentally, despite what has so far appeared to be a successful rehabilitation, it's important to realise that Winona will always be a recovering shoplifter, and that just because she made it through today paying for her high-end hair accessories, tomorrow could all too easily be the day on which the struggle becomes too much, and the unlawful acquisition of a Marc Jacobs bobby pin forces a return to treatment.

• *Beating your staff.* It would be wrong to let an examination of rehab go by without saluting Naomi Campbell's ongoing battle with hitting the help – a disease so niche that it doesn't have a name yet. Maybe we could lobby to get it called Naomi's disease, like all those other rare conditions that so desperately require funding if we are ever to find a cure. Despite several flare-ups, it would not be until 1999 that the strong-willed *Vogue* cover star realised she was battling a serious illness. The diagnosis point appears to have been the moment her former assistant testified that she had been grabbed by the throat and smacked around the head with a telephone by Naomi, while on another occasion madam had threatened to throw her out of a moving car. Her condition exacerbated by bad headlines, Naomi checked into an Arizona clinic to 'find out what was making me do the things I did'. We'll never know whether anyone offered the diagnosis 'because you're spoiled and unpleasant and you basically operate in a consequence-free environment'. What we do know is that recovery is such a long journey, and Naomi has relapsed on several occasions.

• *Having sore feet.* In May 2008, Aerosmith's Steve Tyler – the man once known as one half of hair rock's Toxic Twins – confirmed he had checked himself into a Californian drug rehabilitation clinic. Turns out his feet hurt. 'The doctors told me the pain in my feet could be corrected,' he explained, 'but it would require a few surgeries over time. The "foot repair" pain was intense, greater than I'd anticipated. The months of rehabilitative care and the painful strain of physical therapy were traumatic. I really needed a safe environment to recuperate where I could shut off my phone and get back on my feet. Make no mistake,' he concluded, 'Aerosmith has no plans to stop rocking. There's a new album to record, then another tour.' Bunions permitting.

• *Because you need a backdrop for a magazine photo shoot.* Occasionally, a celebrity will be struck down by a non-specific reputation-laundering-type ailment. Happily, there is a treatment for this, and you really have to doff your hat to the pioneers at the Cirque Lodge rehab facility in Utah, who allowed Lindsay Lohan to stage a photo shoot with *OK!* magazine during her actual stay. Here she was in full make-up looking demure; there she was ostentatiously thumbing through an Alcoholics Anonymous book. Unbelievably, the photos weren't snatched, but set up by Lindsay or her handlers, who went on to share all kinds of pointedly specific detail about the actress's treatment with readers. 'She really is taking it seriously,' ran one of these clinical updates. 'She's replacing LA and smoking with yoga and reading.' Duly noted.

So there you have it: medical science is gamely keeping pace with a rapidly-proliferating array of modern ailments. Sometimes it's even outpacing it – so next time you hear a star racially abusing a disabled person, be gladdened that there will be a treatment facility somewhere out there in which they can battle this most cruel of diseases. Their publicist just needs to locate it.

## Riddle-me-rehab: selecting a rest facility

Contrary to popular belief, the most terrifying challenge for any addiction-plagued star is not facing up to the fact they have a problem. It is the prospect of being taken under Elton John's wing. A reformed addict himself, Elton appears to have anointed himself as the saviour of anyone looking like they're having a better time than him at parties, with former pet projects including Kate Moss's erstwhile boyfriend Pete Doherty, and Robbie Williams, who subsequently paid tribute to Elton's intervention as 'tarnished with the lack of professionalism'.

So no matter how close a celebrity is to rock-bottom, if they have managed to avoid being annexed by Elton congratulations are in order. They've survived the first difficult step. However, it will fall to that star or their people to pick an appropriate treatment venue. If they're a second-generation celebrity their parents will have put their name down for a really prestigious rehab at birth, and they will most likely have made use of it before they were legally able to drive, let alone buy alcohol to bring themselves down off that last speedball. But parvenus must flick through the prospectuses alone – unless they happen to alight on the back issue of *Playboy* in which Ozzy Osbourne offered readers a truly expert, comparative analysis of rehab units he'd sampled over the years. Think of it as the Michelin guide to places in which you may care to suffer withdrawal symptoms.

Stating that he'd 'lost count' of the number of treatment centres he'd graced, the Prince of Darkness began by outlining the specific set of circumstances that would hint the time was right for another sojourn. 'When my ass was on fire,' he explained, 'when I'd fuck someone up or go crazy and everyone was chasing me, and my wife had left home and the kids were screaming and I was never allowed into the house again, I'd check in.'

And so to his ratings. 'Betty Ford is a good one,' Ozzy mused. 'And a place called Promises, in Malibu, which is like a fucking Hollywood camp resort for wealthy fucking lunatics. Hazelden, in Minnesota, is a really hard one. They do not fuck around. I checked out because it scared me. They use a thing called tough love, where they're like: "You fucking piece of shit!" I was like: "I felt like a piece of shit before. That's why I'm paying you all this money. You don't need to tell me every day." Another bad one is a place called Steps that I think closed down. They modelled it after Auschwitz.'

Many thanks to the Black Sabbath frontman for that foray into service journalism, because ultimately, as a celebrity, where you rehab is more important even than where you ski. Having perused that list, all that remains is for the stricken celebrity to fight their demons in private. If, that is, they have the luxury of privacy.

### Televised treatment: what's to feel anxious about?

With so many apocalypse-hastening formats littering the TV schedules, it's always hard to play favourites. But for sheer pseudo-clinical peeping Tommery, do just marvel at VH1's *Celebrity Rehab*, which takes drug-addicted celebrities and films them 24/7 as they receive treatment.

Of course, there are obvious issues with the idea. Like the perennial shock-fatigue thing. How do the producers keep that sort of show fresh, you're probably wondering, when its target audience of jaded, *Schadenfreude*-riddled voyeurs demand a surprise round every corner, or they'll just switch to a rerun of Anna Nicole Smith's caesarean on YouTube instead?

The answer is that they come up with enchantingly audacious new ideas. In 2008, one of the new batch of 'celebrity' patients was

Rodney King. Yes, *that* Rodney King. For any younger readers, Rodney . . . how the hell do you even put this? Rodney was previously the star of a hand-held documentary? Rodney's earlier work provoked a mass response? Rodney is *not* a suitable reality-TV pick?

Let's just turn it over to Dr Drew, the media medic who runs the show, who in *Celebrity Rehab*'s advance publicity said of his patient: 'People are going to see him in an entirely different way.' You mean not in night vision?

But really, who could fail to be encouraged by that 'different way', which at least suggested that unscripted programming executives had decided that the best way to treat people with serious drug addictions is actually *not* to have a bunch of bent cops kick the crap out of them.

Obviously, the latter approach is still being trialled in metro-politan areas around the globe, and none of us would wish to prejudge the findings of that street-level research. But, according to TV network VH1, the best way to help addicts is to have them sign all-encompassing release forms, wait till they begin to be racked by withdrawal symptoms, then film it all for the benefit of a slack-jawed audience who were clearly *in no way done* watching Rodney suffer. You know the bit in his first media outing when he was down on the ground? When the cameras began rolling this time around, Dr Drew lost no time in telling the public that the stars were 'retching on the floor'. This was totally a sequel! Don't leave it so long next time, Los Angeles.

And so to Rodney's co-stars, because it seems apposite to examine upon whom was being conferred a kind of cultural equivalency. There was former Guns N' Roses drummer Steven Adler, Rod Stewart's boy, Sean, a model, and some other people too unknown to list.[3] Oh, and appearing as some sort of life coach

[3] Until this precise cultural moment, the definition of the word 'celebrity' had seemed most dubiously expanded when videorazzi website TMZ covertly filmed Fawn Hall at work in a bookshop. Fawn Hall! If you ever wondered what your favourite stars of the Iran–Contra hearings did next, turns out the formerly shredder-happy Fawn was now working in a bookshop.

was Gary Busey. Seriously, Busey. You may not have realised he was at 'sober sponsor' stage, but there you go.

As for What the Stars of Police Beatings Did Next . . . of course, recovery is about taking the positives. Let's just acknowledge how sad it is that so few performers are able to make the transition from the famously difficult police brutality circuit, all the way to headlining a major television show with faux-clinical benefits. Far from his exploitation being the clearest sign yet of the impending collapse of civilisation, King's graduation to bankable addict should be regarded as a modern American success story, and we can only hope that show producers coerced him into making one of those 'it's been an amazing journey' speeches that are the money shot of all reality-TV shows.

If you can't go along with that, then hunker down. Flood's a-comin'!

## Celebrity mountebanks: quack goes Hollywood

For all the hatred-legitimising charm of the previous pages, however, rehab (televised or in camera) remains just one facet of the celebrity medical experience. And as one in which the celebrity is required to cede control, if only briefly, it remains a means to an end – not a long-term solution. In short, celebrities are much happier when they're the ones wearing the white coats. So roll up your sleeve and be prepared for a lot of little pricks, because it's time to get involved with entertainer-sponsored quackery.

Naturally, any treatment of this subject must begin with an awestruck look at the life – and multiple past lives – of Shirley MacLaine. For several decades, the actress's journey towards the fringes of what might tenuously be categorised as healing has been as hilarious as it has been thorough. If there is a provisional wing of Hollywood crazies, then Shirley sits on its army council.

At any given time, Shirley will be practising a whole clutch of way-out therapies – therapies which expose the woeful limitations of the phrase 'alternative medicine'. Alternative doesn't even begin to cover this stuff. To even touch on them all would take a book in itself, so we're blessed that Shirley pens one of those every few years, allowing her public to keep up with the various nutcases, charlatans and bizarre practices that have drifted into her heightened consciousness since her last literary outing.

Yet it feels wrong not to mention a handful of her amazing discoveries, so get comfortable and we'll begin with psychic surgery. Psychic surgery is often described as paranormal surgery – stay with this – and typically involves the 'surgeon' pressing the patient's skin, but not making any incision. Nevertheless, the practitioner will be able to show his patient and any spectators some blood or tissue which he has 'removed' from the body. It is an illusion the quackbuster James Randi has debunked as pretty easy to achieve if you conceal a blood capsule or perhaps some chicken innards in the palm of your hand, only to reveal them with a flourish when the 'operation' is complete.

It may not shock you to learn that psychic surgery has been denounced around the world as a straight-up fraud that preys upon the desperately ill. And you may find it even less shocking that Shirley MacLaine hasn't taken the blindest bit of notice of that. For a long time she even had a pet psychic surgeon, a Filipino chap named Alex Orbito, whom she introduced to a host of Hollywood stars, and even eulogised in her thought-provoking[4] book *Going Within: A Guide for Inner Transformation*. Having gone under the non-knife with Orbito, she claimed he had removed 'negative energy clots' and 'negative stress clots' from her body.[5]

Because misunderstanding tends to dog the greatest vision-aries, however, Orbito was indicted for fraud in Canada a few years ago. But the case was dismissed due to lack of evidence – something of an irony there, perhaps – and he continues to practise today, as well as operate his 'healing tours' travel agency.

[4] The specific thought it provokes is: she's crazy.
[5] The technical name for this procedure is a 'science-ectomy'.

For her part, Shirley continues to embrace and disseminate new therapies to the masses, with her most recent book extolling the virtues of radionics. Alas, a promotional appearance on the US day-time talk show *The View* was derailed when the author was unable to outline the thinking behind this abstruse branch of medicine, and was only able to flounder, 'I don't know enough about this scientifically to talk about it without looking in my book.'

Clearly, Shirley can't be expected to have the vaguest recol-lection of the various therapies she'd espoused in the book she was specifically promoting, so here's the low-down on radionics. The short version is that it makes psychic surgery look like conventional medicine. The longer version is that it is a way of healing a person from afar. No matter where in the world they are, all you need is some kind of proxy for the absent person. This might be a blood sample, or a hair – theirs or their dog's – some urine, spores, pretty much anything that could be combined with water. Machines called dynamizers and oscilloclasts are involved, but we shan't trouble ourselves with those, with all you really need to know being that the remote healing takes place at some other 'level of reality', where we are all linked by a 'universal mind'. This, the Radionics Association insists, is 'entirely com-patible with modern physics'.

Stranger still, the process is entirely compatible with the MacLaine digestive system, because if one actually consults her book, Shirley claims to have mixed toxins with urine, cleansed the liquid with radionics, and then drunk it.

You may care to take a comfort break at this point.

The thing about Shirl, some might argue, is that she's so demonstrably, enduringly bats that she can't be viewed as much of a public health risk. And certainly, right at the other end of the celebrity advocacy spectrum are people like Lance Armstrong and Michael J. Fox, who have written extensively about their diseases (testicular cancer and Parkinson's, respectively) and have been central to increasing awareness and understanding of these conditions.

It is up to you where you place the former Playmate Jenny McCarthy on this spectrum. But when the anti-vaccinationist spokesmodel can claim on a magazine cover that she has 'cured' her son of autism, you may begin to fret that a seriously worrying amount of power is concentrated in entertainers' hands.

Barron Lerner is a professor of medicine and public health at Columbia University in New York, and the author of *When Illness Goes Public: Celebrity Patients and How We Look at Medicine*. Professor Lerner is somewhat wary of the power celebrities have in matters of public health – often in matters to which they have only the most tangential connection.

'There are agencies that exist that connect celebrities with diseases,' he has pointed out, 'and sometimes these are diseases that the celebrity hasn't even had. We have to be careful when celebrities become spokespeople for certain treatments.' We do indeed, and then there's the related question of how entertainers affect research funding. 'The people who scream loudest get the most dollars. Activists for Aids and breast cancer and the other diseases that have been very successful [in raising funds] would argue that they are trying to expand the whole pie and not take money away from other diseases. But if you look at how disease research dollars are allocated it would not line up directly with mortality. It is based partly on who the celebrity of the moment is and whether or not they've gone to Washington DC to lobby.'

Most crucially, though, Professor Lerner is in no doubt that the public really listens to celebrities on matters of health. He notes that Lance Armstrong is deluged by mail in which people ask him for precisely detailed descriptions of the dosages of his chemotherapy, while Michael J. Fox has reported similar efforts on behalf of fellow Parkinson's sufferers. Both are fastidious about referring people back to their doctors, for which they should be applauded, as should breast cancer survivor Kylie Minogue, who immediately quashed press reports that she was using quackish treatments for fear that other cancer sufferers would believe these stories and risk their recovery.

But it's in discussing a much earlier case of high-profile celebrity illness that Lerner crystallises the most extreme dangers of celebrities speaking out on medical matters. In December 1979, the movie star Steve McQueen was diagnosed with malignant mesothelioma, a highly aggressive lung cancer. Against the advice of his doctors, the actor travelled to Mexico, where he submitted to various unconventional and controversial therapies. His treatment programme was largely conceived by an orthodontist blacklisted by the American Cancer Association. There were coffee enemas, injections of animal foetal matter, untrialled drugs and mysterious spiritual sessions.

There were also, alas, highly publicised first-person updates on his good progress. 'Mexico is showing the world a new way of fighting cancer through nonspecific metabolic therapies,' ran the most famous. 'Thank you for helping to save my life.' As Professor Lerner relates, his miracle testimony appealed to vulnerable cancer patients, who inferred that this was 'a famous guy, who must know what he's talking about, going down to Mexico and getting better'. McQueen, in reality, was not getting better. He was getting far worse, and died soon after – but not before his glowing reports had encouraged significant numbers of seriously ill cancer patients to follow his example.

You're probably thinking that this awful tale is pretty far removed from Shirley and her cavalcade of kooks. And in an ideal world, we could divide this section into two discrete halves: Celebrity Quackery That's Crazy But Basically Harmless and Celebrity Quackery That Could Actually Kill You.

This is not that ideal world. Perhaps because they don't *do* small and low-key, celebrities will make the most outlandish claims for the unconventional treatments they espouse. Godwin's Law states that as an Internet message-board discussion grows longer, 'the probability of a comparison involving Hitler and Nazis approaches one'. In similar vein there is an unwritten law – let's call it MacLaine's Law – that states that the longer a celebrity harps on about a non-evidence-based therapy, the probability that they will suggest it could help cancer sufferers approaches one.

So unfortunately, we can't dismiss celebrity discourse on science and medicine as the consequence-free witterings of an adorable entertainer. Subscribed to at the right moment – when you're in the peak of health but just feeling like a coffee enema could really put the icing on your day – these theories might seem to do no harm. But subscribed to at the wrong moment – for instance, when you're suffering from cancer – these theories can cause serious problems. Serious problems like death. Slavishly copying some celebrity's haircut is funny. It's somehow so much less amusing to ape some celebrity's stridently voiced 'medical' plan, and suffer as a result. Anyone who thinks this is the wages of stupidity should grow a heart.[6]

## Tom Cruise: Renaissance crazy man

No matter how desperately we may care to avoid it, there can be no escaping infamous Tom Cruise's tussle with the American broadcaster Matt Lauer, presenter of America's *Today Show*. It was 2005, and Tom had been on quite the run of public outbursts, ranging from beating his breast about his new love Katie Holmes, and surfing Oprah Winfrey's sofa in demented delight, to condemning the actress Brooke Shields for having the temerity to say that antidepressants had helped her overcome a severe bout of post-partum depression. Shields had already issued a withering rejoinder – 'Tom Cruise did not have a uterus last time I checked' – but when called upon to substantiate his position, Tom was in no mood to draw a line under the subject.

'When I started studying the history of psychiatry,' he informed Lauer with customary intensity, 'I started realising more and more why I didn't agree with psychiatry.' Clearly, Tom Cruise

[6] Shirley could probably put you in touch with some guy who grows hearts.

not agreeing with psychiatry is like a dehydrated man not agreeing with water. But let's allow him to continue.

'I know,' he declared triumphantly, 'that psychiatry is a pseudoscience.'

Now . . . It seems vaguely apposite to insert a reminder of the deeply scientific tenets of Scientology. Very briefly, then, this is what advanced-level Scientologists believe. Seventy-five million years ago, the intergalactic alien tyrant Xenu exiled manifold individuals to Earth, who were then imprisoned in mountains, before being blown up with hydrogen bombs and brainwashed. Their traumatised spirits then clustered around human bodies and continue to do so to this very day, and can only be removed using advanced Scientology. Xenu? Currently held captive in a mountain by a force field.

Now let's rejoin the scourge of pseudoscience, Professor Tom Cruise, who graduated summa cum laude from the University of Batshit. 'Do you know what Ritalin is?' the increasingly agitated actor demanded of Lauer, referring to the widely prescribed treatment for ADHD. 'Do you know that Ritalin is a street drug?'

Lauer stated that of course he understood that there is abuse of all medications – 'Here's the problem,' Tom cut in. 'You don't know the history of psychiatry. I do.' And so it went on. 'There is no such thing as a chemical imbalance . . . There's misinformation. [Brooke Shields] doesn't understand the history of psychiatry . . . You're glib. You don't even know what Ritalin is . . . You don't know and I do.'

Though Tom never did enlighten *Today* viewers as to the nature of Ritalin – or indeed the history of psychiatry – he was good enough to inform them that Brooke Shields could have dealt with her 'depression' (his air quotes) by recourse to vitamins and exercise.

It's the ferocious certitude that sticks in the mind, really, and anyone regarding the exchange as nothing more than a cause for mirth might care to take a sobering look at the comments posted beneath the various clips of it on YouTube. Many people do simply stop to point and laugh at Tom, but a great many others don't. Perhaps they have had bad experiences with psychiatry; perhaps they are suspicious of the modern tendency to suggest a pill is the answer to everything. But a worrying number write things like 'people hating on Tom are just jealous' – and that doesn't mark the episode down as one of the great moments in celebrity medicine.

## Sharon Stone is a medical miracle

Picture a black backdrop, and Sharon Stone's face staring straight into the camera as she utters the following words: 'There's something you should know about me. I'm cold, I'm calculating. I get what I want. If you get in my way, I'll wreak havoc upon you. I can leave you limp, weak, twisted, confused ... If you want to live to see tomorrow, you answer to me, and you answer quickly.' Cue Sharon's bottom lip beginning to wobble as she attempts to hold back tears. 'I ... am ... a ... stroke.'

This is the full script for an advert by America's Heart and Stroke Foundation in 2003. But Sharon's command performance as a cerebrovascular accident – which critics would hail as her finest since she managed to masturbate in the bath in *Sliver* while both her hands remained firmly planted on the sides of the tub – was by no means her first foray into offering public information on medical matters. It was certainly her least controversial.

To Washington, then, in the year 1995, when Sharon was riding high on the success of *Casino*, and a leading breast cancer foundation sought a famous face to front their Race for the Cure charity run. It would be a match made somewhere other than in heaven. The annual fund-raiser had previously been chaired by the likes of Marion Quayle, and would subsequently be helmed by Al and Tipper Gore. But 1995 was the year Race for the Cure went after a real headliner.

Headlines certainly ensued. Who knows what drew Race for the Cure to Ms Stone above all other candidates? Perhaps they made the classic logical error of assuming Sharon's extensive experience in drawing focus onto her breasts made her an excellent choice to draw focus onto breast cancer. Anyways, Sharon agreed to do the run, act as celebrity chair, address journalists about women's health, and show up at marquee fundraising events over the weekend.

Here's how it all went. First off, our heroine missed her flight from California, which had been provided free by an airline as a concession to the charity. The hotel provided was not to her liking, so she booked a suite at the Washington Four Seasons, and declined to attend a scheduled appearance before some eminent doctors. The next day, she effectively bailed out on a press conference, arriving at a packed ballroom just in time to deliver her speech, which was introduced as being about 'wellness, fitness and positive mental attitude'. 'Being a movie star is like being an alcoholic,' ran one of her *pensées*. 'The only way to survive it is one day at a time.' But the peroration seemed to be passing off without incident until . . . well, let's hand over to Sharon.

'I hadn't planned to say this,' she suddenly told the room. 'Four years ago I was told I had cancer, lymph cancer . . . I had a lump in every lymph area of my body. I knew what that meant. Very, very fortunately for me, with a lot of positive thinking and a lot of holistic healing – I say that in a very personal sense because I know that that's a personal approach – I ended up testing negative for lymph cancer, but it took several months, and those months changed my life. And one of the changes during that time is that I stopped drinking coffee, and when I stopped drinking coffee, ten days later I had no tumours in any of my lymph glands.'

Mmm. Without the statistics to hand, it's difficult to say precisely how many more people are killed every year following this kind of celebrity-endorsed kookery instead of proper medical advice . . . But it's probably a fair few more than are snuffed out by, say, bisexual ice-pick murderesses who decline to wear underwear. Whatever the ratio, many experts were unwilling to let it ride, and began flooding the airwaves to denounce Sharon's apparent belief that saying no to espressos is a substitute for chemo.

'Irresponsible statements like that can kill,' one professor told radio listeners, while the American Cancer Society moved to dispel the suggestion that there was any proven link between caffeine intake and an increased risk of cancer. Sensing the way the wind was blowing, Sharon opted to claim she had stated that she had been the victim of a misdiagnosis, and couldn't believe she had been misquoted. And it is totally incredible, isn't it, when you consider that according to *Washingtonian* magazine's exhaustive account of the debacle, there were 'dozens of journalists' and no fewer than ten camera crews recording proceedings.

'The point of all that,' Sharon later floundered of her digression, 'was to try to express some empathy to the condition of vagueness in medicine for women.'

So . . . How did she do in the running race? Alas, despite dressing up in sports clothes and telling her fellow participants that she'd 'been carbo-loading for three years for this', Sharon declined to actually do the run, claiming that the 'media frenzy' would have been more than her security detail could cope with.

## The quacking gets louder

Celebrity medicine is such a fast-growing field that some almost view it as a stand-alone discipline. In fact, the doctor who prescribed methadone to the late Anna Nicole Smith while she was heavily pregnant listed one of his specialisms as 'celebrity medicine'. At the less euphemistic end of things, though, all manner of literature on the complementary medical practices of famous folk exists. Notable horrors in the canon? The expensively produced *It works for me! Celebrity Stories of Alternative Healing*. Ironist rubberneckers may care to dip into this work, if only for the bowel-moving story of how eighties soft-rocker Kenny Loggins ended up marrying his colonic irrigation therapist. It's a real modern romance.

Of course, not all celebrity remedies for serious illnesses involve kooky religions, or take place on some other 'level of reality' entirely. And the ones that don't are arguably more insidious. 'Cancer has been the curse of my family,' Gwyneth Paltrow once announced. 'I am challenging these evil genes by natural means. I am convinced that by eating biological foods it is possible to avoid the growth of tumours.'

Whatever 'biological foods' may be, it's that 'convinced' that worries one. Gwyneth Paltrow's convictions are her own business if the thing she's convinced of is – for example – that starring in *Shallow Hal* was a good idea. But the fact that Gwyneth is good at pretending to be other people hardly means she is within her rights to use her fame to talk about science or medicine. In fact, given her diet-prevents-cancer thesis – a link consistently disproved – we should conclude that she knows the square root of nothing about science and medicine, and has an even more minuscule right to preach to others on the subject. 'Diet cannot prevent cancer,' Ursula Arens, a dietician at the British Dietetic Association, was forced to state in the wake of Gwyneth's unsolicited public health lecture – delivered, unbelievably, at a legitimate cancer research fund-raising event. 'It is reasonable that the risks of some of them can be reduced with certain diets, but some cancers, alas, show no link to dietary factors.'

Indeed, whereas one might regard it as merely a shame if the surgeon general were cast in a movie and ruined it by mugging to the camera, it's morally offensive and dangerous to find Gwyneth gatecrashing a field in which she is completely unqualified. But celebrities' hold over ordinary people grows stronger all the time. Advertisers know that simply associating a star's face with a product shifts myriad units, while the thirst for content means media outlets air celebrity views almost entirely uncritically. All very well, but when this influence extends to flaky medical theories, it becomes a genuine social tragedy.

Let's mention only in passing Madonna's assertion that Kabbalah water 'has gotten rid of my husband's verrucas'. The point is, a celebrity shouldn't even be talking about verruca cures, let alone cancer. But the boundaries are gone. There is now a continuum between celebrities telling people how cutting out carbs got them into a pair of skinny jeans, and telling leukaemia patients how to eat.

It almost makes you yearn for the establishment of some kind of regulatory body. Then again, given that celebrities tend to come out with this stuff during interviews to promote personally enriching projects, perhaps one radical answer would be to treat such outbursts as commercials and subject them to the same censure and legal scrutiny. Madonna was promoting her children's books when she spouted the claptrap about Kabbalah water. Let us dream of a day when a country's advertising standards authority raps her publisher for misleading statements, and bans her from repeating them in public ever again.

Until that moment, though, we have to endure this rubbish, and continue living in a world where Uma Thurman can sing the virtues of 'gem therapy'. Gem therapy, if you please. Any minute now one of these halfwits will be advocating the use of leeches.

## One of these halfwits advocates the use of leeches

Hasn't cinema's Demi Moore always been a force for good? Certainly she has, ever since that time in the mid-Triassic period when she posed pregnant on the front of *Vanity Fair*, providing the inspiration for a thousand copycat celebrations of entertainment-industry fecundity, which will never, ever grow stale as an editorial idea, no matter how many celebrities haul their distended bellies into the photographer's studio of a third-tier celebrity magazine, then meet the camera's gaze with a defiant jut of the chin, in the misguided belief that they're engaged in something to do with empowerment.

And so it is that were you to learn that Demi's blood has been sucked by Austrian leeches, you would naturally assume the reference to be to a movie plotline. At some point, Demi was always going to have to accept that the call from *Inside the Actors Studio* was unlikely to come, and a move into cod-European schlock horror would represent a realistic choice for a woman previously out-acted by a pottery phallus.

So try not to feel too drained at the discovery that the blood-sucking happened in actual real life. In fact, it's something Demi swears by. She took it upon herself to travel all the way to an Alpine spa to have 'leech therapy', and upon her return hastened to David Letterman's sofa to proclaim herself phlebotomy's newest devotee.

'These aren't just swamp leeches,' she explained. 'We are talking about highly trained medical leeches.'

Zikes. Do you think one sucked out her brain? Though any leech permitted to latch on to Demi's silicone exoskeleton would ideally have spent seven years in leech medical school, it appears one unlicensed bloodsucker slipped through the spa's screening procedure – and the result was a pseudoscientific discourse that contrived to make Shirley MacLaine look like Christiaan Barnard.

'They have a little enzyme,' Demi explained, 'and when they are biting down on you it gets released in your blood and generally you bleed for quite a bit – and your health is optimised.' Mmm. *Optimised*. But how? 'It detoxifies your blood – I'm feeling very detoxified right now. We did a little sampler first, which is in the belly button. It crawls in and you feel it bite down on you and you want to go, "You bastard." ' Yes, dear. Then what? 'Then you relax and work on your breathing. You watch it swell up on your blood, getting fatter and fatter – then when it's super-drunk on your blood it just kind of rolls over like it's stumbling out of the bar.'

Then it was on to the full procedure. 'You have to do a turpentine bath first,' which must have been something of a risk for someone largely fashioned from injection-moulded plastic. 'The other thing I found out,' she went on, 'is that leeches don't like hair, so if you are hairy, be prepared to do some shaving or waxing – they much prefer a Brazilian.'

Don't you love how even annelids are body fascists now? These days you need to be no more than a crawling digestive tract to consider yourself too superior to suck anyone who hasn't had a full Hollywood.

But it is Demi's verdict on the treatment that should leave us all too drained to go on. 'I feel,' she muses, 'that I've always been someone looking for the cutting edge of things that optimise your health and healing.' Cutting edge? It's difficult to pinpoint when and where leeches stopped being cutting edge. But let's go out on a limb and say it was ancient Babylon, towards the end of the second millennium BC.

## Kabbalah: rewriting the science textbooks with a big, blunt crayon

One of the most competitive benefits offered by the Kabbalah faith is the promise of immortality. Not spiritual immortality – you can get that anywhere – but *physical* immortality. Rabbi Philip Berg, the former insurance salesman who founded the LA-based sect, wrote an entire book in which he attempted to yolk Kabbalah teachings with some pseudoscientific crap.[7] Modestly entitled *Immortality*, it is a spellbinding work, and suggests that Kabbalah devotees can *change their own cell structure*. Seriously: differentiated cells (specialised cells with a specific function, for instance those that make up heart muscle) can be transformed into undifferentiated cells, which can generate all kinds of new cells. How? Simply by meditating on the seventy-two names of God. And still we waste money on stem cell research.

What this all means, of course, is that the body can literally regenerate itself, and go on living forever. 'Satan has no affinity for an undifferentiated state,' Rabbi Berg explains, 'and, therefore, he cannot bond with the cell.' Did we cover the fact that things like organ failure happen because Satan possesses

[7] This is not the precise wording on the dust jacket.

your differentiated cells? It's pretty obvious when you think about it.

Unfortunately, we don't hear so much from Philip these days – he suffered a stroke in 2004 – but before he was taken ill, the Kabbalah CEO was at pains to spread the word about Kabbalah water, one of the many ways in which one can accessorise one's way to physical immortality. Kabbalah water is standard water that has been given special healing powers through blessings, 'meditation, and the consciousness of sharing'. It retails at £3.95 for 1.5 litres, and can cure Aids and cancer. But not strokes, it seems.

Anyway, not only do the blessings give the water 'a higher molecular order . . . necessary for eternal cell regeneration', but the Kabbalah Centre once went so far as to have the water tested for these properties, under what they claim were laboratory conditions. We shall learn more about this experiment in due course, but for now, be advised that though the results were never published, anywhere, ever, they were conclusive. The water totally had magic powers.

But the Kabbalah Centre has to fight scourges on many fronts, and so it is that its leaders have developed a response to the problem of nuclear waste, which several of the movement's leading lights have claimed is responsible for the spread of Aids.

Indeed, Kabbalah rabbis like Berg and his sons are given to interrupting prayers and leading their devotees in chanting the names of nuclear power plants. 'Chernobyl, Chernobyl!' is a particularly popular one, with one journalist reporting he had seen Madonna and Guy Ritchie turn eastwards, and dutifully bellow it out during a visit to the London Kabbalah Centre in 2005. On another occasion, a BBC journalist observed Ritchie and 2,600 other worshippers chanting 'Chernobyl, Chernobyl!' at a TV image of a giant rotating atom. This is said to help 'heal the problem of nuclear waste'.

So: miracle water and chanting the names of nuclear power stations. It was probably inevitable that at some point the

Kabbalah organisation would attempt to fuse these two . . . *technologies*, would you call them? . . . and so it was that in 2003, they hit upon the idea of pouring a certain liquid into a lake near Chernobyl. Result? No more radiation![8]

Apologies. That is a callous oversimplification. To give the Chernobyl experiment its full due, we must go back to the start of this decade, when an august body named the Oroz Research Center was established in New York. Please don't read anything into the fact that it was registered to, and presumably funded entirely by, the Kabbalah Centre in Los Angeles.

According to its own, self-effacing account, the Oroz Research Center was 'a 23rd century' facility.[9] 'Our revolutionary products hover on the cutting edge of tomorrow's medical-science break-throughs,' declared the centre's promotional material. And the marquee product was something called Orodyne solution, 'a revolutionary radioactive decontamination agent that neutralizes and decontaminates both high and low levels of radioactive waste in natural water bodies, nuclear reactors, and other applications'. Orodyne was developed by Oroz's director himself, one Dr Artur Spokojny – the very chap who had conducted the experiment that 'proved' Kabbalah water's magic powers. Dr Spokojny (who, worryingly, moonlights as a real-life cardiologist) produced a report which purported to show before-and-after photographs of water molecules which had been Kabbalistically blessed. His conclusion? 'We have reversed entropy and reversed the second law of thermodynamics.'

No doubt, no doubt . . . Back to Orodyne, though, which was such a top-secret formula that the Oroz Research Center didn't

[8] If you didn't hear about it, that was because the government and the Illuminati didn't want you to.

[9] Why does one picture a cramped, rented box room, with all calls taken by an answerphone whose message began 'Thank you for calling the Oroz Research Center! Unfortunately, all of our professors are closeted in the laboratory wing at this time. Please leave your name and number and a research fellow will get back to you shortly . . .'?

want to give away too much about it. They would only say that it was a liquid compound, and that it could also be used to treat gynaecological problems in livestock such as sheep and cows. So, your basic nuclear physics and animal husbandry crossover.

No sooner had Orodyne's discovery been announced than things began to get even more interesting. Oroz declared it had conducted a decontamination experiment which had 'delivered unprecedented results'. The 'landmark study' had involved introducing Orodyne solution into Lake Glyboke – a body of water inside the Chernobyl exclusion zone. As for these unprecedented results, the cynics would say that Oroz's total failure to publish them might have caused the credibility problem, and it's a little hard to press the point what with the Oroz Research Center having vanished without trace by 2006.[10] And despite repeated calls and emails to his New York cardiac practice during the writing of this book, Dr Spokojny himself seems unwilling to speak further about his momentous discovery.

But as the old saying goes, cynicism is the enemy of radioactive magic – so can we please just take this one on trust? Madonna was certainly willing to.

It is not for us to speculate on the chain of communication that resulted in Madonna being told about the Chernobyl 'experiment'. But she soon began granting interviews in which she hinted she was ready to make the leap from corset-clad mock-crucifee to nuclear physicist.

'One of the biggest problems that exists right now in the world is nuclear waste,' began one such peroration, 'and that's something that I've been involved with for quite a while with a group of scientists – finding a way to neutralise radiation, believe it or not.'

Not. But continue.

'I can write the greatest songs and make the most fabulous films[11] and be a fashion icon and conquer the world, but if there isn't a world to conquer, what's the point?'

---

[10] Maybe someone poured magic water over it?
[11] !

Well, it's probably a crazy suggestion . . . but to entertain? Or will only a Nobel now do?

'I've just come to a place in my life where I'm trying to really see what the big picture is,' Madonna intoned, 'and where my energy is better spent, and [nuclear waste] is one area I'm really concerned about.'

Just how concerned would become apparent. From a series of civil-servant briefings, it transpired that the Ciccone-Ritchies (as they then were) had lobbied both the British government and the nuclear industry, at the highest level, over the groundbreaking, mysteriously unpublished Orodyne experiment. Madonna began with Downing Street, calling the prime minister's office directly. Alas, a precisely minuted record of the conversation is tantalisingly unavailable, but an anonymous government official was good enough to give a flavour. 'It was like a crank call,' he briefed the *Sunday Times*. 'The scientific mechanisms and principles were just bollocks, basically.'

Masterfully, Downing Street judged the magic water to be a matter for the Department of Trade and Industry, and a former DTI official was on hand to gloss this phase of proceedings to the *Sunday Times*. 'She relentlessly pursued people,' ran this official's account. 'She wanted to get this Russian scientist to explain it to civil servants.'

A Russian scientist? Dr Spokojny, we presume – but his high-level presentation was not to be, as the Queen of Pop was shunted from department to department in a strategy designed to prove that while the liquid could cure radiation, it had no chance against Whitehall bureaucracy. 'It was a case of pass the parcel,' the civil servant revealed delicately.

Quite understandable. Yet this was not the only avenue of attack. The couple were also attempting to engage British Nuclear Fuels Ltd, the government-owned national nuclear industry. The body subsequently confirmed that they had been cold-called by a Mr Ritchie, who also wrote them a series of letters to which he appended what he imagined to be scientific papers.

One senior BNFL executive informed Guy that the scheme completely defied the laws of physics – but this was not enough to discourage the *Swept Away* auteur from further pressing the point. And why not? He knew this bloke who had reversed the second law of thermodynamics using only his bare hands and a couple of blessings/meditations/drops of sheep dip. So persistent was the mockney auteur that in the end, BNFL were forced to refer him to their executive director of technology.

Ultimately . . . well, for reasons probably related to top scientists being 'can't-do' people of closed mind, BNFL were unable to find any scientific basis for Dr Spokojny's claims. The last recorded mention of Madonna and Guy's nuclear project came in 2006, when one of their spokespeople would only reveal 'I don't think it is top of the list of things they are working on at the moment'. What you wouldn't have given to see *that* list.

What do you think would happen if you cold-called a government department and told them that magic sheep medicine could neutralise nuclear waste? In an ideal world, it would trigger the welfare state's fabled safety net to close around you like a mantrap, leaving you suspended in mid-air till a kindly mental health professional arrived.

In the real world, it would simply get the phone put down on you – unless, that is, you are a famous singer, in which case hours of government time would be wasted hearing out you and your quarter-witted husband, even when your proposition is so luminously ridiculous that a seven-year-old child with a chemistry set could dismiss it in under a minute. Does this feel like a good use of your taxes?

Does it feel right that the same people who have repackaged 'having lots of affairs' as 'sex addiction' are the very ones quacking on about how leukaemia patients should live? Of course it doesn't. Celebrity endorsement is nothing more than advertising without regulation. But cancer treatment isn't analogous to a perfume choice or a high-end watch, and the sooner celebrities are banned from making such pronouncements in the course of promoting their work – or more achievably, the media stop reporting them – the safer humankind will be. These people aren't doctors. They don't even play them on TV.

# CELEBRITY PARENTHOOD

'The joys of parents are secret, and so are their hopes and fears: they cannot utter the one, nor will they utter the other.'

Francis Bacon

'Once a week I do the school patrol, where you get the kids out of the car and get them to their classes. People get out of the car and high-five me and say: "You are great for doing this!"'

Pamela Anderson

In a life in which everything else is taken care of by someone else, gifting a child to the world is one of the most important decisions a celebrity can take.

Whichever method the celebrity chooses to avail themselves of the child – by biologically spawning it; by adopting it; by renting a womb in exchange for a mansion and eternal silence – something momentous is afoot. They are subdividing as a magical entity. If the parent is sufficiently famous, the baby will be a celebrity itself from birth, and hopeful of making Forbes's Hollywood child power list before its first birthday. Either way, it should be introduced to the world via a glossy photo shoot, for which its parents will be paid anything up to $10 million.[1]

But at zygote stage, all that feels very far away to your average expectant entertainer – though of course there's no harm in signing the deal now. You'll be too busy with other things later on.[2]

---

[1] You know, for its 'college fund'.

[2] In fact, you'll have people to be busy for you with whatever those things are.

There is something deliciously idiosyncratic about the way in which a celebrity handles pregnancy and birth. It's not just that certain private hospitals offer specifically tailored packages (breast implants out in the last trimester to prevent stretching, then replaced – after the C-section at eight months – while you're under for the tummy tuck). It's more that they will be the first person ever to have had a child. The traditional quote from a newly offsprung star runs along the lines of 'you can't imagine how amazing it feels when you first hold them'.

By that stage, of course, they'll already have been on a thirty-six-mile run, weight loss being the key goal once someone has checked it's got a full complement of toes. From then on, the child is a constant source of joy, right up until the moment it develops its drug problem.

During our travels through this specialist reproductive field, we'll learn how easy it is to confuse adopting one African child with saving *all* African children – and we'll review perhaps the most insane performance of a birth plan in human history.

In the meantime, though, the whole incredible journey is best summarised by Joan Collins's TV-presenter daughter, who once announced: 'I came home the other day with new nail varnish on and Miel said, "Lovely nails, Mummy." Then she took my hands and kissed each nail one by one. What can you say about something like that? It's worth all the pain.'

You may need an epidural in your head for this one.

## Acquiring a celebrity baby

Though exotic adoption is gaining an increasing hold upon the celebrity imagination, it's important to remember that old-fashioned pregnancy and birth are still popular within the entertainment community.

Not *that* old-fashioned, naturally. In these progressive, enlightened times, many expectant fathers want to buy a little something that says to their partner, 'I'm with you on this.' And when it came to what we can only refer to as the confinement of his beloved Katie Holmes, Tom Cruise was no exception. He purchased his own ultrasound machine.

Yes, those who thought he'd go for the Winnie-the-Pooh mobile were left with egg on their faces when the actor announced he had enabled himself to monitor continually the progress of his unborn child. Predictably, there was disquiet among so-called medical experts who wondered whether too many such scans are potentially harmful to a foetus. The outcry would probably have been greater had not the prevalent public assumption been that that thing strapped to Mommy's belly was just a series of cushions in ever increasing size differentials. Scientology's messiah baby was believed to be being incubated in a development pod at the Church's desert compound, and watched over by a twenty-four-hour Operating Thetan guard. Cruise could sonogram with impunity, particuarly as he'd pledged to donate the machine to a hospital after the silent birth insisted upon by the Church, presumably with any unsettling evidence wiped off its hard drive.

Yet silent or otherwise, mere childbirth tends not be anywhere near enough of a performance for most people connected with the entertainment industry. As Rod Stewart's wife, Penny Lancaster, explained after the nativity of their first son: 'We doused the placenta in tea tree oil and placed it in a hole we'd dug in the garden, and shovelled in some earth . . . After that we all jumped on the top and flattened the ground. It was symbolic, a little resting place for it.'

As a mere spectator to the main event, however, Matthew McConaughey must be saluted for delivering one of the most epically self-centred accounts of a celebrity birth – courtesy of *OK!* magazine, to whom he had sold the first pictures of little Levi. If Levi's arrival had been a movie, Matthew would have got pre-title billing and his girlfriend wouldn't even have made fifth card. It would be: 'Matthew McConaughey presents . . . Matthew McConaughey . . . in a child by Matthew McConaughey.'

It wasn't just the continued use of the 'we' pronoun, exemplified by such gems as 'we ended up having an epidural'. It was Matthew explaining: 'We found a great rhythm. Contractions started kicking in. I sat with her, right between her legs. We got tribal on it, we danced to it! I was DJ-ing this Brazilian music . . . I learned – and no one tells you this – but having a baby is a bloody, sweaty, pukey, primeval thing!' He's right. No one tells you this.

Still, for the birthing ritual to end them all, you will need your passport, as our mission takes us all the way to darkest Africa . . .

## Apocalypse Brangelina: the horror! the horror!

You'll be familiar with certain megastars' practice of having stores close their doors so that they can have the place all to themselves. Imagine if they could do that with a whole country. Great news: they can.

Back in 2006, Brad Pitt and Angelina Jolie opted to give birth to their first biological child in Namibia. They did this for a variety of reasons which can be broadly summarised as 'total affectation'. The Holy Family of showbiz just *had* to have a great nativity story.

Two months ahead of delivery, the couple and their two other, adopted children headed to the seaside hamlet of Langstrand, and set about weaving their African dream. The image offered to the public was that of two Hollywood idols roughing it in the Third World. The reality, not altogether surprisingly, was that the couple had rented the entire local five-star hotel. As for the eventual birth, which US tabloid readers may have pictured taking place in a mud hut, with only a witch doctor for assistance . . . that in fact occurred in a first-class clinic, under the auspices of the obstetrician Angelina had flown over from Los Angeles.

But we're racing ahead of ourselves, because the big birth had a really packed undercard. In the weeks leading up to it, Angelina's bodyguard was charged with assaulting a restaurant owner, shortly after having been widely reported as informing local photographers: 'If I find anyone getting a picture of Jolie I will fucking smash someone to pieces. I'm not joking. I'll fucking put someone in the hospital. Tell your friends.' This charmer was in charge of a huge, armed security detail, who cordoned off roads, used pepper spray, chased away locals, and generally disported themselves as renegade law enforcers.

As the pageant unfolded, the local governor's declaration that 'we don't want them to be harassed' was superseded by increasingly strong-arm tactics. This one was now way above his pay grade. Government-backed security teams conducted house-to-house searches of Langstrand, apparently on the suspicion that locals could be shielding or concealing members of the world's media.

Though it's difficult to cite the the precise point at which the situation tipped over into dark farce, you'd probably locate it around the moment that the Namibian government began enforcing a no-fly zone over the stretch of coast on which the couple's hotel lay. To repeat: *a no-fly zone*. Congratulations, Namibia. You have ceded control of your airspace to the star of *Tomb Raider*.

The Namibians are wonderful people, as Brad and Angelina were good enough to tell the world – but the feeling was not entirely mutual.

'Never in my life have I seen two individuals exercise so much power here,' was the furious verdict of Phil ya Nangoloh, executive director of the National Society for Human Rights, Nambia's foremost human rights organisation. 'They effectively captured the state.'

It got worse. Halfway through their stay, Leon Jooste, Namibia's tourism minister weighed in. '[Brad and Angelina] never asked for anything,' he explained. 'They simply said to me: "Listen, things are getting a bit out of hand." So I spoke to a bunch of people within government. For a small country like ours, with a small economy and a growing tourism industry, this is of major marketing value for us. What we've done is that every time they've got an appointment with a photographer or a journalist they contact me and tell me that "Mr So-and-so" is coming, and I contact the Ministry of Information and Broadcasting, and they contact the Ministry of Home Affairs, and they inform the immigration department.'

What could be simpler?

Futher light was shed after investigations by the *Pretoria News* in South Africa, who reported that 'the Namibian embassy in Pretoria has told journalists seeking visas for Namibia to [cover the birth] that they must have permission from Pitt and Jolie in writing before they will be allowed into the country'.

As a bewildered *Washington Post* wondered: 'Surely Hollywood stars can't dictate who enters and leaves a sovereign state?'

But of course they can. A little less time in the underground parking garage, *WaPo*, and a little more down the rabbit hole, and we should get you up to speed on the state-sponsored deep-throating of entertainers. Like the tourism minister said: it's a marketing opportunity. And if a few basic freedoms have to be trampled in the cause of getting a little star power behind your sovereign state, them's the breaks. Weirdly, however, there were those who remained doggedly unwilling to toe this line.

'Imagine if a celebrity couple controlled England's borders,' was Nangoloh's exasperated take. 'This is very anti-democratic.' He drew attention to the case of a South African journalist who had both camera and passport confiscated, adding pointedly: 'This time it wasn't apartheid rulers restricting his freedom of expression, but government officials in thrall to Brad and Angelina.'

But on it went, with Nangoloh stressing that the government could be tempted to use the precedent for future political crackdowns, and pointing out that unwarranted door-to-door searches and the deportations of journalists were actions only constitutionally permitted in the event of a threat to national security or public safety. 'The presence of Angelina Jolie and Brad Pitt in Namibia does not elicit any concern for national security such that the deportation of reporters could have any lawful or constitutional basis,' ran his thunderous verdict. 'If anything such deportation in this fashion constitutes a very grave embarrassment and threatens to bring Namibia's democratic status into serious question.'

The key thing to keep reminding oneself of is that Angelina does not style herself as a stereotypical Hollywood diva who'd think nothing of turning an entire country into a VIP room. She is a strident liberal who actually has part of the UN declaration on human rights tattooed across her neck.

'Ms Jolie is a goodwill ambassador for the United Nations,' Nangoloh observed acidly, 'yet she seemed to tolerate the removal of human rights that are guaranteed by the UN.'

And thus the Jolie-Pitts allowed their African adventure to play out: with its central characters sliding into exploitative, arrogant, indulgent lives, above the laws and conventions by which they are bound back home. Basically, just a better, televised version of what always tended to happen when white people colonised Africa. But this was a celebrity birth plan, not a Joseph Conrad novel.

In its way, though, the entire ridiculous performance suggested another acid-inspired take on *Heart of Darkness*, wherein we observers are bidden to take the role of Marlow.

Think about it. To deepest Namibia they were drawn, where a mysterious renegade had established what newspapers genuinely began calling 'a compound'. The Kurtz in question was obviously Angelina, swollen to Brandoesque proportions and holed up with Brad.[3] Were they preparing for marriage, or birth, or a military coup? Conflicting stories were floating down the river. Some said Ms Kurtz was operating a kind of crazed autocracy, imposing her own laws on the local populace. One paparazzo, dispatched to photograph the couple with extreme prejudice, tunnelled his way into the fortress, and was reportedly beaten even more senseless by Ms Kurtz's bodyguard. Where would it all end? Well, unless we were much mistaken, it all seemed to lead into the heart of an immense darkness . . .

[3] He loves the smell of nappies in the morning.

Anyway, to compound the horror – and to kill any last suggestion that the government was anything less than utterly prostrate before this pair – the Namibian president wrote Angelina a thank-you letter before her departure. 'For the first time ever,' gushed Sam Nujoma, 'our entire nation can agree on something – how wonderful it is that you chose Namibia for your special day. You didn't just birth a child but a new era for our new country. If we are the UN's baby, then you, as one of its greatest supporters, are among its founding mothers.'

Jesus wept . . . For her part, Angelina returned to the United States and promptly granted an exclusive interview to CNN, portentously billed as 'Angelina Jolie: her mission and mother-hood'. 'The borders were drawn in Africa not that long ago,' Angelina explained during the course of this ludicrous soft-soaping. 'These people are tribal people. We colonized them . . . They have just recently learned to govern themselves . . . And we need to be there to really support them at that time, to help them to understand how better to govern.'

To recap those 'how to govern' lessons: subject populace to house-to-house searches, deploy unnecessary force and restraint, muzzle media, implement draconian border controls, and violate human rights legislation. While Angelina was giving CNN her prescriptions for a post-colonial world, one Namibian farmer was offering his own evaluation of her stay to the *New Statesman*. 'The restricting of local and international press, and this pseudo-royal attitude, are the exact opposite of what Namibia needs,' lamented Tomas Lorry. 'People who, for years, tried to build a democratic society can only shake their heads at this.' And all so an actress can have her baby in the 'cradle of civilisation'. As Nangoloh put it: 'We have around 150,000 orphans in this country, and a lot of crime. I want to know how much money was wasted protecting two actors.' He demanded an inquiry into the whole affair, but was denied it.

So next time Angelina flaunts her 'know your rights' tattoo, remember this: you have the right to completely ignore her.

## Michael Jackson dares to be different

All of which is one way to have a baby. But before we move from the low-key business of birthing biological children to the international psychodrama of rainbow adoption, let's pause to applaud a certain celebrity who has declined to be fitted into these standard models of child acquisition, and has carved out for himself a third way.

Yes, of all the spellbinding tales of celebrity parenthood, perhaps the most amazing is the Michael Jackson Is Allowed To Have Kids story. No matter how many narrative twists threaten to derail it, this one has the magical ability to regenerate itself and keep reminding you just what crazy looks like.

It all began back in 1996, shortly after the breakdown of Michael's first marriage, to Elvis Presley's daughter, when dental nurse Debbie Rowe married the most famous man on the planet in a small private ceremony at which the best man was an eight-year-old boy.[4] In fact, Debbie was at the time already pregnant with the happy couple's first child, the wholly Caucasian Prince Michael. He was followed in 1998 by another little Caucasian baby, only this time the stork's gift was a girl, whom they named Paris. Well, one says 'they' – according to his own account, Michael was so delighted with his new daughter that he cut the umbilical cord in the delivery room, picked Paris up and ran straight out of the hospital, never to return – with the little darling still covered in blood. He later realised he was also trailing the placenta.

What went wrong in Michael and Debbie's marriage? Gosh, it's always so hard to know. For a while they were the perfect nuclear family, in a Chernobyl kind of way, but approximately ten minutes after Paris had been born they agreed an amicable divorce, in which Debbie waived all rights to the children, including those of visitation.

---

[4] Friend of the groom, obviously.

They would live with Daddy in his adult fairground, and wear scarves over their faces in public. In return, Debbie would receive a house in Beverly Hills and a staggered payment of $8 million. Hey – it happens a lot with second marriages. You're more realistic.

And as Debbie explained in court documents, she would only be 'an intrusion on their life, and they're going to have enough intrusions as it is. I'm absolutely around if Michael ever needs me, if the children need me for a liver, a kidney, a hello, whatever.'[5]

But what of Blanket, the adorable stunt baby who exploded onto the public stage in 2002 when Michael encouraged him to crowd-surf off a Berlin hotel balcony? Well, Blanket's provenance is shrouded in mystery, but he does complete the Caucasian hat-trick for Michael. And acccording to one magazine interviewer who observed Blanket with his father, Michael is quite the paterfamilias.

'Very quietly,' they wrote, 'with very few words, he was able to communicate to his son what was appropriate to do and what not.' No doubt, no doubt. God knows, if Michael Jackson had a parenting superpower, it would be boundary-setting. And yet, it's somehow bitter-sweet to hear news that Blanket is still very much under Daddy's non-opposable cartilage composite.[6] Ever since that audacious airborne debut, many have nurtured hopes that the young lad would take a good hard look at his life, gain wisdom from his subsequent encounter with Martin Bashir, grow in strength and confidence, reject his bed-rug appellation, and eventually come to realise the importance of overthrowing his father. Like Luke Skywalker when he goes to the Dagobah system, only with Bashir in the Yoda role.

Until that day comes, Blanket remains in Michael's care, with the deposed King of Pop declaring: 'I always had this tug in the back of my head, the things I wanted to do – to raise children, to have children.'

[5] If only she had a spare nose.
[6] Hereafter, 'Daddy's thumb'.

And happily, his child-molestation trial freed up his time to realise that ambition.

## The celebrity adoption trend

At long last, then, to celebrity adoption, the tiger economy of celebrity parenthood. Hard to believe now, but there was a time when it was associated with the likes of Joan Crawford, whose adopted daughter Christina penned the seminal abuse memoir *Mommie Dearest*, and who maintains to this day that 'it was complete and total hypocrisy between the public and the private. She adopted us for the publicity.' Later, of course, there was rainbow tribe earth mother Mia Farrow, who for so long averred that she and Woody Allen had the perfect domestic arrangement – she living on one side of Central Park, and he on the other. Alas, the shine on this one oxidised slightly when Woody began a relationship with her adopted daughter, and for a few years celebrity adoption was without the poster family it deserved.

Angelina Jolie single-handedly changed all that, when in quick succession she adopted a Cambodian boy and Ethiopian girl. Adopting photogenic children was once again fashionable – and in this incarnation the goods were acquired overseas, allowing the celebrity to conflate adoption with vague notions of charity. The more obscure the country of origin the better, with early adopters of the adoption trend including Madonna, who selected a Malawian boy in 2006. Soon pretty much everyone was filling awkward silences on the red carpet by suggesting that somewhere out there was a picturesque foreign kid with their name on it.

Here was Lindsay Lohan indicating it looked like fun; there was Gwyneth Paltrow declaring that she and her husband were 'open to adoption'. 'I do feel we're so fortunate,' Gwyneth explained, 'and we kind of owe it to humanity.'

A decade ago, the notion of the Paltrow-Martins having run up a debt to the human race that could only be worked off by annexing an orphan might have jarred ever so slightly – but such is the adoption trend's extraordinary traction that it seems a perfectly reasonable statement to make in the course of promoting a motion picture.

Pretty soon, Angelina was inviting the world to understand the complex social engineering problems she faced, on one occasion breaking a three-second silence to explain why she finally felt she could have a biological child with Brad Pitt, as opposed to simply purchasing another one from a willing Third World orphanage.[7]

In what we must assume was a tacit confirmation that she and Brad were recruiting and spawning a highly specialised child black-ops unit, Angelina announced she eventually saw that 'a biological child would not in any way be a threat'.

More destabilising to the command structure is the suspicion that other people might be stealing the Pitt-Jolie thunder. When Madonna's adoption of a Malawian boy appeared to be becoming mired in problems, Angelina was quick to serve up sympathy with a garnish of undermining.

'Madonna knew the situation in Malawi, where he was born,' she told an interviewer. 'It's a country where there is no real legal framework for adoption. Personally, I prefer to stay on the right side of the law. I would never take a child away from a place where adoption is illegal.'

The first, but certainly not the last, instance of adoption-upmanship had occurred. Where will it all end? Trend forecasters would no doubt concur we're headed for a competitive adoption-off, in which one celebrity would simply telephone another and rasp: 'I hear there's a lotus-eating, mystically powered golden child available somewhere in Tibet. Race ya!'

---

[7] Just kidding. Angelina and Brad always go by the normal procedural channels when selecting a photogenic infant to join their rainbow brood, with the only cost incurred being the standard registration papers. Anyone on the Pitt-Jolie memorial wings around the world will confirm this. Thereafter, all that remains is to change the foundling's name to something more suited to its new parents' daffy take on the world. One to undergo such rebranding was a Vietnamese boy, who at the age of three could hardly have been expected to be attached to the name Pham. Either way, he's now called Pax.

## How can ostentatious celebrity adoption be a bad thing?

Draw near, darlings, and prepare for selfless people to be mis-understood: because it turns out the celebrity adoption trend hasn't been quite the boost for the world's most disadvantaged children that various stars would have you believe.

In fact, psychologists from Liverpool University began claim-ing extraordinary things after taking a lengthy scientific look at problems that we all know can only be solved by self-regard and cod spirituality. Their study – published by the British Assocation for Adoption and Fostering – warned that the number of children left in orphanages is actually rising because of what they referred to as 'Madonna-style' inter-country adoptions.

'Some argue that international adoption is, in part, a solution to the large number of children in institutional care,' stated Professor Kevin Browne, a senior researcher. 'But we have found the opposite is true.' Their research showed that the surge in international adoptions by Europeans did not only leave more children in their own countries in institutional care, but 'closely linked to the Madonna effect', Professor Browne confirmed, 'we found that parents in poor countries are now giving up their children in the belief that they will have a "better life in the West" with a more wealthy family'.

Was that an oblique reference to little David Banda, the Malawian boy Madonna began adopting in 2006? Being in possession of a living father, little David was indeed only orphan-effect – although the quality of the product is so good these days that you can hardly tell the difference. As for African naivety . . . that was surely no longer a problem. Thanks to a relentlessly managed media campaign, we knew by this stage that Madonna had really put in the hours with his birth nation, who on her first visit basically acted like a bunch of rubes.

'People started to say my name and they had never heard of Madonna,' madam explained to the Associated Press. 'And in

Chichewa, the word "madonna" means "distinguished white lady", so I think they got very confused.'

Of course, the disorientation is easily explained by the fact that Africa receives its celebrity vanity projects on a time lag. Malawian coffee tables were only just beginning to groan beneath copies of Madonna's 1992 book *Sex*, so – for a few heady months – the unsophisticated natives might have struggled to square this respectful epithet with the arch-backed lady in a bobtail-trimmed G-string allowing a dog to go down on her on page 36. However, they were advised to keep faith and stay with the project: Madonna's anilingus phase was soon followed by her cast-me as Evita phase, during which the Distinguished White Lady's demure, 1940s first-lady pose undoubtedly made her worthy of the name.

But back to the point in hand, and the concern – voiced by many – that celebrities see international adoption as a moral crusade, akin to saving all of Africa's children. 'I will give David an education and a chance for a better life,' declared Madonna, 'and what better way to go back and help his own people, and help [Malawi] and be a voice for the people, than to be able to first have a life and be educated?'

Is there something slightly odd about raising a child to inherit your own messianic tendencies? Only time will show.

### 'My most challenging role . . .'

As you're aware, once any celebrity has given birth, it falls to them to decide which publication should be given an exclusive tour of what can be described both technically and colloquially as their crib. Selling pictures of your baby to the highest bidder is one of the most precious moments in a child's early development, and getting it wrong could have far-reaching repercussions.

But once the selling of the baby has been successfully negotiated, it behoves you to tell the world what amazing parents you are. Celebrities will often profess that parenthood is their 'most challenging role'. Few, though, make it seem as much of a real-time, publicity-blitzed Oscar campaign as Angelina and Brad. Barely a week goes by without the pair offering yet another sermon on – or exclusive photo of – their perfect family. That said, the pair are beset by problems. At one point – between the adoption of Pax and the exclusive photos of Angelina breast-feeding their twins in bed that Brad took for the cover of *W* magazine – the man of the house delivered a keynote address on the difficulty of getting one's household furnishings to keep pace with the demands of a rapidly expanding brood of infants.

'We made a nine-foot-wide bed that's just big enough,' Brad informed an anxious public. 'One more and we'll have to go to eleven foot.'

Was there any happy news for specialist quilt-manufacturers? 'We're not done,' he went on. 'They say: "Any plans for a fifth?"And I say, "And a sixth, and a seventh, and an eighth, and a ninth." That's my answer.'

So, two foot per child . . . By Brad's calculations, the advent of the ninth foundling will necessitate a bed nineteen foot by at least six, with a mattress surface area of 114 square feet, the magic number that will finally trigger an emergency UN session on Pitt-Jolie proliferation, and end this enchanting trolley dash once and for all.

In the meantime, is there something cruelly disingenuous about Brad and Angelina's weekly insistence on sharing every detail of their domestic life with a world slack-jawed at its own comparative inadequacy? Well, almost every detail. They will speak of 'chaos'. They will speak of 'muddling through with a lot of laughter'. Yet not once has either of them spoken of 'the SWAT team of nannies which enables us to have six children under the age of eight, but still shoot at least two pictures each every year'. And is there a point at which this modulates from disingenuous smugness into a real unkindness towards the aforementioned ordinary people?

Of course, they're not alone. 'I just love getting up for my kids in the middle of the night to feed them or soothe them,' says Pamela Anderson. 'Motherhood is so sexy,' says Uma Thurman. And Halle Berry. And Catherine Zeta-Jones. 'I love ironing his little romper suits,' simpers Liz Hurley. 'It's hard,' Nicole Kidman used to tell interviewers. 'You know, I'm a single mother.'

Anyone who has ever read such protestations – and has resisted being swept along by the implication that Kidman would spend every minute with her little angels if only she didn't have to do this damn blockbuster and pocket another $20 million – might find solace in *The Mommy Myth*. Authors Susan Douglas and Meredith Michaels, mothers themselves, declared themselves 'fed up with the myth – shamelessly hawked by the media – that motherhood is eternally fulfilling and rewarding, that it is always the best and most important thing you do, that there is only a narrowly prescribed way to do it right, and that if you don't love each and every second of it there's something really wrong with you'. They identified three key groups in the 'new momism'. The celebrity mothers, with their perfectly airbrushed domestic tableaux. The panicky mothers for whom scare stories about psychotic day-carers or devilish vaccines are concocted. Then the monster mothers, with their wretched, multi-fathered, antisocial, yobbish spawn, the failed states of maternity and a warning to us all. And it is a rigid little caste system, because no one ever describes Christie Brinkley, for example, as having three children by three different fathers.

Meanwhile, we demonise the past while hopelessly romanticising it. Poor 1950s housewife, we say, denied the chance to have a career, too – while adding a whole extra roster of duties the old girl never had to perform. Leave your kids to walk to school? What kind of a paedophile-baiting she-devil are you?

Believe it or not, hundreds of thousands of children are born every day. Yet many celebrities – like the new parents you'd rather not get cornered by at a party – think they are the first people it has ever happened to. This would be fine, did our culture not elevate their pronouncements to a level that can only engender inadequacy in the humble worker bees going through the same thing.

As the images of celebrity mothers have proliferated, so the rules for parenting have become stricter, until any woman unable to hold down a glittering career, find the birth 'magical', expand her child's mind in the cradle and look a million dollars while she is doing it is a failure – and possibly a danger to her kids.

But this is not merely a concerted right-wing attempt to drive women back into their homes. It has become part of the very fabric of celebrity culture, the defining media explosion of our times. Celebrity spokesmothers have white sofas and toddlers. They do not mention childcare. They make every scrap of Thanksgiving dinner or Christmas lunch themselves. And of course, the size zero ones *always* polish off trays of mince pies.

Even the liberal media demands this kind of 'down-to-earth' detail from the stars it interviews – perhaps because we have tried to normalise celebrity. For some reason, we need to feel that celebrities are going through all our problems – and still finding time to have fabulous, stratospherically successful lives. Which, one might argue, makes the whole business pretty self-loathing.

# CELEBRITY JURISPRUDENCE

'The rule of law is better than the rule of any individual.'

Aristotle

'I own Malibu.'

Mel Gibson, to his arresting officer

All men are equal before the law. You know, in a way. Even Michael Jackson has been called for jury service, but was excused, presumably on the basis that he couldn't readily be slotted in to a jury of anyone's peers. Does he have peers? They remain undiscovered.

In the first instance, of course, that means that like all their fellow citizens, celebrities require protection by law. But whereas your average Joe will often claim to feel let down by the law, the police will gladly go the extra mile where entertainers are concerned. We're not just talking about how many police officers it takes to handcuff Paris Hilton,[1] or why a Supreme Court judge was once prevented from attending an international law summit at a New York hotel while a posse of US marshals ushered in Angelina Jolie. We're talking about things like the FBI actually investigating reports that a contract hit had been put out on Britney's ex-husband, Kevin Federline. Fo' real, yo! In 2007, a spokeswoman for the FBI's Los Angeles Field Office confirmed: 'We received information, which was not specific and uncorroborated, and we shared it with local authorities who pursued it further.'

---

[1] Although the answer to that question is five.

Where to start? The spokeswoman declined to elaborate on the subsequent investigation, but the threat would probably have been handled by the FBI's crack Playa Hater unit, whose frantic search for clues would have taken them swiftly to the texts of Kevin's commercially disappointing 2006 rap album, *Playing With Fire*. As they combed the lyrics, federal investigators would doubtless have alighted on a track called 'America's Most Hated' as a source of credible leads as to who exactly might have a grudge against an almost elaborately idle ex-house husband.

'Tabloids tried to screw me/Magazines try to kill me/But I'm nasty/Too fuckin' slick and sly,' runs this snapshot of Kevin's existence. 'You gonna need a big army/If you comin' for me.'

We may assume that was the Code Red. The second these words were scanned, Delta Force operatives would have been dispatched to embed themselves in the garden of Kevin's Malibu home, trigger fingers just itching to dispense justice the minute this 'big army' – or perhaps just a disgruntled *Playing With Fire* purchaser acting alone – should steal up the lawn, bent on putting a cap in Kevin's indolent ass for lacking the rhymecraft to pair 'hoes' with anything better than 'stoned' in his otherwise thoughtful rumination on life as late-capitalist America's most polarising cultural figure.

And then? Well, we will probably never know what went down among those palm trees. All the FBI will now say of the threat is: 'We looked into it. It was not credible.'

So rest easy. Unless it involves an open-and-shut case of reckless endangerment by the paparazzi – in which event it will be ignored – any vague complaint by a celebrity will be exhaustively investigated, usually with a number of solicitous house calls. Primarily, though, celebrities run up against the law when they break it, or when they need to use it to sunder themselves from the person they married. Neither, as we shall see, is an especially pretty sight.

## Celebrity divorce: the start of a beautiful severance pageant

Sometimes, celebrities stop loving each other.[2] Yet for a tribe so vocal about their love, the transition into open hatred can be an awkward one. One week you're telling interviewers about your fairy-tale kingdom; the next you're wrestling Prince Charming for control of it.

For instance, the 2006 announcement that beach-based polymath David Hasselhoff and his wife Pamela were to split was greeted with sadness. When two people find the pressures of a high-profile union too taxing, it is a stain on all our characters, and you really hope they can patch things up, maybe after a Relate-sponsored road trip in David's loquacious Pontiac TransAm, Kitt. That car always gave sound advice. Alas, hopes turned to dust just the second the couple's respective attorneys began describing the divorce as 'amicable'. As we will discover, amicable is your go-to vocabulary for a publicist who knows things are getting ugly but still fantasises they can keep a lid on them. Unfortunately, it has a lexical nemesis. And nothing lets daylight in on celebrity magic like the words 'in court papers filed Tuesday . . .'.

Thus the Hasselhoff marital boat went down on the iceberg of the Los Angeles superior court records department. The band did not play on.

In court papers filed one Tuesday, Pamela alleged that David once broke her nose, and detailed a number of incidents including one where 'Petitioner told me that he was going to break through my security gate, drive his car through the house, beat the door down and go into the house and take my jewellery and sell it'. The allegations were denied by the couple's respective lawyers, with David's issuing a statement from his client in which he explains 'the only person who broke my wife's nose is her plastic surgeon'.

Yes, it was amicable all right.

---

[2] And often, it's your fault.

This is the thing with all celebrity court papers. What should have been a beautiful, private spousal assault or prescription-drug addiction suddenly becomes public. How cheapened the phrase 'erectile dysfunction problem' becomes when it is plucked from a bedroom screaming match and deposited in documents freely available from a court clerk.

Just look what happened to the Minnelli-Gests. One minute Liza and her 'music producer' husband David were making the most intimate and soulful commitment as a wedding sold to *OK!* magazine – at which Michael Jackson and Liz Taylor were guests of honour – would allow. The next, their union was being dissolved in a legal slanging match involving allegations of undisclosed homosexuality, of undisclosed herpes, and of failure to con-summate the marriage.

Yet as an illustration of the sheer futility of war, little in recent years has really touched the parting of Charlie Sheen and Denise Richards, a divorce for which rubberneckers were advised to cancel all engagements, and settle into a good seat. As the pageant moved into its beguiling second act, things were getting more amicable by the hour, with the Sheen-Richardses speeding way past the Hasselhoff-Bachs, leaving only the Basinger-Baldwins to beat in the race to be Hollywood's most shame-free sundering. One document laid before the judge was a series of emails from Charlie to Denise, in which the actor outlined various reasons she might want to 'go cry to your bald mom', whom we learned was undergoing chemotherapy at the time.

'You are a pig,' he observed. 'A sad, jobless pig who is sad and talentless, and, um, oh yeah, sad and jobless and evil and a bad mom, so go fuck yourself, you sad, jobless pig.'

Was Denise currently employed? It was difficult to read between the lines. Clearly, the outgoing Mrs Sheen's response would have to be considered – and profoundly public. By some mysterious design, it took the form of an anonymous reminiscence to the *New York Daily News*, detailing the time Charlie had purchased a $6,000, life-size, anatomically correct cheerleader doll, and attempted to persuade two female companions to enjoy a foursome with him and his pom-pom-toting latex friend. They declined.

'Charlie got so mad that he ran the girls out of his house,' the source obligingly elaborated. 'Then he took a meat cleaver and chopped one of the doll's hands off. He and his bodyguard tried to dispose of it, like it was a real body. They wrapped it in a blanket and drove around in the middle of the night till they found a dumpster.'

Of course, it wasn't all hand-ectomies borne of sexual frustration. There was the time Denise told an interviewer she'd asked Charlie for a sperm donation, but not because she wanted another child. 'It was to make his girlfriend Brooke jealous,' she explained blithely. 'Make her think that I wanted to get back together.' Or the time Charlie called Denise the N-word in a voicemail subsequently leaked to the media. Or, indeed, the time Denise explained to *In Touch* magazine that the couple's three- and four-year-old daughters were in therapy, adding powerlessly 'It's very sad that they need to be there, but they do for now.' And the time she went to court to throw out Charlie's objections to her using their daughters in a reality-TV show which centred on her 'life as a working single mom in Hollywood'. Wait – 'working'? Oh, right . . . Working on a reality-TV show.

That show would become the E! reality legend *Denise Richards: It's Complicated*, so you will rightly surmise that Denise won. Sadly, we don't know precisely how, because the judge heard the case in private, believing that 'the welfare of the children trumps freedom of information'. Still, let's all be glad it doesn't trump the TV networks' desperation for unscripted programming, and look forward to season six of the show, provisionally entitled *Rehab Mom*.


## The Hilton Prison Experiment

Like its Stanford predecessor, the Hilton Prison Experiment gave the world a terrifying glimpse of the ease with which even well-adjusted members of society can adapt to playing out the darkest punitive fantasies.

In June 2007, the world prepared to break a butterfly on a wheel. Paris Hilton – whose only crime was to be a drink-drive sentence-violating heiress of negligible moral code and almost mesmeric stupidity – was sentenced to spend forty-five days in LA's Century Regional Detention Facility in downtown Lynwood. By court order, Paris was due to surrender her sweet freedom to tip knickerless out of nightclubs, to expand her menagerie, and to drone 'that's hot' at low-income families with whom she had been billeted while filming her TV show, *The Simple Life*.

The celebutante may have continued her red-carpet engagements till the end, but greater Los Angeles seethed at the miscarriage of justice, and area police remained on high alert – terrified that the anger might spill over into the city's traditional, jurisprudence-inspired rioting. As the hour of Paris's lockdown drew near, the canyons echoed with the wails of her fellow citizens. Was there something they could do? Some Swarovski-encrusted ribbon they could pin to their drab civilian garments, some petition they could sign to underscore the fact that this will, like, so not stand?

The answer was simple. The answer was never to give up hope. One did not speak of hope for a dramatic last-minute intervention by Arnold Schwarzenegger. The Californian governator's wandering hand was not believed to be hovering over a telephone, ready to issue a pardon on the basis that he didn't fight against countless androids to live in the kind of screwed-up society where rich white girls go to jail.

No, hope was how we would choose to see the correctional experience that awaited Paris.

And in looking for a cinematic precedent to help Western civilisation make sense of it all, it was vital to avoid sacrificial parables. None of us wished to sit through *Cool Hand Paris*, in which one celebutante's ultimately doomed rage against the machine involved her having to swallow fifty eggs before being finally broken. Clearly, only one prison movie could be our guiding light. It was time to amass popcorn and drinks you could windsurf on, and take your seats for *The Lynwood Redemption*, an updating of its *Shawshank* forerunner, which is consistently voted one of the best movies of all time.[3]

For our notional *Lynwood Redemption*, Morgan Freeman must surely reprise his famous Shawshank narration:

'I must admit I didn't think much of Paris first time I laid eyes on her,' Morgan would drawl gruffly over grainy footage of the gates clanking shut on our latter-day Andy Dufresne. 'Looked like a stiff breeze would blow her over.' And for a while it would look as if it might, as we followed Paris's disturbing treatment at the hands of 'the Sisters', a group of inmates for whom the word 'turnout' does not refer to a well-attended bar opening. 'I wish I could tell you that Paris fought the good fight, and the Sisters let her be,' Morgan would intone ruefully. 'But prison is no fairy-tale world.'

And so it isn't. Yet in this uplifting tale, Paris would unveil skills that would make her indispensible to her jailers – getting them guest-listed for exclusive nightclubs, and putting them in touch with chihuahua breeders – before eventually pulling off her escape and burrowing all the way back to the VIP booths of West Hollywood. As the original's trailer ran: 'Fear can hold you prisoner. Hope can set you free.'

So ... how did the Hilton Prison Experiment actually play out? Attempts to cast her as a political prisoner having fallen on stony ground, it was merely days before the incarcerated socialite was using her phonecard to call the famed broadcaster Barbara Walters. Having described the iron-barred cell in which she was billeted as 'like living in a cage',[4] Paris told Barbara that she had found God.

'I'm not the same person I was,' she told Walters down a crackling phone line, presumably while other inmates queuing

---

[3] By morons.

[4] Yet another surplus 'like' in the never-ending Hilton monologue.

for the use of the jail's communications facilities drew their fingers across their throats: the prison gesture for 'I'm awfully sorry, but I need to make contact with the guard bringing my meth in tomorrow. Would you mind winding things up sometime before lockdown?'

'God has released me,' Paris went on. Upon her actual release, she revealed to Larry King that she had spent the hours between lockdown and reveille pledging herself to the Almighty, and wished to announce two landmark charitable schemes divinely guided by His hand. One: a 'transitional home' for women released from the jail, to break the recidivist cycle. And two: the establishment of the 'Paris Hilton Playhouse', where sick children would enjoy toys and clothes donated by Paris and friends.

And really, what wasn't to love about a Paris Hilton Playhouse, where young sufferers might don a pair of Nicole Richie's cast-off Manolos and play at falling drunkenly out of the Wendy houses customised to look like miniature LA nightspots, or crash their little pedal cars into strategically placed shrubbery, in healing play scenarios that should swiftly make them forget all about their mortality?

Alas, despite having been so convincingly found, God some-how managed to give Paris the slip again. How else to explain a life resumed exactly as it had always been? As for a ribbon-cutting date on the two charitable projects . . . Does the Paris Hilton Halfway House today ring with the sound of liberated laughter, as recent releases clink their Goin'-Straight-o-Tini glasses together and pledge themselves to their sister and mentor? Even now, are brave little infants forgetting about their impending death in the Paris Hilton Playhouse, where they are encouraged to spend afternoons sticking Play-Co-Cayn in Lindsay Lohan's generously donated skinny jeans?

This is going to be painful for all of us. But you need to understand that sometimes celebrities say things they don't mean. Sometimes they say them because they're tired, or upset, or on *Larry King Live* . . .

Listen, the short answer is that Paris remains busy with other stuff, OK?

## Naomi Campbell: fashion's Josef K

The almost balletic familiarity of events makes this a mystery play for our times. The arrival of a dishevelled minion at the police station, the filing of a report alleging demented assault, the spokesman's assertion that it is all 'a misunderstanding'. The coincidence of these three circumstances can only mean one thing: Naomi Campbell has been accused of beating the help again.

We have explored elsewhere the scientific basis of the supermodel's condition, but for now, suffice to say that the woman who describes Nelson Mandela as her 'spiritual grandfather' has long battled a compulsion to hit those in her employ for perceived instances of domestic inefficiency.

Brave as this fight has been, there have been innumerable occasions upon which the power to resist this brand of personnel management has eluded Naomi, and she is once again plunged into a Kafkaesque legal nightmare as a result. Space could never permit a full round-up, so we must be impossibly brief.

She first pleaded guilty to assault of her personal assistant in 2000, the weapon in question having been a telephone. In 2003, a former assistant sued her for throwing a phone at her during what was described as 'a tantrum'. In 2004, her maid claimed to have been slapped around the face: Naomi countered that the maid had started the fight. In 2005, her personal assistant alleged Naomi had smacked her around the head with a BlackBerry, while another associate accused her of coming over 'like Mike Tyson' after they wore the same dress to an event.

But in 2006, Naomi succumbed to the most debilitating bout of her illness. Not only was she arrested on suspicion of assaulting her own drugs counsellor, but a former housekeeper sought damages from Naomi, whom, she claimed, was 'a violent super-bigot'.

The one that really stuck, however, was her New York maid, Anna Scolavino, filing charges of civil assault and battery, alleging Naomi had beaten her around the head with a crystal-encrusted phone after she couldn't find a particular pair of Stella McCartney jeans for her mistress to wear on *Oprah*. The maid required hospital treatment, and a bloodstained uniform bearing the monogram 'Miss Campbell' was impounded as evidence. Naomi's lawyer, David Breitbart, actually complained that his client was so rich that bail being set at $3,500 was 'an insult'. He argued that she needed to retain her passport to honour an existing commitment 'to visit Nelson Mandela'.

The case raised a lot of important questions. Like: where were Naomi's damn jeans? Would 'failure to locate denimwear' count as mitigation in the New York courts? Would Lady Justice rule in favour of our tactile heroine? Her blindfold isn't the best news for a winsome supermodel, but those scales at least suggest it helps if you're thin. Naomi herself opted to face down the allegations with the dignified humility that had become her trademark. She accused the maid of stealing the jeans herself. She was photographed in a T-shirt reading 'Naomi hit me . . . and I loved it'. In the end, though, her attorney took the difficult decision to enter a guilty plea, claiming he wished to spare his client the media spectacle of a trial. Thus David set his sights on community service – though not without pre-emptively rejecting the street-sweeping humiliation that had been recently dished out to Boy George. In his view, Naomi could only work in an enclosed environment such as a hospital. 'It's so upsetting,' he fretted to reporters, 'that someone who has devoted so much time to charity is being despotised.'

Well, quite. And yet . . . was there something vaguely concerning about that despot reference? Was there a hint of trouble to come in Naomi's lawyer casting her as a resistance fighter, mounting regular political protests against the injustice of maids being unable to find her stuff?

Yes. Yes, there was, and it became apparent on the first day of

Naomi's community service at the New York Sanitation Department. She had struck a deal to *turn the entire event into a cover story for* W *magazine*. In a measure of Naomi's contrition for the violent assault which had landed her there in the first place, she opted to have famed fashion photographer Steven Klein shoot her arriving on the job, every day, in progressively more outlandish outfits.

'What I wear walking into my community service has no connection to what I'm going to do when I get inside,' was Naomi's opening line in her *W* diary. 'This is how I dress, and this is how I carry myself. What do they expect me to do – walk in looking all drib and drab? I've never looked drib and drab in my *life*.'

'I'm not allowed to bring my cellphone in,' was her first major gripe. 'Though all the other people doing service seem to have theirs.'

Mmm. Maybe they aren't there because they attempted to brain people with them. But it was Naomi's wholly predictable delight in life's simpler pleasures which struck the most amusingly hollow note.

'I find solace in sweeping,' she explained to *W* readers. 'I have no other responsibilities. I have no phone. I have time to think. I just have, you know, peace. I'm getting very protective of my pile of rubbish – kind of the way I feel about my Hermès handbag or my Louis Vuitton. I keep looking around to make sure no one is crossing into the area I was assigned to sweep.'

Thank God they dis-phoned her.

The joy, alas, was tempered with frustration. Despite turning up to work each day in six-inch Louboutin boots and haute couture, and 'getting all these calls from designers and stylists asking me to wear their clothes', Naomi despaired that anyone had even noticed her outfits. 'I find out that the press is turning this whole thing into a fashion show by commenting on what I was wearing,' laments one entry. 'I say my prayers and rush to the shower. It's freezing outside. Really cold, so I wear a Giuliana Teso fur coat . . .'

Perhaps the saddest vignette finds Naomi being made powerfully aware that bowing and scraping does not come as standard in normal life.[5] 'When I get out of the car,' she related, 'my bodyguard grabs my bag and just hands it to someone. It turns out it was a policeman. I'm not treating the police like they are my valet – like the papers will say later – it's just that I'm used to gentlemen. Obviously I'm wrong.'

Obviously. And therein lay the takeout lesson of her community service: if being Naomi Campbell is wrong, then which of us wants to be right? All that remained was one final, Sanitation Department-appropriate costume change. 'I slip on the silver sequined Dolce & Gabbana demi-couture gown that I packed in my bag this morning,' concludes her hard-hitting exposé of the criminal justice system. 'I put it on lying down so I can't be snapped by the paparazzi, who can see in the window. When I get outside, they start screaming, going crazy, as I get into my friend Giuseppe Cipriani's silver Bentley.'

As madam concluded: 'I've paid my debt to society.'

The question is really how long people wish to be part of that society, when it humiliates celebrities for the most trivial infringements of laws prohibiting one from being totally wasted and in charge of a motor vehicle, and takes their 'special circumstances' into account only 96 per cent of the time. Moving forward, as that irksome modern expression runs, it is time to begin carving out a new system of entertainer jurisprudence.

Just as the rabbinical court, the Beth Din, is invested with certain powers in Jewish communities, wouldn't it make sense to establish a semi-autonomous system in which celebrities could be judged? In its earliest inception, a 'jury of one's peers' meant just that: farmers were judged by twelve farmers, peasants by twelve peasants and so on. As the celebrity class towers further

[5] Even more powerfully aware than she must have been when she was beating her maid.

and further above the dowdy civilians who underpin it, the time has surely come for entertainers to be judged only by other entertainers, who understand the special pressures and burdens of being, say, a humanitarian with an underperforming retinue of domestic staff.

Should this new system prove successful, there is no earthly reason it should not be expanded, until a celebrity-specific penal code is drawn up, which looks leniently on activities such as high-end shoplifting or drug-fuelled pursuit of a minion, but throws the full weight of the book at you if commit some unforgivable transgression. If you get fat, basically.

# CELEBRITIES AND THE MEDIA

'A cynical, mercenary, demagogic, corrupt press will produce in its time a people as base as itself.'

Joseph Pulitzer

'She's not pregnant!'

*Now* magazine's caption to an up-skirt photo of Britney Spears, showing menstrual blood on her knickers

What is the role of a free press in this brave new celebrity world? If you guessed it is something to do with bringing you pictures from glamorous red-carpet events, along with the odd scandal, you really need to move out of the dark ages.

If you answered: to go through its bins and confect stories about its denizens being pregnant or on the verge of death from an Aids-related illness; to publish wild rumours with made-up quotes from 'anonymous sources'; to hound mental patients as they're taken from their homes on a gurney, and then endanger the progress of the ambulance to the psychiatric ward; to stick their cameras up the skirts of young women and not be arrested as they would were they civilians engaged in the same pursuit; to euphemise grotesquely focus-pulled shots of a celebrity's inner thighs with the ubiquitous 'STARS: THEY'RE JUST LIKE US!' headline; to cover all this stuff, endlessly, at the expense of news about war, government, the economy... then congratulations. Doesn't it feel great to be right?

Where there was once a relatively small pool of entertainers whom the world would agree were stars, there now exists a virtually limitless number of people upon whom the description 'famous' can be conferred. Words strain, crack and sometimes break under the pressure, so the media has coined new ones to keep pace with the fast-evolving new breed of persons of note: celebutante, sublebrity, popwreck.

But however you want to classify your stars, the noughties has been the decade in which it stopped being about them winning, and became about them losing. This is the age of the trainwreck.

The media's brand of celebrity-watching is now indistinguishable from *Schadenfreude*. Were an in-his-prime Jimi Hendrix to perform today, he would simply find his sweat patches ringed in some magazine or other's weekly 'Circle of Shame' feature, probably accompanied by a teeth-grinding caption: 'Ewww! He may be experienced – but Jimi's not deodorised.'

In the 1991 documentary *In Bed with Madonna*, the singer's then boyfriend Warren Beatty observed darkly that 'she doesn't want to live off-camera, let alone talk', and the film was seen as a watershed in the level of access the public were given to a celebrity. *In Bed with Madonna* now looks like a piece of infinitely reserved Victoriana. People have seen Paris Hilton perform fellatio in night vision. Internet-enabled fans are never more than two clicks away from a Britney Spears up-skirt shot.

So then to Britney, arguably the ur-trainwreck, whose imploding life is a staggeringly powerful sales tool. Ill-advised marriages, breakdowns, rehab, knickerless exits from cars, custody battles, videorazzi chases, public insobriety episodes, kerbside tears – she's ticked them all, and remains an enthralled world's most popular Internet search term. 'If there was no Britney, would all web traffic stop?' a senior editor at Yahoo once wondered. 'I would hesitate to give her that much power, but it's hard to argue with the facts.'

## Your dramatis personae

Before we dive into the noble business of news gathering and delivery, you should make yourself aware of the key players who shape the public discourse. Or to put it another way: Britney Spears is the bear. Meet the sticks.

• *Paparazzi*. The borderline criminal behaviour of these 'news photographers' is too well worn to need a retread, but suffice to say the reckless driving, trespassing, and behaviour calculated to incite grows exponentially worse. At its best, paparazzi photography can offer up a valuable news image, like the *National Enquirer*'s snap of O. J. Simpson wearing the Bruno Magli loafers he said he'd never owned, of which fewer than three hundred pairs were sold in the United States, and whose bloody imprint was found at the scene where his ex-wife and her friend were brutally murdered. This happens about once every 278 blue moons.

These days, paparazzi photography mainly keeps the reader up to date with the key details of a celebrity's existence, allowing them to exclaim: 'My God! I see Kate Beckinsale's been to Starbucks again.' For large sections of the print media, this is what we call 'content'. It eases out stuff no one wants to read, or isn't given the chance to read, like hints that the world economy might not be as buoyant as can only be implied by the fact that the first three pages of a newspaper show pictures of Paris Hilton buying a puppy.

• *Videorazzi*. The same as paparazzi, only their medium means you get to hear the stuff they say to bait the celebrity – or sublebrity – into giving them the rise that gives them their 'content'. *See* TMZ's cameraman asking Kim Kardashian's brother, 'Hey – did you watch your sister's sex tape?'

• *Headline writers*. These guys whip 'content' into shape, by squinting at a picture of a starlet with a slightly convex bloat to her stomach, and slapping the enquiry 'BUMP-THING TO TELL US?' across it. Alternatively 'BABY BUMP OR LADY LUMP?' The question mark is crucial. Like the word 'riddle', it conceals the fact the publication has absolutely no idea about a subject it is nonetheless covering as a news story. *See* 'J-LO LOVE SPLIT RIDDLE'.

• *Celebrity journalists*. Latter-day alchemists, who can turn a chance remark or camera angle into a major news event. And so it is that features are entitled 'Paul auditions FIVE beauties to be the third Lady McCartney', when they should correctly be entitled 'People with two X chromosomes Paul McCartney has recently spoken to'. Crime reporters anxious that their stories should make the paper have resorted to inserting extraneous celebrity angles into stories. Thus the first paragraphs of a *Sun* story about a woman killed by an unknown attacker inform you that she was 'murdered just yards from Jerry Hall's £10m mansion'. About 1500 yards from it, but you've got to sex this thing up somehow.

• *Celebrity bloggers*. Like journalists, but with even fewer checks and balances upon their valuable work. Meld news and comment via the Ben Bradlee-esque device of scrawling the word 'gay!!' across a photo of a teen star.

• *Anonymous sources*. The very lifeblood of celebrity journalism, without whose concerned – and almost always completely fabricated – leaking we would never know just how close to the edge is every last person who has ever made a success of themselves. Intriguingly, they talk in that way that only anonymous sources do. You know: 'they were all over each other – they didn't care who saw', or 'it's desperately sad – but we can only stand by and watch'.

• *Celebrity magazine editors*. The puppet masters who sit atop this pyramid of ordure. No matter how palpably wrong they are proved in their endless cavalcade of split/hook-up/pregnancy/death stories, you will never once see a correction or even an acknowledgement that this week's cover is a direct contradiction of last week's.

• *Publicists*. The relationship between publicist and the media is vaguely attritional, and you may even have heard either side exclaim that the other side lying 'undermines trust in the whole system'.[1] To help you sift your liars from your liars, publicists are the ones who will deny a divorce rumour for weeks, on the record, until the couple finally go public, with a statement penned by said publicist, in which they will blame 'media pressures' for the split.

[1] This is impossible. There is less than zero trust in the whole system.

When Boris Becker separated from his wife Barbara, the pair cited 'media pressures', presumably forcing huge payouts from bookies who'd blamed his knocking up that woman in a restaurant broom cupboard.

- *'Experts'*. The hordes of business-hungry plastic surgeons, 'body-language professors' and doctors who have never treated the star upon whom they are passing opinion, but without whose gravitas no anonymously sourced celebrity story could be without. They either charge for their quotes, or regard them as promotional devices which will turn them into mini-fameballs themselves. Strings of garlic should protect against them.

So, now you've met your tour guides, it's time to remind yourself what their savage, malfunctioning universe looks like.

## Celebrity magazine editors – they're just like us!

Remember, kids: celebrity magazine editors wield huge power, and that makes them public figures too. Perhaps the best way to examine our magazine editors is on their own terms, in their own argot, and with their ghastliest trademark: fake concern. Our data sample is a single week in British celebrity magazine publishing – the first week of August 2008, to be precise, as you can verify if you care to consult the bound volumes in your national library.[2]

Time, then, to analyse the preoccupations of 1 August 2008, dateline London. First up, Lisa Burrow, of *Closer* magazine, which sported cover lines such as 'Insecure Cheryl – Starving to get attention', 'Stressed Jordan – Surviving on apples and ice cubes', and 'GMTV's Penny Smith – I wasted my 20s worrying about being fat' (Whyever do women feel like Penny did?). But it was the

---

[2] Do people still archive this stuff? If so, we need to find a way of informing future historians that there were many people living in the early twenty-first century who were acutely ashamed and embarrassed by it all. It's just that no one ever learned how to make that whole silent majority thing into a viable business model.

editor's thoughtful letter to readers about Amy Winehouse that really impressed.

'We're all used to seeing horrific pictures of Britain's most talented junkie,' began Lisa, sweetly addressing the ennui, 'but the one below is quite shocking.' Great. Don't run anything that won't raise our pulses, yeah? Lisa couldn't understand why Madame Tussaud's had that week unveiled a waxwork of Amy 'minus the dirt, cuts and bruises'. 'It helps neither Amy nor any impressionable fans to portray her as anything less than a physical wreck,' she explained.

A close pal of Lisa's told this book: 'It's desperately sad – we don't know whether Lisa's so dangerously thick that she thinks this is "help", or whether she goes home, looks in the mirror and it actually cracks in disgust. If Amy Winehouse dies, Lisa will fart out some leaden prose about how no one could help her, even though her magazine did its best by paying the photographers who hound Amy every minute of her miserable life. Lisa might even read this and think "you don't understand addiction", not realising that "publishing wildly intrusive pictures of seriously sick people" isn't a recognised treatment either. It's funny how she's always sticking in lines about celebrities "taking responsibility" for their actions, when she's so utterly incapable of taking responsibility for her own. I've taken the difficult decision to speak out because I'm terrified she thinks her magazine's something other than a drain on society.'

Also starring in our randomly drawn data sample is *Reveal* editor Michael Butcher, who that week led his publication with a story entitled 'Britney: my boys or my sanity' – an article which contained precisely *no* quotes from recent mental patient Britney Spears. A media-whore medical expert who should be struck off told this book: 'Michael is exhibiting all the signs of a compassion-ectomy. And after last year's lobotomy, pals fear he's becoming addicted to surgery. It might be because he's bald and perhaps pathetically grateful for attention – but there is a serious possibility that he thinks his opinion's worth something.

I'm speaking out because I want him to get help before it's too late.'

And completing our line-up of mag hags was *Heat* magazine's Julian Linley – who won the week's douche-off for publishing long-lens pictures of Britney Spears *in her own home*. They showed Britney's son picking up a packet of her cigarettes and her taking it out of his hands in the next frame. Lest you failed to grasp the import of this fleeting moment, *Heat* let an *anonymous Internet commenter* gloss it.

'Even with supervised visits this bitch can't be trusted with her own kids,' ran this *message they lifted from a paparazzi website*. 'Her baby is playing with a lighter in front of her [he wasn't] but she is too worried about looking perdy to notice what the fuck he's doing [she wasn't].'

Why did *Heat* publish what they describe as this 'horrified message' from one of 'Britney's critics'? A source close to the magazine confided to this book: 'Julian is in denial about what a poisonous little prick he is. It might even be a medical condition – but pals say he refuses to seek help. He tells himself that only intellectual snobs could take issue with this kind of editorial line. He'll say "our readers want to know about Britney" or "we're giving our readers what they're interested in". Don't forget that in 2007 *Heat* printed a sticker of Jordan's disabled son saying, "Harvey wants to eat me". Presumably that was originally justified on the basis that "our readers" would be amused by it – so he's literally ceded editorial control of the magazine to people who laugh at disabled children. It's heartbreaking. Even sadder, someone at *Heat*'s job is circling celebrity body parts and writing the word "Ew!" across them. They're so ashamed of the way they earn a living that they tell their parents they work in animal porn.'

Not this book's words, Julian: the words of one of your close pals. And that about wraps up our play'n'learn Circle of Shame feature, but you should return to it in spirit every time it feels right. Publication dates for these enchanting periodicals vary – but the basic formula never does.

## Entertainment news on TV: neither entertaining, nor news

Like the press, the television media has honed an arsenal of tricks that allow them to cover wholly unsubstantiated stories. So if the media has confected a row, say, or speculated wildly on what one half of a celebrity divorce is saying to the other, there is no need for on-air pundits to anchor their 'expert views' in facts. They take to the airwaves to discuss who is *perceived* to be winning the row – which may of course be non-existent. This sleight of hand has the added bonus of making the pundits feel that they are not gossiping on-air about matters that should in no way concern or even interest them. They are offering a professional opinion on a public relations story. They are showing you the workings of Hollywood.[3]

Though this pose could be exposed for what it is by a child of ten, ten-year-old children do not anchor news channels, and so it is that studio guests will discuss last night's pictures of a gurney-strapped Britney in tones that suggest that they are offering expert commentary on the latest fluctuations in the oil futures market. And because entertainment is now deemed serious news, the networks will gladly show footage of the gurney and its poor, discombobulated passenger. As long as you can maintain that wholly convincing tone of fake concern, you could pretty much screen stolen pictures of a celebrity cutting their wrists on their own bathroom floor.

Any victories for dignity? Well, you'd probably have to count a small coup by the late Anna Nicole Smith's lawyer, which made him one-for-three after failing to secure custody of her remains, and failing to have produced the sperm that fathered the gazillion-dollar heiress's daughter.

In 2007 – after Anna Nicole's untimely death – Howard K. Stern finally used his powers for good and successfully blocked the sale of what can only be described as a somewhat specialist piece of

---

[3] They are being 'meta-scumbags'.

film memorabilia. Namely, a video of the breast-enlargement operation the erstwhile Playmate underwent in 1994, performed by a Texan surgeon who subsequently attempted to sell it to an LA-based souvenir dealer or any interested TV networks. You'd assume it to be the type of product whose sale is traditionally preceded with the words: 'For you, sir, I do have something at the back of the shop . . .'

Alas, one particular genie was already out of the bottle, and even Howard couldn't then turn his weirdo-avenger energies to eradicating every copy of a second film showing Anna Nicole's Caesarean section – a fairly involved task following her decision to sell it to US TV show *Entertainment Tonight*, whose way-more-unconscionable decision to broadcast it has ensured it lives on in the Internet's least Elysian fields.

You may well be feeling it's time for you to take your bath now – and so it is, though you should know that this is a six-bath chapter, and you never really scrub the dirt off. As Elizabeth Taylor, a star accustomed to the mores of a different age, recently exclaimed: 'Some audience out there – don't ask me who they are, but there are millions – they like scandal. They like filth.'

## Death pools. Hey – it's a living

And so to death pools. Once the preserve of the more esoteric corners of the Internet, speculating on when a given celebrity is going to die is now a wholly acceptable way for the world's celebrity tabloids to face down the August news slump, combining their customary blend of painstaking investigative work with stuff you go to hell for even thinking.

Take an August 2007 issue of *Globe*, whose Pulitzer-courting cover offered a timely reminder that journalism is not simply the first draft of history. It is also the first draft of tragedies that haven't yet happened. Readers were invited to feast their eyes on a nuanced think piece entitled 'WHO'LL DIE FIRST?', wherein 'psychologist and leading age expert' Dr Lillian Glass waved her witch doctor's staff over various celebrity lifestyles and asked: which of their lights will be snuffed out soonest?

Here goes, then. According to Lillian, the kind of therapist you just have to pray has no contact with actual patients, 'Ailing Liz Taylor will outlive wild child Lindsay Lohan.' Yes, the hard-to-kill Dame was judged to be capable of flogging her self-inspired jewellery on cable TV long, long after Lohan has graduated to the great blow-fuelled car chase in the sky. Lindsay had just the four years left, according to Dr Glass, who according to her website specialises in 'self-esteem issues' and is the author of a book called *I Know What You're Thinking*.[4] Further tomes designed to extract a wedge from the miserable are *Toxic People*, and *50 Ways My Dog Made Me Into a Better Person*, which we'll imagine is quite the *Brothers Karamazov* of any bookstore's Mind Body Spirit section.

By Lillian's expert reckoning, there was good news for fat-free fertility miracles Nicole Richie and Angelina Jolie, who could see sixty, though Michael Jackson's fragile exoskeleton was predicted to shatter fatally before the decade is out. Sad news too for Barbra Streisand, judged to have cried 'farewell tour' once too often, while Oprah Winfrey was permitted to preach her sacred doctrine of closure till 2013. And with 'just a few years' left in him, George W. Bush was being tacitly advised to break ground as soon as possible on what promises to be the smallest presidential library in American history. We leave Britney Spears till last, as the *Globe* giving her just five more years contrived to look like favourable coverage next to that of their 'concerned' news-stand colleagues.

### Power lists: a way for the media to waste its power

Listicles – lists dressed up as articles – are now a mainstay of the news media, allowing journalists the illusion of having produced an article without any of the tiresome effort, research, or basic news judgement usually involved. Your guests will never know!

---

4 Do you? In which case, choose your weapon.

Even in a world drowning in subjective and fist-gnawingly cretinous rankings, however, the power list stands out as a classic of the genre, with *Forbes* now even printing an annual rundown of Hollywood's Top Tots, wherein the infant offspring of various celebrities are pitted against each other. In 2008, Suri Cruise edged out Shiloh Jolie-Pitt, though both could easily be displaced by any number of nappy-clad scions of the great entertainment houses.

But if you're looking for the dumbest list in a field this crowded, then you want the December 2007 'Power and Influence' issue of *Details* magazine, in which cover star Kevin Federline was named the seventh most powerful man under forty-five years of age – *on the entire planet*.

First Britney Spears's backing dancer, then her husband, then her ex-husband, and then this: Kevin's rise has been so meteoric that conservative estimates suggest he will enslave us all by 2010, and elevate his 'dawgs' to an all-powerful kitchen cabinet – a bro-ligarchy, if you will – while awarding entire continents to girls who, in the words of his since-remaindered rap album *Playing With Fire*, 'go down like a fresh pair of panties'. The star once known as the sun will be officially extinguished in early 2011; Earth and its remaining inhabitants will perish shortly thereafter.

For the time being, though, it was your duty to salute Kevin, whose empire stretched from the PlayStation all the way to the sofa, behind which Little Sean Preston and Little Jayden James were allowed to play with matches and refined sugar products while Daddy notched up another Madden NFL personal best. Though this painstakingly assembled seat of power would appear to have had no obvious revenue streams bar the monthly alimony cheque bearing the greeting, 'Smoke up, loser! Kiss kiss, Britney', it is a testament to our thriving meritocracy that the self-styled pimp clocked in on the *Details* rankings a full place above Muqtada al-Sadr. Yes, the Iraq-based radical Shi'ite cleric could only manage eighth spot, presumably marked down for an absence of cod-mystical tattoos and his failure to 'bring it' in console-related activity. Wii *House-to-House Fight 07*? K-Fed was taking him *down*.

It was bad news, too, for YouTube founders Steven Chen and Chad Hurley, in thirteenth spot, and there were tears before bedtime in Syria, whose president, Bashar Assad, limped in at twenty-one. Nothing was upsetting the *High School Musical* imperium, though: a bunch of dancing kids topped the entire list. To repeat: the list of the most influential men on the planet under the age of forty-five.

But it was K-Fed's showing that effectively skyrocketed the exercise to No. 1 in the list of Stupidest Power Lists Ever – a position previously held by British *GQ* for claiming that David Beckham was more powerful than Rupert Murdoch.

Still, another issue of one of our finest magazines had hit the streets, while its staff and thousands like them bemoaned the inexplicable decline in print media sales, and those featured congratulated themselves on an influence of which they were already well aware. You returned to your horizonless life of eternal servitude; they awaited the call from the Bilderberg Group.

## Body mass: a matter of international importance

Of all the celebrity magazines' obsessions, though, there is one whose relentless pounding is pan-seasonal, and could never be confined to a single annual index. That obsession concerns fluctuations, perceived or otherwise, in the body weight of people who work in the entertainment industry. Though it is a closely guarded publishing secret, there is an immutable law which states there is a finite amount of fat in the celebrity universe, that cannot be created or destroyed, merely transferred from one star to another. The chronicling of this endless migration of adipose tissue is one of society's noblest callings.

Some celebrities collude in it, offering their exclusive weight-loss secrets to a public they hope will not discern the lipo scars, or speculate on precisely when they had the gastric band fitted. Others are not so lucky, and should a single extra pound be discerned upon their frame will find long-lens photos of themselves engaged in day-to-day tasks captioned with headlines such as 'FAT-NEY SPEARS: LOSING THE BATTLE . . . AND THE WILL TO LIVE?'. To help ease the pain, imagine this primal pageant glossed in the familiar tones of a Discovery channel wildlife documentary. 'Following the birth of her fawn,' the narrator might whisper over paparazzi footage of Britney purchasing a frappucino, 'the female Spears faces a gruelling struggle. The summer of crop tops is over: swaddled in baby weight, she must now nurture the fawn, provide coitus for the already restive Federline, and shed the surplus pounds if she is to keep up with the rest of the herd and get into something by Roberto Cavalli in time for the MTV awards. The odds are slim . . .'

Well, at least something is, and so on. Tragically, the Fates will usually have decreed it is too late for Britney. She will very likely also adorn the cover of another second-tier celebrity title, perhaps next to the headline 'STARS LOSING THE FAT WARS!' As for the ensemble feature inside, the tone the magazine will attempt is that of a well-meaning friend who recently read *The Dummies Guide to Tough Love*, and is now mainlining truth serum.

An unnamed 'source close to the troubled star' will say something helpful to the narrative, such as 'Britney feels she has nothing to live for and she doesn't care how repulsively fat she gets or what a shadow of her former self she becomes. It's so sad.'

That anonymity . . . It's not that one doesn't believe the *In Touch* reporters wouldn't do anything to protect the identity of their esteemed sources, but you have to hope they weren't forced to linger too long in the underground parking garage to secure the information. 'Follow the money!' their non-existent Deep Throat might whisper. 'She's spending it all on hot dogs!'

## Publicists' excuses, and excuses for publicists

There's a passage in Bret Easton Ellis's novel *Lunar Park*, in which the author's publicist attempts to explain Ellis's drug-related failure to show up to book readings. 'After a pause [the publicist] would answer with his now customary vagueness. "Um, fatigue . . ." A new tack: "Why did Bret postpone this whole leg of the tour?" Another long pause before "Um, allergies."' The excuses grow weaker, until he is reduced to claiming in barely a whisper: 'Food poisoning.'

In Hollywood, at least ten publicists will be making this type of call every day, with varying degrees of success. When it works, you don't hear about it. When it doesn't, as in the case of Lindsay Lohan's questionable commitment to the filming of the movie *Georgia Rule*, you get a bigwig like James G. Robinson, CEO of Morgan Creek Productions, firing off a letter to the star herself. Immediately leaked to the *Smoking Gun*, Mr Robinson's billet-doux moved up through the gears with lightning speed.

'Dear Lindsay,' it began. 'Since the commencement of principal photography on *Georgia Rule*, you have frequently failed to arrive on time on set. Today you did not show for work (all day). I am now told you do not plan to come to work tomorrow because you are "not feeling well". You and your representatives have told us that your various late arrivals and absences from the set have been the result of illness; today we were told it was "heat exhaustion". We are well aware that your ongoing all night heavy partying is the real reason for your so called "exhaustion". We refuse to accept bogus excuses for your behavior.' How could Robinson have been so sure the excuse was bogus? It probably didn't help that Lindsay was photographed clubbing till the small hours that very night. And almost every other.

Publicists get a bad press, but occasionally – and mostly when the matter's none of our business anyway – their refusal to cave in to the facts is so dogged that it tips beyond mere euphemism and becomes something genuinely creative. In this spirit, let us salute one practitioner of the craft's comment on Jude Law and Sienna Miller's disbanded relationship. One week in 2005, their travelling circus had docked in Paris, where, according to several reports, Sienna ran screaming into a restaurant in which Jude was lunching with an unnamed woman, and proceeded – in full public view – to drop to her knees, place her head in his lap, and plead, 'Don't go, don't go.' Or, as the encounter was summarised by her publicist: 'Sienna had arranged to meet Jude in Paris for lunch and it was all very amicable.'

As previously indicated, you know things are really bad when you hear 'amicable'. 'Amicable' is how Jerry Hall and Mick Jagger's split was described about twelve minutes after it was established he had impregnated some Brazilian model. Indeed, the Sienna denial can sit proudly by rebuttals so perfectly formed that including the question that inspired them is superfluous. Take the 1996 classic: 'No, Dannii [Minogue] has just been doing a lot of chest exercises recently.'

However, even that pales next to the response to the actor Eddie Murphy being arrested with a transvestite prostitute in his vehicle on Santa Monica Boulevard: 'Eddie is a humanitarian. He was merely talking to the woman [*sic*] in an attempt to persuade her not to continue with a life of vice.'

Clearly, we were being encouraged to think of Mr Murphy as the William Gladstone for fallen shemales, and the actor himself soon shored this impression up – with an explanation which handily excused all the subsequent transvestite accounts of trysts with Eddie that were looming. 'I'm just being a nice guy,' he explained. 'I was being a good Samaritan. It's not the first hooker I've helped out. I've seen hookers on corners . . . and I'll pull over . . . and they'll go, *Oh, you're Eddie Murphy, oh my God*, and I'll empty my wallet out to help.'

Less amusing was one publicist's answer to enquiries after Mariah Carey posted a confused rant on her fan site, hours before she was admitted to hospital with bandaged arms. 'Mariah did break some dishes,' her flack breezed, 'and may have cut her foot in the process.' Mmm. Let's play out on a lighter note, with a retreat on the initial denial that Princess Diana had made three hundred silent phone calls to a married art dealer. The princess, it was conceded when the calls were indeed traced to her private line at Kensington Palace, was 'in the habit of' ringing Oliver Hoare, 'and it's possible that she may have replaced the receiver when he didn't answer . . .'.

One has to feel a certain disappointment that no star's publicist has yet found the chutzpah to use the line: 'Oh no, that must have been his evil twin . . .'

## Bins: trash talking

People often describe Hollywood as a strange beast. By which they mean it has unnaturally taut skin, glazed eyes, and a vast, sore-infested underbelly.[5] Thanks to clever camera angles, Hollywood is usually seen from the neck up, but every now and then something threatens to expose the whole hideous body shot. You are hereby advised to gird yourselves in protective clothing. We're going into the bins.

When did the focus of celebrity journalism shift from the red carpet to the dumpster? Well, one watershed was reached in 2004 when two French 'photojournalists' held an exhibition of the contents of celebrity trash cans in New York. Being French, they declined to see themselves as invasive parasites. 'For us, it's really *socialogique* and *archealogique*,' one of them explained loftily. 'If in the next fifty years the work that we do is helping people, students, to understand our society, then we will win what we intend to do . . . Some people, they think we are like paparazzi. They are wrong. You have to think a little bit. We are sure of one thing: this is a real portrait of our society.' Quite . . . The most talked-about exhibit came from the bin of CNN host Larry King. It was an adult nappy wrapper.

So, people mused, Larry King wears adult nappies. What a telling glimpse into the psychology of a man whose life's work has been inserting himself into the colons of other notable – but wait! What was this? A formal statement – oh please, *no* – from CNN

[5] Sharon Osbourne would probably play it in a movie.

host Larry King, on the matter of the adult nappy wrapper. It was not his adult nappy wrapper. He does not wear adult nappies. He would not know what an adult nappy looked like.

Had Larry's publicist intervened – one had to assume she was on a residential remedial course – she would probably have sighed that this breed of journalism is forcing dignity into the gutter. And she'd be partly right. But just as coppers and criminals speak the same slang and drink in the same bars, so these entertainment hacks and the industry players they cover bathe in the same swamp.

For two decades, Anthony Pellicano was known as 'private investigator to the stars', mainly because 'PI to the stars, their agents, lawyers and studio heads' sounded unwieldly. But that was the scope of it. When Michael Jackson wanted dirt dug on the family of the boy who accused him of child molestation in 1993, he went to the Pelican. The same with the late, appetite-driven producer Don Simpson when he had a spot of bother with a receptionist. Routine celebrity bin search? Pellicano was the man for you. It may be painful, but you need to let go of the idea that *Magnum P.I.* was *cinéma-vérité*. Unless we all missed the episode where Tom Selleck dons his rubber gloves to separate Liz Taylor's used tissues from her empty medication bottles.

Unfortunately, during an investigation into legendary *Under Siege* actor Steven Seagal, Pellicano overstepped the line, warning off a journalist by placing a dead fish on her car windscreen, which had been cracked by what looked to her like a bullet hole. When the FBI raided his office they found almost two billion pages of phone-tap transcripts, several homemade bombs, and sufficient plastic explosives to bring down a passenger jet.

The resultant trial found Pellicano guilty on seventy-six out of seventy-seven counts of racketeering, wiretapping, conspiracy, wire fraud and identity theft, while a subsequent court outing convicted him for further wiretapping offences. But it was the industry figures who had employed him – oblivious of his illegal methods, they claimed – that were the real boldface names. We're not talking TV extras. Those questioned, though never charged, over their practice of paying Pellicano to dig dirt on everyone from hugely powerful rivals to mere *New York Times* journalists included former CAA/Disney/AMG boss Michael Ovitz. Ovitz's performance on the stand was particularly emetic. 'I wanted all kinds of information,' he whined. 'I had no one feeding me information ... All I wanted was a graceful exit from this business.' A business he described as 'very much like high school'. High school with bombs? Also spoken to by investigators were Paramount chairman Brad Grey, Universal president Ron Meyer and legendary entertainment lawyer Bert Fields. Your basic dream merchants.

Turns out that if you're in the business of selling people a dream, you tend to be a pretty nightmarish person. So next time you see Larry King soft-soaping an A-lister, just consider the armies who've schemed and cheated to get Larry the gig, and the armies scheming and cheating in the hope he never gets another, and the armies of 'journalists' attempting to get his bin to yield up another secret in the dead of night. On the bright side, at least you know he's not wearing a nappy.

The traditional news media may be on its knees, but celebrity journalism is a near-lawless growth sector where even unauthorised refuse collection is seen as an activity that knits you into the tradition that produced Woodward and Bernstein.

Where is the skill in inventing stories about an entertainer's children? What does it behove humanity to divide all female entertainers into those who are either too fat or too thin? What utility a circled sweat patch? It would be comforting to think that, given their daily refusal to answer any of these questions, a certain strata of 'entertainment journalists' eventually succumb to that haunted look worn by foreign correspondents who've been there for the exhumation of mass graves – the thousand-yard stare that says 'I've seen stuff I can't unsee'. They don't, unsurprisingly. Because once you lack sufficient human compassion to stop baiting a psychiatric patient even as she weeps on the kerbside, you are no longer documenting the problem. You *are* the problem.

Back then to Britney, whose poor, shaven-headed spectre looms large over this chapter because she embodies the logical end of these 'news values'. More than any living celebrity, Britney has been hounded in the name of entertainment news, eventually into mental illness. Frantic attempts to gain ownership of her breakdown reached epic proportions, descending into a kind of Britney arms race, in which warring titles competed to amass the most damning assessments of her condition – and you can see why. In 2008, *Portfolio* magazine estimated that Britney Spears was worth at least $75 million a year to the American media – and between $110 million and $120 million to the US economy as a whole. One day in the midst of her dramas, she emerged from the house into the customary scrum of paparazzi and videorazzi wearing a T-shirt. Its slogan? 'I am the American dream.'

Paging Arthur Miller . . .

# CELEBRITIES IN THE FUTURE

'Men, it has been well said, think in herds; it will be seen that they go mad in herds, while they only recover their senses slowly, and one by one.'

Charles Mackay, *Extraordinary Popular Delusions and the Madness of Crowds*

'With the whole light-years thing, what if I come back 10,000 years later, and everyone I know is dead? I'll be like, "Great. Now I have to start all over."'

Paris Hilton on her planned space mission

Way back in 1961, the social historian Daniel Boorstin warned that public life had become overrun with 'pseudo-events', meaningless confections given a counterfeit life by the media. Defining a celebrity as 'a person who is known for his well-knownness', he argued that stars were human pseudo-events, whose constructed images and semi-scripted narratives are sufficiently hypnotic as to distract millions from reality. Today, you will not be especially shocked to learn, Boorstin's name is seldom used without the epithet 'prescient'.

In 2008, with the world in the grip of an economic crisis whose reach and severity is likely to be the stuff of nightmares, the most popular Internet search term was Britney Spears. For the fourth consecutive year running.

The Internet was once supposed to short-circuit the institutionally powerful, giving rise to a new, roots-up form of discourse, connecting people who might not otherwise be able to capitalise on their common cause. Yet it has made celebrities more celebrated than ever. It has enabled vast herds of humankind to congregate in search of the latest mundane update on how an entertainer is spending their weekend. And it has proved a state-of-the-art disseminator of pictures of Paris Hilton's knickers.[1]

Contemplating the hold celebrities exercised on the popular imagination even in the early 1960s, Boorstin concluded that stars 'provide that "common discourse" which some of my old-fashioned friends have hoped to find in the Great Books'.

Today, the suggestion that celebrity is a religion scarcely raises an eyebrow; although any emphasis on redemptive narratives has given way to a relentless obsession with the downward spiral, where fame is just a staging post en route to the real destination – infamy.

So where now? The Book of Revelation might seem the obvious answer. But on the basis that we've already met enough fifth horsemen on our travels, our business here is merely to extrapolate a picture of the impending celebrity future from the evidence and indicators we have at our disposal. Things like trends in celebrity doll-making, or a Russian parliament debate about Madonna, or the star-studded passenger manifest for the first commercial space flight.

And having run the rule over these, you will likely conclude that those who predict the imminent bursting of the celebrity bubble do so more in hope than expectation. The celebrity of the future will be bigger, faster, stronger – and even more alluringly influential.

In terms of achievable goals, perhaps entertainers' immense power and influence might become subject to conventional forms of regulation. For instance, those celebrities who mention drugs on chat shows should be required to state when they are paid huge fees by the pharmaceutical giants who make them. You know, the little things.

[1] Or lack thereof.

But if you truly want to know the answer to the question 'How screwed are we?', you need simply take a look at the Britney Industrial Complex, with a single LA paparazzi agency claiming the bear-baited singer accounts for 30 per cent of its business. Take a look at the Jolie-Pitts' ability to effectively close a sovereign state's borders to reporters. Take a look at the ever swelling ranks who queue outside convention centres to audition for TV talent shows, testament to a whole Western generation's assumption that fame is a basic human right.

Contemplating these Boschean hellscapes, you will realise that you already know the answer. The entertainers have won. Even as Britney Spears loses, the culture that spawned her and feeds off her wins. The best response? Seek out like-minded individuals and start your own gallows-humour-fuelled resistance movement. Failing that, lay in supplies of duct tape and canned goods. It's unlikely to be pretty.

## Celegislators: the Fifth Estate

When third-tier Backstreet Boys and Muppets are already designated expert witnesses by United States congressional committees, you may be wondering how much lower we can sink in enabling celebrities to hijack political debate. Well, should things continue in this vein, legislative bills will soon stop seeking celebrity endorsement, and begin actively requiring it. Before the reading of any prospective piece of legislation, a minimum of twelve celebrities must be seen drinking appletinis and shrieking about the imminent launch of their next project in the halls of the relevant country's legislative body. 'Oh my God! I heard, like, *no one* showed up for "Universal Healthcare" except a couple of reality sublebrities. That baby is so totally dead in the water.'[2]

Fanciful? Perhaps, but as far as your showbiz-addled legislative

---

[2] Goody bags may well be offered as incentives.

future goes, we're going to need a new -topia prefix. Dystopia just won't cut it.

Major lobbying firms are already allocating more and more resources to the business of attracting celebrities to their causes. The most audacious leap forward has been taken by the prominent Washington lobbyist Jarvis Stewart, who in 2006 launched a service providing entertainment clients with advice on political participation, catering for everything from specific fund-raising requests to that most charmingly vague of modern aspirations: wanting to get one's voice heard in Washington. Stewart's firm went right to the heart of the beast and opened a West Coast office in LA's Century City, whose stated aim is to offer 'strategic management services to recording artists, celebrities, record labels, studios, and others in the entertainment community. Services include counseling entertainment clients on their political participation, such as contributing to and endorsing candidates, and assisting them in developing and articulating their philanthropic interests to the media, contributors, and policy decision-makers.'

How has this sainted mission been received by the traditionally self-effacing entertainment community, who for too long have languished in voiceless disenfranchisement? 'The same thing Jarvis does for Verizon he can do for Jay-Z,' was the judgement of one impressed record executive. 'Jarvis can teach them how to play on the political stage.'[3]

As for the vision nurtured by Jarvis himself, the lobbyist told a *Details* magazine profiler that he imagined bringing Kanye West to Washington and scheduling talks between the hip-hop star and a conservative senator. 'How about Trent Lott?' he wondered. 'Wouldn't that be fantastic? I'd be a fucking rock star. I'd have everyone licking my ass if I got Kanye West to meet with Trent Lott.'

---

[3] But can he teach the CEO of Verizon to rap? Or does his Pygmalion formula only work one way?

What can you say? Other than to simply thank heavens that as stars continue to exercise their constitutional right to remain less silent than the rest of us, there is a whole new generation of wildly appealing back-room players, working in ever more ingenious and determined ways to assist them.

## Loser-generated content: the future of celebrity merchandising

As far as watershed moments in celebrity merchandising go, the one to watch was the response to one of the most profoundly disturbing episodes in the tragic picaresque of Britney Spears's life. In mid-February 2007, Britney went AWOL from rehab and, after the obligatory late-night paparazzi chase, eventually lurched into a cheap hair salon in the San Fernando Valley. Because the owner had refused, Britney shaved her own head, before wandering off in search of a tattoo parlour. 'I don't want anyone touching me,' she explained distractedly to the tattooist. 'I'm tired of everyone touching me.'

Within one calendar week of the incident – and let's hope the industry will eventually eliminate that sloppy time lag – it was possible to purchase a commemorative Britney Spears Rehab Doll. 'Britney Shears' read the cute pink packaging, which encased a barefoot, jogging-bottomed Britney complete with shaved head and a vacant expression. Oh, and she was wearing a straitjacket. The box also contained a padded room diorama, to assist smirking ironists in displaying their new toy.

Looked at dispassionately – and how else did anyone examine this sweet little curiosity? – the Britney rehab doll appeared to herald a new generation in toymaking, being one of the first to be created in response to a developing news story. Satan willing, the product will open the market for big-ticket items that should make ideal Christmas purchases for fashion-forward youngsters. Hopefully, in time, we'll see a scale replica of the Promises rehab facility in Malibu, where the absence of a fourth wall will allow children to position their injection-moulded idols in group-therapy sessions, perhaps overlaying their interaction with adorably naive imagined dialogue.

Another logical expansion would be to market models of fashionable Hollywood nightspots, allowing inquisitive doll owners to learn through play the precise number of bathroom visits that triggers an attack of 'exhaustion', while an elder brother's Action Men could be co-opted into the role of circling paparazzi, ready to thrust tiny plastic cameras up the Velcro-fastened miniskirts of our figurines as they emerge onto the pavement. Face it, the inhumane figurine market is ripe for commercial exploitation. And, as the manufacturers like to justify such moves, if we don't do it, China will.

## Celebrities: soon to be literally shaping your world

Now that Gwyneth Paltrow has launched a website where she issues regular, unsolicited directives on how to 'nourish your inner aspect', it's clear that celebrities are keen to take charge of our emotional landscapes. But wouldn't it be amazing if there was a *physical* citadel designed by celebrities, a sort of giant vanity project built by modern-day slaves, unconstrained by the fetters of democracy and propped up by hot, black oil money?

Faustus, party of one? Your table is ready. Come fly to the United Arab Emirates – not literally, of course, one couldn't be seen dead anywhere so vulgar – a destination we shall classify as the Helldorado of the Middle East. And that's a tough field.

Recent times have seen a shift in construction policy in the desert kingdom. Not content with building hotels in the shape of palm trees, or God, or Mammon, the powers that be in Dubai and Abu Dhabi have decided that what the place really needs is buildings actually designed by celebrities, and to this end they have commissioned all manner of stars to take to their drawing boards.

Thus Boris Becker is to design a Dubai beach resort in the shape of a sea turtle. Mies van der Rohe manqué Pamela Anderson is to build an eco-hotel in Abu Dhabi, which is a bit like building a yoga retreat in Basra. And undead Chanel auteur Karl Lagerfeld is creating some sort of Coco-inspired Sesame Street on Isla Moda – Fashion Island – which is part of the charmless man-made Dubai archipelago, The World. Commissioning Karl are an outfit called Dubai Infinity Holdings, who declare that the designer's exquisite work 'transcends demographics'. As only a £100,000 haute couture ballgown can.

Still, how cavalier of Dubai Infinity Holdings to even acknowledge the existence of 'demographics' in Dubai, where stately pleasure domes are in fact built by a demographic best described as 'modern-day slaves'.

Before we come on to that, however, we should mention that the most high-profile star contracted to play architect is none other than Mr Brad Pitt. Having spent years lecturing interviewers with his thoughts on architecture, Brad has always been a hotter version of George Costanza – who, you may recall, spent most of *Seinfeld* wishing he was an architect. George once claimed to have designed 'the new addition to the Guggenheim'. Amusingly, then, it has emerged that Brad is genuinely being allowed to design not just an addition, but a whole building in Dubai. He will expand his burgeoning moral relativism portfolio to the emirate, creating an entire resort whose centrepiece is an 800-room, five-star hotel complex. 'Whilst acting is my career, architecture is my passion,' Brad told the world upon the inking of the deal. 'Selecting this development as my first major construction project has been a simple decision.'[4]

Our matinee-idol project manager has yet to release a scheduled completion date, and yet, and yet . . . On the basis that Brad's stated desire was to build a 'socially conscious' building, we must assume that he is somehow unaware of the uniformly horrible conditions in which the armies of labourers who work on this perpetual building site are forced to live. Perhaps his people

[4] In that it's the only such offer he has ever received?

could do the requisite basic Internet search for him and decide whether the risk of 'SLAVE LABOUR BUILDS BRAD HOTEL' headlines is really worth the 30 million pieces of silver, or whatever the going rate for building a pretentious theme park is these days.

Were they to engage in this type of research, they, and any other celebrities thinking of phoning in a Dubai real estate project for a huge pay day, would soon discover that the migrant workers who turn their vanity projects into bricks and mortar are housed in desert labour ghettos, to which they return after sixteen-hour days and queue behind the communal pans to make a meal out of such impeccably sourced ingredients as a single onion and a lump of bread. These indentured servants' passports are almost always held by the firms who have shipped them from countries such as Pakistan and Afghanistan, and any form of labour union is outlawed. According to UN estimates, there are up to 300,000 strictly segregated illegal workers in the emirates. Should Brad's people find their interest piqued by such delights, they may also care to look at the many reports from Human Rights Watch on working conditions in the UAE, which utterly condemns the practice of bonded slavery by which people's holiday homes are built.

On the off chance he bothers to do any of this, will the actor perform a U-turn? We probably shouldn't get our hopes up. In the end, you see, all of the above has to be set against the lure of being able to hand out business cards reading simply 'Brad Pitt: starchitect'.


## Madonna's log, star date 2009

But what happens when the world is not enough? Now that entertainers have conquered the globe, whither their expansionist dreams? Why, the International Space Station, of course – the low-earth orbit research facility upon which earthling governments have lavished in excess of $100 billion since 1998, but whose lack of a celebrity angle has earned it derision throughout the galaxy.

For a heady period in 2006, it looked as though all that was to change. Madonna was on tour in Russia, and it emerged that between the nightly round of crucifixions, nun-humpings and Kabbalah lectures, she had found time to indicate what kind of sights she wished to see. Red Square? Lenin's Tomb? The Winter Palace? Apparently not. Her ladyship had, confirmed Russian member of parliament Alexei Mitrafanov, 'expressed a desire to go into space and board the ISS'. But of *course* she had.

Very likely, you will have assumed that the Russians treated this request with the contempt it deserved, or told Madonna to get in line behind the ragtag collection of billionaires / billionaire scientists/Malaysian competition winners who have already committed to pay a $30 million-odd fee for the privilege. In which case, you will have assumed wrong.

Mitrafanov immediately put the prospective scheme before a plenary session of the Duma, and a motion was duly tabled. It was official: the Russian parliament really was going to spend legislative time deciding whether or not an extraterrestrial research facility, jointly run by the world's various space agencies, was due a pop-star house guest. They'd had a look at the calendar and thought 2008 or 2009 seemed a time when all parties might be able to synchronise diaries . . . But honestly. What in the war of the worlds were they thinking?

'It would be a serious event,' Mitrafanov insisted, despite having sanctioned an event that appeared the very essence of stupid, 'considering the TV coverage and the fact that it will coincide with elections in the United States and Russia.'

Could we at least rely on the boffins themselves to put the kibosh on the idea? 'We are aware of today's debates in the State Duma as to the proposed flight by Madonna to the International Space Station,' a Russian Space Agency spokesman soon announced. 'Taking into account her good physical preparedness, the dream of Louise Ciccone on a space flight could be realised in 2009.' (Russian Orthodox Christians decline to refer to her as Madonna.)

Not quite the withering dismissal we were looking for. In fact, news agencies seemed unable to find anyone who didn't think that Madonna's mission would be the crowning glory of the space race. How could this be? Did we really spend $837 trillion to provide a backdrop for a Madonna video? Wouldn't it have been quicker to paint a giant bullseye on the earth's face and transmit the binary code for 'We lack ambition: please invade us' into the further reaches of the galaxy?

While superior life forms were mulling their options, however, sense at last prevailed, and the Duma voted against the motion.

All for the best, perhaps. Given the subsequent cooling of relations between Russia and the West, there was every reason to suspect the proposed Madonna space mission was in fact a fiendish plot to destabilise Western culture. Having shepherded her into an escape pod, the Russkies might have permitted the Queen of Pop one live broadcast, a disco version of 'Space Oddity', before severing her ties to the space station and letting her drift helplessly into outer darkness while the world watched powerless below.

## Celebrities in space: far from the final frontier

You know the episode of *Dallas* where Pam wakes up and finds Bobby in the shower and realises she dreamed an entire series? Well, it would appear that humanity has slept through an entire series of very important meetings – because it turns out we're sending Victoria Principal into space.

Set your faces to stunned, because the woman who gave Pamela Barnes Ewing such subtly shaded life in the classic show will be a passenger on the first commercial space flight. Once again, the only reasonable response is: is this planet now actively courting invasion by more intelligent life forms?

Inevitably, the flagship mission is being run by entrepreneur turned alien-baiter Richard Branson, who has spent recent years gradually unveiling the various bits of hardware that will send his

SpaceShipTwo craft 360,000 feet above earth. At one of these big reveals, somewhere in the Mojave Desert, Dame Victoria Principal was in attendance, and asked – to much applause – 'Will Virgin Galactic have any women pilots?' Victoria holds an earthling pilot's licence, so make of her nightmarishly loaded question what you will.[5]

There will, naturally, be all sorts of stars attached to this mission to the stars. After all, how utterly *meaningless* would it be if there weren't? Celebrities who are either signed up, have expressed strong interest or have been offered free seats include Principal, Tom Hanks, Stephen Hawking, Robbie Williams, William Shatner, Paris Hilton, Lindsay Lohan, Morgan Freeman, Madonna, Dave Navarro, Prince Harry and Lieutenant Ripley herself, Sigourney Weaver. We've all heard about exploring the final frontier. Say hello to the advance party.

Still, at least they've got Lieutenant Ripley on board. And Freeman to provide an elegiac voice-over should any *Titanic*-style malfunction occur. But really, wouldn't it just be quicker to contact 581c, that other, recently discovered planet that scientists believe could sustain life, confess we're too terminally stupid to make use of our world, offer them all our natural resources at a fire-sale discount, then switch on *American Idol* and await death?

That debate, alas, does not top the Virgin Galactic agenda. According to its senior executives, a flight could take place in 2010, and the $200,000-a-ticket mission will give these travellers 'a more philosophical view of our place in the universe'. Way to go, celebrity thinkers! And you know what? If just one of these blowhards comes back espousing the philosophy of 'How many starving Aids-ridden Africans would $200,000 help?', then the mission will so totally have been worth it.

[5] What Virgin Galactic won't have, incidentally, is anybody attempting to join the 68-mile-high club. The company have confirmed they turned down $1 million from an outfit which wished to film a zero-gravity porn movie. Oh, humankind! Such is the scope of your ambition.

Still, let's begin the search for positives – starting with the choice of personnel. The academic and visionary science-fiction author Isaac Asimov described space exploration as 'the only chance of escaping the destruction of all that humanity has struggled to achieve for 50,000 years'. And suddenly, one is struck by a very real sense that if one had to distil all of humanity's achievements over the past 50 millennia into a single being, it would be Victoria Principal.

Here, after all, is a humanoid who has spent the best part of two decades waging a courageous war against gravity, at one stage even going so far as to marry her plastic surgeon. Who knows what she could achieve in space, where she would be freed from the pull of Newtonian forces attempting to drag her breasts southwards?

The only sadness, for we economy-class rejects watching the mission by videolink from earth, is that we will be unable to experience vicariously the wonders of space by gauging Victoria's simulcast reactions to the view from her window seat. Truth be told, expressions do not scud across Victoria's visage like so many variformed clouds. She can basically do 'surprised' and 'asleep', and 'asleep' actually looks a lot like 'surprised', except the eyelids come halfway down, the eyeballs roll back, and for twenty minutes she stops trying to sell you her miracle moisturiser range.

To avoid any potentially fatal misunderstanding during the flight, mission control should probably avoid arming Lieutenant Ripley.

And there we must leave our celebrities, skyrocketing into the thermosphere, perhaps under the impression that their perfume lines and unsolicited medical directives are the sort of commodities our superior civilisation might usefully gift to other life forms as yet unknown.

What a topsy-turvy planet they leave behind. Once upon a time, celebrity excess was cited as evidence of moral decline. Rock stars spun out on drugs were held up as corruptingly decadent.

Today, though, who is the more totemic embodiment of a society gone awry? The stoned actor, or the one we've charged with solving a refugee crisis? The rock star arrested for onstage lewd behaviour, or the one using the UN lawn to sell luxury handbags? The celebrities aboard the spaceship are emissaries from a Bizarro world – a planet where the entertainers are formulating aid policy, and backing legislative bills, and dominating the news media to the exclusion of almost everything else.

Indeed, wistful philosophers might view the craft and its precious cargo as a perfect time capsule of early-twenty-first-century earthling preoccupations. Perhaps in the future, idealistic explorers will come across its wreckage, half buried in the post-apocalyptic landscape, and in that single agonising moment realise the self-destructive futility of all human existence.

But then, you've seen *Planet of the Apes*. You know how this one ends.